Talking Sociology

THIRD EDITION

Talking Sociology

Gary Alan Fine

University of Georgia

Allyn and Bacon

BOSTON   LONDON   TORONTO   SYDNEY   TOKYO   SINGAPORE

Senior Editor: Karen Hanson
Editor-in-Chief, Social Sciences: Susan Badger
Production Administrator: Annette Joseph
Production Coordinator: Holly Crawford
Editorial-Production Service: Laura Cleveland, WordCrafters Editorial Services, Inc.
Cover Administrator: Suzanne Harbison
Cover Designer: Dorothy Cullinan
Manufacturing Buyer: Louise Richardson

This book is printed on
recycled, acid-free paper.

Library of Congress Cataloging-in-Publication Data

Fine, Gary Alan.
 Talking sociology / Gary Alan Fine. — 3rd ed.
  p. cm.
 Includes bibliographical references.
 ISBN 0-205-13755-5
 1. Sociology. 2. Social problems. 3. United States—Social
policy—1980– I. Title.
HM51.F535 1993
301—dc20   92-20712
                                                                                      CIP

Printed in the United States of America

10 9 8 7 6 5 4 3 2 1   97 96 95 94 93 92

Text Credits

pages 21–23: from Stephen T. Wagner, "America's Non-English Heritage," *Society*, November-December, 1981, pp. 37–41, 43. Published by permission of Transaction Publishers, from *Society*, Vol. 19, No. 1. Copyright © 1981 by Transaction Publishers.

(Continued on page 219, which constitutes a continuation of the copyright page)

To
Mary Roszak

My Student
My Son's Teacher

The Chain of Knowledge Is a Circle

Contents

Acknowledgments   xiii

■ **INTRODUCTION**
Murder and Martyrdom   1

The Social Order   5
The Libertarian Point of View   6
The Conservative Point of View   9
The Social Democratic Point of View   11
The Structure of the Text   14
For Further Study   17
Notes and References   18

■ **CHAPTER ONE**
Culture: Should Elementary School Children Be
Taught in Their Native Language?   19

The Conservative Point of View   24
The Social Democratic Point of View   26
The Libertarian Point of View   27
Hispanic Education and Social Research   29
Culture and Bilingualism   31
Questions   32
For Further Study   32
Notes and References   33

■ **CHAPTER TWO**

Socialization: Should Parents Be Allowed to Hit Their Children However They Wish?   35

The Social Democratic Point of View   38
The Conservative Point of View   41
The Libertarian Point of View   43
Child Abuse and Social Research   45
Spanking and the Socialization Process   47
Questions   47
For Further Study   48
Notes and References   49

■ **CHAPTER THREE**

Deviance and Social Control: Should Drug Use Be Legalized?   51

The Conservative Point of View   56
The Libertarian Point of View   57
The Social Democratic Point of View   59
Marijuana and Social Research   61
Social Control, Deviance, and Drug Use   63
Questions   65
For Further Study   65
Notes and References   66

■ **CHAPTER FOUR**

Human Sexuality: Should Adolescents Engage in Premarital Sexual Intercourse? Should Contraceptives Be Distributed in High Schools?   68

The Conservative Point of View   73
The Social Democratic Point of View   75
The Libertarian Point of View   76
Premarital Sex and Social Research   78
Human Sexuality, Adolescents, and Society   80
Questions   81
For Further Study   82
Notes and References   82

■ **CHAPTER FIVE**

Economy and Stratification: Should the Government Regulate Businesses to Protect Endangered Species?   85

The Social Democratic Point of View   90
The Libertarian Point of View   92
The Conservative Point of View   94
Sparrows and Social Research   96
Environmentalism and the Economy   98
Questions   100
For Further Study   100
Notes and References   101

■ **CHAPTER SIX**

Gender Roles and Sexual Stratification: Should Women Be Permitted to Serve in Military Combat?   103

The Social Democratic Point of View   106
The Libertarian Point of View   108
The Conservative Point of View   110
Military Women and Social Research   112
Gender Roles and Military Service   114
Questions   115
For Further Study   115
Notes and References   116

■ **CHAPTER SEVEN**

Race and Ethnicity: Should Minorities Be Given Preferential Treatment in Hiring?   118

The Social Democratic Point of View   123
The Libertarian Point of View   125
The Conservative Point of View   127
African-American Unemployment and
    Social Research   129
Race Relations and Preferential Hiring   131
Questions   133
For Further Study   133
Notes and References   134

■ CHAPTER EIGHT

Family: Who Should Be Allowed to Adopt?   136

The Libertarian Point of View   141
The Conservative Point of View   143
The Social Democratic Point of View   145
Transracial Adoption and Social Research   147
Adoption and the Family   149
Questions   150
For Further Study   151
Notes and References   151

■ CHAPTER NINE

Education: Should Books in Public Libraries Be Censored?   154

The Libertarian Point of View   159
The Conservative Point of View   161
The Social Democratic Point of View   163
Pornography and Social Research   164
Censorship and Education   167
Questions   168
For Further Study   168
Notes and References   169

■ CHAPTER TEN

Work and Organizations: Should Corporations Be Allowed to Give Employees Lie Detector Tests?   171

The Libertarian Point of View   176
The Social Democratic Point of View   178
The Conservative Point of View   180
Organizational Control and Social Research   181
Work and Organizational Control   183
Questions   184
For Further Study   185
Notes and References   185

■ **CHAPTER ELEVEN**

Aging and Medicine: Should Euthanasia
Be Permitted?   187

The Conservative Point of View   192
The Libertarian Point of View   194
The Social Democratic Point of View   196
Senility and Social Research   197
Aging, Medicine, and Euthanasia   199
Questions   200
For Further Study   201
Notes and References   201

■ **CHAPTER TWELVE**

Social Movements/Collective Behavior: Can Civil
Disobedience Be Justified?   203

The Libertarian Point of View   207
The Social Democratic Point of View   209
The Conservative Point of View   211
Moral Development and Social Research   213
Social Movements and Civil Disobedience   214
Questions   216
For Further Study   216
Notes and References   217

Acknowledgments

■ With each subsequent edition, the number of individuals who deserve thanks for bettering a manuscript grows. Ira Reiss, D. Stanley Eitzen, Ramona Asher, Albert Chabot, Dennis Teitge, Maurice Garnier, Michael Bassis, Ira Cohen, T. S. Schwartz, John Taylor, Rick Hargraves, and Rene Wildermuth helped improve this work through their comments. Judith Ann Williams, Randy Stoecker, Sari Fried, Nancy Wisely, Kendra Butler, Lori Ducharme, and Christopher Vacek have served ably as research assistants sniffing out clever quotations as if they were truffles—a metaphor that pays heed only to their powers of investigation and not to any similarity to our porcine colleagues. With the advent of word processors, I haven't had to burden secretaries with the need for typing and retyping, but I do wish to thank Sandra Gary for her skills in helping me print out some of this material. I would also like to thank Charles Ogg, Emerson College, and Meg Wilkes-Karrader, University of St. Thomas, for their review of the manuscript of this edition. Finally, thanks to Al Levitt, formerly of Allyn and Bacon, who convinced me, over several fine dinners, to write this book, and, later, to Karen Hanson, who persuaded me that revisions were in order.

Talking Sociology

INTRODUCTION

Murder and Martyrdom

- *What would you die for?*
- *What would you kill for?*

Before reading on, spend a few moments pondering your answers. Is there anything for which you would either give up your life or take the life of another?

Would you be willing to die to prevent your child from dying? Would you kill to prevent your sister from being raped? Would you lay down your life to prevent a military invasion of the United States? Would you murder an oppressor to end brutality against your ethnic, racial, or religious group? Around the world, young people, in most respects identical to you, are choosing to die and to kill for their beliefs. Americans were willing to die and to kill to gain independence from the British, to defeat the Nazis, to control the Viet Cong, and to liberate the Kuwaitis. We have died in struggles for union rights and civil rights. We have executed murderers, lynched those accused of crimes, and knifed members of rival gangs.

Yet, if you compose a list of what you would die or kill for, the list is likely to be short. If you are like most students I have asked, the only answer you will give has to do with individuals for whom you have intense personal feelings. You might kill someone who attacks your family. You might choose to take a risk in giving birth to a child. Of course, not everyone would assent to these hypothetical emergencies, but many would. Some would agree that they would pick up arms and lay down their lives for the sake of national defense against a hostile enemy, if asked by our government.

Few of you will name a cause that you might kill or die for. Americans today do not care enough about causes, even those they deeply believe in, to take or give a life. Yet, when we read the newspapers we learn that people around the world are doing just that. Whatever you might think about the morality of terrorism, admit that these terrorists have a passion for their causes. Many Protestants and Catholics believe that who controls those six counties of Northern Ireland is literally a matter of life and death. Most Americans think of Great Britain and Ireland as civilized democracies, both with good governments. Protestantism and Catholicism are both respectable religions; some of our best friends belong to each. Because they cannot understand these intense nationalistic or religious impulses, most Americans see this violence as silly, futile, and tragic. The terrorists on each side do not share our perspective, and the violence shows no signs of ending. We look, for example, at India, Sri Lanka, Iraq, the Philippines, Peru, Cambodia, Lebanon, Haiti, Armenia, Yugoslavia, Zaire, Togo, Somalia, South Africa, and Italy and see essentially the same thing. People do care enough to kill and be killed, even when, from the view of outsiders, their deadly crusades are pointless. One of the goals of the so-called New World Order, propounded by President George Bush, is to cause the rest of the world to think about political problems in the pragmatic fashion preferred by Americans, draining disputes of physical force.

Consider two important political issues in the United States. The fight over the passage of the Equal Rights Amendment is history. That constitutional amendment, which meant so much to so many women, was defeated by enough state legislatures to prevent its passage. Significantly, during the decade in which the Equal Rights Amendment was a political battleground no one was killed, no one took her or his own life. Although the passage of the amendment was vital to many women, women did not feel it appropriate to assassinate state legislators who opposed them, and no woman saw fit to become a gasoline-soaked martyr for the cause. This political moderation is in sharp contrast to the battles for suffrage in Great Britain and the United States during the first two decades of the twentieth century, where these campaigns included acts of violence. Although it may be repulsive to consider the tactical value of a well-placed bomb, terrorists consider this to be a legitimate strategy.

The civility shown by those who hold strong beliefs does not apply only to progressive causes. Many members of the pro-life (anti-abortion) movement believe that each year some 1.5 million babies are being *murdered* in the United States. Surely such genocide—as some have termed it—is ample reason for direct political action. Yet, the pro-life movement, with rare exceptions, has worked within the conventional political rules with few overtly violent acts. Only recently through "Operation Rescue" have the opponents of abortion turned to mass civil disobedience. Although there have been a few bombings of abortion clinics, these are uncommon and the "murderers" themselves go unpunished. Each day pro-life activists let thousands of innocent babies go to their deaths without putting their lives and freedom on the line. Why?

In suggesting that Americans do not see murder and martyrdom as acceptable political alternatives, I do not imply that we should. We are not politically deficient because we lack a tradition of organized political terrorism. Presumably this relative (but not total) lack of collective violence is a reason for our political stability. Americans are largely pragmatic and centrist in political outlook. We vote overwhelmingly for two parties that often seem not to have "a dime's worth of difference" between them. Perhaps this is a reason for the low intellectual level of our political campaigns. This is particularly striking when we consider the broader range of political beliefs acceptable in Great Britain, France, or Canada. While we should not ignore the real differences between the Democratic and Republican parties, their basic values and policies are similar. Both claim to believe in a strong national defense, a social security system, aid to the needy, support for the arts, nuclear arms reductions, and free enterprise. The two parties differ in the level of funding for these programs and in the way specific programs are administered; however, when we consider them in light of the range of possible alternative political policies, our two major parties are huddled very much in the center. Each wishes to convince voters that it is the real centrist party, the party of moderation. When a Barry Goldwater or a George McGovern is nominated, he is overwhelmingly defeated. Socialist, nativist, populist, and libertarian parties have had little success in selling their nostrums to the American people.

Because of the success that the two parties have had together in making the United States strong at home and abroad, most voters feel that the general centrist positions of the major parties are correct. Furthermore, Americans have accepted the idea that compromise and civil discussion are more effective than forcing their opinions on others. Americans typically are pragmatic in their political orientations and avoid all-encompassing ideologies, despite strong opinions on many issues. We seem more concerned with getting the job done than with the larger questions that surround the immediate problem. Americans tend not to be much concerned with what George Bush called "the vision thing."

Of course, there are other good reasons for not wanting to kill—and be killed. Some accept the principle that nothing is as valuable as life and that there is no excuse for shortening it. In days of the Cold War, some claimed that it was better to be Red than dead. No political issue, these thinkers believe, can take priority over the destruction of human life—a point emphasized by the Indian revolutionary Mahatma Gandhi and his followers who believe nonviolent demonstrations and civil disobedience can achieve the same end. The popular response to the August 1991 Soviet coup provides cheer for those who believe that massive peaceful protest can defeat tyrants, although the repression at Tiananmen Square in Beijing indicates that such victories are by no means certain. In theory, we all probably agree with this approach, but whether we believe it will routinely work depends on our view of human nature. Debates over the death penalty reveal this strain: Many people would prefer not to have the state involved in the killing business, but others feel that it is needed to protect the rest of us.

I used killing and being killed as an opening gambit to indicate how strongly some people feel about social issues and political ideology. (I have no desire for students to raise arms.) Yet I wonder whether our American lack of ideological concern is a good thing; how far can political pragmatism be pushed before it becomes a willingness to accept any policy so long as it is nicely packaged? I wrote this book to expose students to the philosophical bases of social life. Sociology is the proper place to begin to understand underlying questions of social order.

I believe that people are better off if they are consciously aware of their basic principles, that is, those beliefs and values that structure how they view the world. In the terms of social critic Thomas Sowell, in his book *A Conflict of Visions*, these constitute "visions" of society. From these basic principles, attitudes toward particular issues can emerge in logical and consistent ways, to the extent that psychology allows. Most people do not have strong feelings about human nature or about the role of the government in individual affairs. I assume that many students have never considered these two issues in any detail, yet most students do have beliefs on particular social problems. Since I believe that these two issues, human nature and government intervention, are at the heart of sociological understanding, they deserve to be considered in detail.

Over three centuries ago, the British moral philosopher Thomas Hobbes raised an intriguing and important question that continues to haunt sociologists: How is social order possible? In other words, why, in a world of individuals with their own needs and personalities, is society as orderly as it is? Just as the physical world rarely fools us, the social world (perhaps a little less consistently) rarely surprises us. We usually know what to expect from our fellow citizens. How, in a world of over four billion people, do we so neatly fit our personal routines together? The answer that a person gives to this puzzle of social order depends on how he or she evaluates human nature, and from this answer one can draw conclusions about how people should be governed.

People do not go through their daily routines constantly aware of these fundamental questions; people generally act on the basis of immediate circumstances and options. While this is fine for small decisions, such an approach presents difficulties when we confront momentous decisions. These decisions may be erratic or inconsistent since they derive from immediate concerns and not from basic principles. Some critics have suggested that U.S. economic and foreign policies lurch from position to position to position, depending on what the public is most clamoring for and how close it is to an election. We try to control inflation just when inflation is subsiding, only to push the country into a recession; we deal with rising unemployment by establishing social welfare programs, which increase inflation; or we stimulate the economy by cutting taxes, which leads to increased deficits, solved by raising taxes. Conservatives support high deficits when it is in their political interest; liberals support massive arms buildups when this is what the public wishes to hear.

A dilemma inherent in a pragmatic approach is one of morality. The pragmatist sees problems in their immediate setting but often without concern for their long-term consequences. Some solutions may be morally wrong, even though they are more effective than others. For example, sterilizing "genetically deficient" individuals might decrease the incidence of mental retardation; yet, many who believe this is possible to institute would reject this policy on moral grounds. Such forced sterilization may be wrong, even though it works. Ethics may take precedence over technical efficiency.

Finally, by considering issues only pragmatically, we are prone to ignore universal sociological principles. Sociology strives for insights with general relevance. What sociology can tell us applies to more than narrow, local problems, but rather addresses a wider range of concerns. As we shall discuss later, the sociological perspective of *functionalism* allows us to understand many social spheres. The same can be said of an alternative approach, *conflict theory*.

Do not make too sharp a distinction between decisions based on principles and those based on the needs of the moment. Many sociologists believe the world is too complex to be completely dominated by any single set of principles or ideologies. No theory can account for "every sparrow's fall."[1] We should be sensitive to each of the sometimes contradictory principles that are widely held. Many claim that no single set of beliefs can possibly hold all the answers. Whether or not this is true, political reality typically means that some principles must be compromised. Politics is, after all, the art of the possible, of learning to make adjustments to the wishes of others. Although you should be aware of your principles in making decisions, this does not mean you should always blindly and coldly act on those principles. Pragmatism is not a dirty word: In a democracy, it is essential to reaching consensus.

The Social Order

There exist many possible prescriptions for how society should be ordered. Each society, each tribe, each nation has at least one, sometimes several, ways of seeing its world. In this book I will examine three of the most common views in American life: libertarianism, conservatism, and social democracy. I do not claim these are the only three perspectives that Americans hold, but they do have several things in common that make them good subjects. First, each presents a reasonably consistent and complete view of human nature. Second, each contains within it the principles by which a government could make policy. Third, each of these views is accepted by a significant number of Americans, and elements from each have penetrated the general, pragmatic political view. Finally, each perspective described here is consistent with democratic government. Certain important philosophies that are not readily amenable to democracy are not considered, such as communism (Marxist-Leninism), fascism, or benevolent monarchy. In addition, I consider only "western" political philosophies; those of the great empires of China, Japan, India, Persia, Mexico, Peru, and West Africa are ignored.

I don't pretend to discuss the details of the three approaches that I have selected. Each is a complicated point of view with many nuances of thought and objective. There is no single, correct interpretation of any of them. I only try to capture their basic ideas. Keep in mind while reading the following descriptions that few people are "true believers"; most individuals pick and choose the best ideas from each philosophy. Furthermore, it will be helpful for you to read these points of view sympathetically. In other words, try to see the world from each perspective. After reading, ask yourself which view you find most appealing and why. Why do the other two approaches seem wrong? Ask your study partners and classmates the same questions.

This book will not tell you that one approach is more correct than any other. If I can give you something to think about, something to argue about, and something to help you understand the buzzing, booming social order a little better, then I will have accomplished my purpose. Ultimately, I want to prod you into thinking about your basic assumptions, your visions about the world, and how your assumptions lead to positions on important contemporary issues. Although sociology is, in some measure, a science grounded in empirical investigation, it is also a branch of social philosophy.

The Libertarian Point of View

Of the three approaches, the libertarian perspective is probably the easiest to describe, as libertarians pride themselves on their logical consistency and principled positions (which reach absurdity in the eyes of critics). Libertarians hold individual freedom as their highest value. They believe that each person should have the right to do what he or she wishes, if it does not directly coerce or interfere with the freedom of others. The libertarian strives to uphold individual rights in all ways. Although we tend to think of a single liberal/conservative dimension, libertarianism falls outside of this schema with its belief in governmental nonintervention in all realms of human affairs, economic as well as social.[2]

Although many social democrats and conservatives hold public office, few strict libertarians do. One reason is that libertarians are often perceived as extremists who are unwilling to compromise. This stems from their reliance on pure logic, cold logic, some might call it, to make their case. For instance, the 1992 Libertarian Party platform endorsed the following programs, which most Americans would find difficult to accept: (1) eliminating all restrictions on firearms and weapon ownership (presumably, although not explicitly, including nuclear and chemical weapons); (2) ending government payment for psychiatric or psychological treatment; (3) eliminating all antipornography legislation; (4) ending all government operation and subsidy of schools; (5) abolishing the Consumer Product Safety Commission, the Environmental Protection Agency, the Federal Aviation Administration, and the Food and Drug Administration; and (6) ending all government regulation of nuclear power. In conventional political terms, libertarians are very conservative on economic issues (ultimately opposing all government regulation of businesses) and very liberal on social issues (allowing any and all acts that do not directly harm another person). How, you might ask, have libertarians come to adopt such views?

These positions are derived from the libertarians' understanding of human nature, especially the belief that individuals are largely responsible for their own actions, and they subscribe to what many call the "Protestant Ethic." If people are successful, it is because they have the skills that enable them to be successful: They have chosen to be successful. They are hard working, sincere, honest, diligent, and educated. None of these traits are inherited but are acquired through personal effort and moral strength. Of course, the libertarian would not deny that some things are hereditary, but those are seen as less important. Likewise, the libertarian does not deny that some individuals have social handicaps such as race, parents' income, and sex; however, the libertarian believes that in a fair society discrimination would not exist and, anyway, people should be able to overcome these obstacles without government help. This may strike some as naive, but it follows from a belief in free will. (We would do well to recall in all the philosophies we examine matters of degree, rather than absolutes.) The libertarian believes that people are rational decision makers, relatively free to do what they wish; success or failure in this life is due to one's own efforts. The libertarian believes you are free to get an "A" or "D" in this course, and the fact that you attended a poor high school, or just split up with your lover, or that your grandmother recently died, does not alter your own responsibility for the grade you receive. The libertarian, of course, has no objection to voluntary charity and other forms of communal support, but these must not be coerced.

From this belief in individual effort follows the libertarian's view of government. The libertarian assumes, in Henry David Thoreau's words, "that government is best which governs least." Since people have the knowledge and ability to make themselves happy and successful (if they choose to), it follows that government can best serve its citizens by maximizing their freedom. This position derives from the writings of eighteenth- and nineteenth-century British liberals, such as Adam Smith, John Stuart Mill, and Jeremy Bentham, who mistrusted the power of the state. These thinkers, and others who followed them, raised the individual to a pinnacle of power in the social universe. They also believed reason would ultimately provide the means by which human beings could live happily with each other. If everyone would try to maximize his or her happiness, without infringing on the rights of others, the world would be a nice place in which to live.

The greatest sin for the libertarian is coercion. Although they recognize that some people can coerce other people (muggers or rapists, for instance), libertarians' primary concern is the power that is taken away from individuals by the government. Although at first this concentration of power might seem innocent—someone has to provide for national defense and for a police force to prevent anarchy—power can easily be misused. As the American revolutionary Thomas Paine wrote in *Common Sense* (1776): "Society in every state is a blessing, but government, even in its best state, is but a necessary evil; in its worst state, an intolerable one." Libertarian economist Murray Rothbard uses the metaphor of the state as "a criminal band" to explain the libertarian philosophy.[3]

As a result, the libertarian believes passionately that the government should not entangle itself in the private lives of its citizens. If a person wishes to have sexual relations with a (willing) sheep, so be it. If someone chooses to use heroin or commit suicide without involving others, that is no cause for concern. The government should not protect people from themselves. Thus, rape is not a crime against the social order but rather a crime that violently eliminates the right of a woman to refuse intercourse. All crimes are crimes against individuals, not against society—an argument to which the conservative would object.

One problem in libertarian theory concerns the boundaries of coercion. When are a person's rights infringed? A libertarian believes people should be allowed to play music if they wish, but suppose they do this at 3:00 in the morning in your dormitory. Are they infringing on your rights? There are no easy answers to these conflicts of rights. The libertarian, more than the conservative or the social democrat, is likely to side with the actor rather than with the person being inconvenienced by the act.

In the realm of economics, the libertarians' position is laissez-faire (translated from the French: "leave it alone"). This concept, derived from the writings of eighteenth century Scottish economist Adam Smith, refers to the theory that the government should not attempt to manipulate the economy. The economy is best stabilized through the laws of supply and demand. When more people want something, its price increases. Price increases will typically increase the supply (because of the hope of increased profit) and will decrease the demand, and this increased supply and decreased demand will, in turn, decrease price. When the government subsidizes a product or action by interfering with the free market (such as through tax breaks), more of that will be produced than could be justified by the natural demand. The economy should operate by the rational decisions of free people. This assumes a "free" market, not one artificially controlled by large monopolies or cartels. Social democrats are likely to object to laissez-faire economics and government nonintervention on this point because, they claim, the market is not really free.

Another problem with libertarian theory is its border with anarchy. Indeed, anarchy is closely related to libertarianism, with the primary difference being that the libertarians accept the fundamental right to property, whereas most (left-wing) anarchists do not. In emphasizing freedom, the libertarian deemphasizes equality and order. The libertarian would qualify this by saying that with rational human beings working together for their common ends, order will emerge, and that equality means only equality of opportunity, rather than equality of outcome. Equality of opportunity is always present in libertarian theory because of the free will inherent in life. The great virtue of libertarians is their lust for freedom; their great failing is their cold-hearted lack of compassion for their neighbors who simply cannot keep up.

The Conservative Point of View

Ambrose Bierce, in his *Devil's Dictionary*, defined a conservative as "a statesman who is enamoured of existing evils, as distinguished from the liberal, who wishes to replace them with others."[4] There is some truth in this sardonic comment. Conservatives do have a high regard for the tried and true, and fret about the new and untested.

The term *conservative* is derived from French political thought during the Napoleonic era and refers to a guardian of principles of justice and the nation's civilized heritage. Conservatism largely originated from opposition to the radical changes brought about by the French Revolution. Sociologist Robert Nisbet, in tracing the history of sociological thought, makes a cogent case that sociology is derived from conservative political thought with its love for community, order, and authority, although relatively few sociologists today would define themselves as politically conservative.[5]

Russell Kirk, a leading conservative theorist, argues that conservatism is not really a political system or an ideology.[6] He makes this claim because conservatives are in favor of preserving what has come before, that is, whatever has worked for a society in the past. Thus, a Peruvian conservative would legitimately differ from a Swiss conservative, who would differ from a Kenyan conservative. Unlike the libertarian, who has the same principles wherever she or he might be, the conservative's policies are based on the society in which he or she lives. As Alexander Hamilton noted: "What may be good in Philadelphia may be bad at Paris and ridiculous at Petersburgh."[7] If an innovation (e.g., Social Security or enforced racial equality) has proven successful, despite the original opposition of the conservative, the conservative will now support it. Conservatives do not suggest that any single set of policies is necessarily superior.

Kirk, making particular reference to British and American conservative writings, points to a set of "first principles" that are shared by most conservatives.[8] I shall draw heavily on his analysis.

Unlike the libertarian who sees human beings as fundamentally rational and basically decent, conservatives believe that humans are imperfect. Human nature is faulty and, as a result, no perfect social system can ever be devised. The conservative sadly concludes that all we can hope for is a reasonably happy, just, and fair society. Finding absolute goodness is no more likely than finding a unicorn. The human lot (perhaps due to "original sin") is to live in a world where some evil, misery, and unfairness exist. We can't eliminate pain; we can only hope to control it. The conservative perspective is most likely to present human beings in an unflattering, pessimistic fashion. They are apt to agree to some extent with the seventeenth-century British moral philosopher, Thomas Hobbes, that human beings without government to control them are destined to live a life that is "solitary, poor, nasty, brutish, and short."[9] This belief in the weaknesses of human nature leads the conservative to accept the rightful place of a variety of social institutions to control these excesses.

Most conservatives include God in their social equation. That is, they accept the existence of a "transcendent moral order"—moral authority that cannot be challenged by other people.[10] Conservatives reject the libertarian credo that individuals should do their own thing. They believe in a moral authority that is set by divine principle or "natural law," an issue that emerged in President Bush's nomination of Judge Clarence Thomas to the United States Supreme Court.

Conservatives also accept the value of social continuity, preferring the devil they know to the one they are yet to meet. They believe most changes are for the worse, and so changes should be made gradually, cautiously, and often not at all. The church serves in some regard as the model for the state. Just as theology changes very slowly—after all, it is supposed to be God's will—so should secular law. The radicalness of revolution, particularly of the French and Russian revolutions, is profoundly frightening to conservatives. Implicit in conservative thought is a deep respect for the past. The wisdom of the past has been replaced by the foolish babble of the present. This romanticism for what has come before leads some to claim that conservatives are reactionary. Yet, it is not so much that conservatives revere particular historical figures; rather, they revere the trial-and-error learning to which they are heir. In eighteenth-century conservative philosopher Edmund Burke's words: "The individual is foolish, but the species is wise."[11]

Finally, conservatives share with libertarians the belief that everyone should not be treated equally. While social democrats wish to minimize class divisions, conservatives believe that classes produce a healthy diversity in a society. Leveling of classes leads to a stagnant society. If all people are equal, there is no need for anyone to exert himself or herself to do better; motivation is lost. Furthermore, conservatives cherish the existence of other social institutions besides government. They see the church, the community, and the family as particularly important social forces that have authority equaling or surpassing that of the government. The state, on the other hand, is a secondary or artificial institution, not derived from the natural relations of human beings.

For the conservative, government is not the evil that it is for the libertarian; it is just secondary. When other social institutions have failed, then government must intervene. As a result, conservatives often believe government involvement should staunch the tide of moral decay and, as long as the economic system is functioning, allow businesses to operate on their own without government regulation. The conservative is not afraid of the fact that some people are poor and some people fail; these unfortunate facts simply represent the natural diversity of a social system.

Unlike social democrats, who admire a just and strong government, and libertarians, who mistrust all governments, conservatives are neutral toward government. It is simply not the most important thing in society. While government is needed to preserve order, it is weakened by the frailty of human nature and doesn't compare with natural, primary organizations. The conservative's greatest virtue is order and, according to Russell Kirk, their particular vice is selfishness—the desire to let things rest in a way favorable to them. Despite popular stereotypes, conservatives are no more anachronisms than social democrats are wild-haired firebrands.

The Social Democratic Point of View

Of the three philosophies, the least clear and most broad is what I have termed social democracy. Although some Americans are proud to call themselves libertarians and conservatives, few Americans call themselves social democrats. In the United States, such people will typically refer to themselves as liberals or progressives, and will be called leftists, left-liberals, or socialists by their opponents. After the 1988 presidential campaign, liberal, once a term of honor, has become scorned by many as the dreaded "L word."

None of these terms really do justice to this social and political approach. Perhaps liberal comes closest, but the history of the word is so muddled up with libertarianism that it does us little good. (Some of the founders of libertarianism were known as liberals.) So, I have chosen to use a European term to refer to this group of Americans. In Germany, the major left-liberal party is known as the Social Democratic Party. In other European countries, the leading party on the noncommunist left is a social democratic party—committed to democracy but also to a strong, involved government. Although this term does not precisely fit the American situation, it is the best available. I have combined an uneasy blend of contemporary liberalism, welfare-state economics, democratic socialism, and progressive democracy. More than the other two approaches, the social democratic perspective casts a wide net, possibly slightly too wide.

Unlike conservative theory, social democratic philosophy accepts the possibility of the betterment of human nature. It is not that people are naturally good, but they can be made to be good. Social policies can bring out the best in people. This perspective can be seen most clearly in the social democrat's fight for civil rights legislation. The social democrat starts with the assumption that all people have been created equal and that they should be treated equally. Of course, in the tough, cold, real world they are not treated in this way. Thus, in the early 1960s social democrats vigorously and successfully fought to have the U.S. Congress pass a civil rights law that would outlaw discrimination in restaurants and other places of public accommodation. They believed that by preventing whites from segregating racial minorities, this would increase the toleration among the races. Social democrats believed that changing laws would eventually produce a change in attitudes—that stateways precede folkways. In this case, at least, the philosophy worked. For example, white southerners, forced by law to eat at the same coffee shops with black southerners, discovered that the moral order of society did not come crashing down. When they were forced to desegregate, southern politicians such as George Wallace discovered that they really did not mind blacks as much as they thought they would. Civil rights legislation provides a textbook case of how government involvement led to positive moral outcomes and a presumed improvement in human nature.

Perhaps most central to the social democrat's philosophy is the positive role of government. President Andrew Jackson provides a wonderful metaphor that captures the social democrats' attitude: "There are no necessary evils in government. Its evils exist only in its abuses. If it would confine itself to equal protection and, as Heaven does its rains, shower its favors alike on the high and the low, the rich and the poor, it would be an unqualified blessing."[12]

State power need not necessarily be scary; it can increase human happiness. Likewise, change need not be the fearsome foe pictured by the conservative. Although some changes can be harmful (no one is in favor of every possible change), other changes, even radical ones, are sometimes for the best. The social democrat sees the multitude of crimes committed by a multitude of governments as not necessarily characteristic of every strong government. The obligation of the government to promote equality and justice must take priority. In this desire for equality, the social democrat parts company with the libertarian and the conservative who welcome the diversity of a class system, a social system in which some succeed and others fail.

Behind this belief in equality lies a different view of motivation. Social democrats believe that people will work hard because that is the right thing to do. Unlike the conservatives who are constantly complaining about the many people who will try to cheat on welfare and try to get by without working, the social democrat believes that there are few people like that. Most people have strong internal moral compasses, and while they are not perfect, they do have good hearts. The social democrat ultimately paints a rosier picture of human beings than does the conservative. The problems for the social democrat are those traditional social arrangements that prevent people from living happily and equally: racism, social inequality, gender discrimination, and prejudice against old people, people of a different nationality, sexual orientation, or religion, and the like.

Ultimately, the primary problem for the social democrat is poverty; poverty destroys human dignity. In the words of Democratic presidential candidate Adlai Stevenson, "a hungry man is not a free man."[13] This reflects the attitude of the social democrat who is concerned with insuring that government takes an active role in preventing these offenses to human dignity and in working against poverty.

One of the problems with such a broad category as the social democratic perspective is that adherents have different attitudes about what is the appropriate governmental response to poverty. Some (the welfare-state liberals) wish to restrain the government's effect on the market to as little as is necessary to cure the symptoms of poverty. Such people favor a collection of welfare programs to help those who are disadvantaged because of their position in society. They also believe government should play an active role in combatting the excesses of business. On the other side, some democratic socialists consider it appropriate for the government to manage large segments of the essential industrial and service economy of the nation. Thus, in Great Britain, the government controls the railroads, much heavy industry, medical practice, and other areas of concern to the people as a whole. Some areas are left to private industry, but often these are not the most central industries and services. Critics have noted inadequacies of government intervention in all its forms and wonder whether an efficient government is ever possible.

In the area of morality, the social democrat often stands with the libertarian, although some who are called neo-liberals have begun to sound more like some conservatives. Since private institutions of religion and the family have no special position in social democratic thought (as they do for the conservative), the government should allow a full flowering of life-styles. Morality is personal and relative, while economic insufficiency is public and objective. Morality is a matter of individual choice, whereas economic position is related to the social structure. Since morality has no special place in society, the social democrat thinks it unwarranted that some groups suffer discrimination by others because of differing beliefs and practices. For example, the social democrat finds it easy to support legislation prohibiting discrimination against homosexuals. Discrimination poses a structural barrier to the well-being of these citizens. A group's right to protection takes priority over an individual's freedom to discriminate.

The leading virtue for the social democrat is equality. All social democrats believe in the equality of opportunity, and many believe in the equality of outcome as well. There is a point below which a society should never let its members slip—a view not shared by the extreme libertarian or conservative. Just as equality is the social democrat's virtue, envy is the weakness. Some say that social democrats are envious failures who wish to grab from the successful those rewards they have not been able to win through personal efforts. Social democrats who are personally successful may be accused of being naively optimistic, painting too rosy a picture of those they wish to help. Redistribution of wealth is particularly appealing to those who have little; just as the status quo is appealing to those with much to lose.

The Structure of the Text

In the remaining chapters we will examine twelve controversial social issues from these three major standpoints. The issues were deliberately chosen to reflect major sociological concepts, those found in most textbooks for introductory sociology and social problems courses. Each chapter has a sociological concept for which the question asked is a reflection. So, for example, when discussing culture, I ask whether Hispanic children should be taught in bilingual education programs.

Each chapter begins with a short discussion of how the relevant concept has been treated in sociological writing. This does not replace the discussion in the text or in class but rather provides a basis for the discussion that follows. I try to present the major concept in a straightforward and simple fashion. In order to provide continuity among the concepts, I will typically include in each chapter some discussion of the three major theoretical approaches to sociology: functionalism, conflict theory, and interactionism.

Functionalists see society as similar to a living creature. By this they mean that all of the systems (or "organs") of society are interrelated. The life of that society is a result or "function" of the interplay of these systems (for example, religion, the family, the economy, culture). The functionalist is likely to emphasize consensus and stability in a society. A smoothly functioning society is a stable society that is a happy society. While functionalists do not totally ignore change, they tend to deemphasize it and see it as a threat to the functioning of the society, something that disturbs the systems in society. The functionalist believes that each system has a role in preserving the society and that, when functioning properly, its form is best suited for its tasks. Furthermore, systems should mesh without conflict. For the functionalist, conflict should be avoided; it is perceived as dysfunctional because it undermines the existence of society. Thus, it is easy to see why functionalism is often seen as a conservative approach to society, although as a group of talented young sociologists (labeled Neofunctionalists) argue, this conservative bias is not inevitable.

Of course, it is not always easy to see what the function of a social system is; as a result, functionalists distinguish between manifest and latent functions. The *manifest functions* are those that are easily observable. The family has a manifest function in providing for the systematic moral socialization of children. *Latent functions* are those that may be unintended and unseen. Some suggest the family has the latent function of preserving the sexual division of labor, of keeping women out of the work force. The problem with this approach is that one person's latent function may be another's oppression. Functionalism with its orientation toward the status quo may be charged with having an ideological bias in favor of the dominant classes.

Conflict theory contrasts with functionalism. Contemporary society for the conflict theorist leaves a sour taste. Just as consensus is basic to the functionalist, struggle and change are basic to the conflict theorist. This approach emphasizes that the existence of rival groups with contrary interests is inevitable and even healthy by preventing a stagnant society.

The conflict theorist is prone to ask: Who gains from current social arrangements? How are opposing groups trying to change systems or society? In practical terms, these sociologists tend to side with those whom they see as oppressed, so the conflict approach can easily be linked to the social democratic philosophy in its desire for change.

Interactionism, the third major theoretical approach in sociology, is less overtly political than the other two. Interactionism focuses on the relations among individuals and the meanings these relations have for the participants. It suggests that the society has no inherent meaning but that individuals give meaning to events. A gunshot, for example, means nothing by itself; whether it is part of a murder, a prank, a hunting expedition, or a suicide depends on the context. Likewise, a minister and a drill sergeant will define a "curse" in very different terms; it will be the same word but with very different significance, provoking very different reactions. The interactionist believes that meanings can change over time and in negotiation with others. In the recent past, two men hugging in public would have been censured; today such behavior is tolerated. Even those who might condemn this action if they assumed that the two men were gay would quickly change their attitudes if assured that the two were long-lost brothers. Behavior is subject to change in interpretation at a moment's notice.

Crucial to interactionist theory is the belief that human beings have the power to define their own world. Unlike the functionalist and the conflict theorist, who both emphasize structure, the interactionist is likely to point to the power of individuals to create their own sets of meanings. It is because of this emphasis on the power of the individual that we can liken interactionism to libertarianism; although, in this case, because of the generally apolitical stance of interactionism, the connection is tenuous.

After examining each broad sociological concept, there is a general examination of the chapter question. I present some background material that will allow you to make sense of the fuss. Each question is controversial and, while it cannot be dealt with in as much detail as the disputants might provide, I sketch a brief description of the basic issue. That section is followed by a discussion of how proponents of the libertarian, conservative, and social democratic points of view address the question. I have chosen to present the approaches in no particular order, choosing as the first perspective that which seems to be the most vehement about the issue under discussion. This is fair because the order in which one makes an argument affects the way in which an audience will respond. By changing the order of discussion, I provide some semblance of balance.

I do not pretend to have provided an exhaustive treatment of any of these subjects; I hope only to give you enough material for debate and controversy and to make you consider the basis of your own beliefs. I do not encourage you to accept any particular perspective or, for that matter, any of the perspectives. I recognize that Marxism has not been adequately covered; neither have many non-American ideologies. Because of the breadth and diversity of each philosophy, some who hold that view may disagree with portions of my discussion. This may, in part, be due to my errors of understanding, and, in part, may be attributed to the difficulty of describing a complex philosophy in simple terms. In presenting these issues, I have attempted to draw from a wide variety of sources, some of which rarely appear in reputable sociology textbooks. I have chosen quotations that are written in a lively fashion and that capture the essence of an argument in a memorable way. Some of the sources make strange bedfellows, but at least I try to change the sheets frequently.

I then turn to a research case study that relates to the question being discussed. My goal is to demonstrate how various styles and methodologies of research can be used to examine these theoretical questions. While the studies selected represent a variety of approaches to social problems, each is respectable. Even though the assumptions of each will be held up for scrutiny, they represent a collection of the best research studies that sociologists have to offer. (You might wish to read the original version of each of them.) The point I wish to make here is that the debates I present are not mere idle speculations, but are empirical questions that researchers can study. Although the research will not provide a solution, it will help us recognize the dimensions of the problem.

The final section of each chapter connects the sociological concept with the particular question I have addressed. Here I raise the basic issues that underlie the specific question. So, in the chapter that deals with race relations, I ask the possibly horrifying question: What is so wrong with discrimination? It is my belief that unless we understand the foundations of our beliefs, we cannot hold them strongly and steadfastly. While these broad questions are not destined to be answered satisfactorily, at least they have been raised, to fester or flower in your mind and in discussion. Do not forget that sociology ultimately is based on questions of human nature and addresses questions of how the social order should be organized. With that in mind, "Let the wild rumpus start!"

For Further Study

Conservative

Buckley, William F., and Charles R. Kesler, eds. *Keeping the Tablets: Modern American Conservative Thought*. New York: Harper & Row, 1988.
Kirk, Russell, ed. *The Portable Conservative Reader*. New York: Penguin, 1982.
Murray, Charles. *In Pursuit: Of Happiness and Good Government*. New York: Simon & Schuster, 1988.
Nisbet, Robert. *Conservatism*. Minneapolis: University of Minnesota Press, 1986.

Libertarian

Bergland, David. *Libertarianism in One Lesson*. 3rd ed. Costa Mesa, CA: Orpheus Publications, 1986. (Available from Libertarian Party headquarters)
Friedman, Milton. *Capitalism and Freedom*. Chicago: University of Chicago Press, 1962.
Hazlitt, Henry. *Economics in One Lesson*. New York: Arlington House, 1979.

Machan, Tibor R., ed. *The Libertarian Reader*. Totowa, NJ: Rowman and Littlefield, 1982.

Social Democratic

Bellah, Robert N., Richard Madsen, William M. Sullivan, Ann Swidler, and Steven M. Tipton. *The Good Society*. New York: Knopf, 1991.

Galbraith, John Kenneth. *The New Industrial State*. Boston: Houghton Mifflin, 1969.

Mansfield, Harvey C., Jr. *The Spirit of Liberalism*. Cambridge: Harvard University Press, 1978.

Wolfe, Alan. *Whose Keeper?* Berkeley: University of California Press, 1989.

General

Nisbet, Robert. *The Sociological Tradition*. New York: Basic Books, 1966.

Sowell, Thomas. *A Conflict of Visions*. New York: William Morrow, 1987.

Wolfe, Alan, ed. *America at Century's End*. Berkeley: University of California Press, 1991.

Notes and References

1. Thomas Sowell, *A Conflict of Visions* (New York: Morrow, 1987), p. 15.
2. "All That's Not Left Is Not Right," *Reason* (October 1986): 16.
3. Quoted in Mark Paul, "Seducing the Left: The Third Party Wants *You*," *Mother Jones* (May 5, 1980): 47.
4. Ambrose Bierce, *The Devil's Dictionary* (New York: Dover, 1958), p. 24.
5. Robert Nisbet, *The Sociological Tradition* (New York: Basic Books, 1966). See also Everett C. Ladd, Jr., and Seymour Martin Lipset, *The Divided Academy: Professors and Politics* (New York: McGraw-Hill, 1975), pp. 107-115, 369.
6. Russell Kirk, ed. "Introduction." *The Portable Conservative Reader* (New York: Penguin, 1982), p. xiv.
7. Quoted in Thomas Sowell, *A Conflict of Visions* (New York: William Morrow, 1987), p. 34.
8. Ibid., pp. xv-xviii.
9. Thomas Hobbes, *Leviathan* (New York: Collier, 1962; original ed., 1651), p. 100.
10. Kirk, *The Portable Conservative Reader.*, p. xv.
11. Kirk, ibid., p. xvi.
12. President Andrew Jackson's message to Congress vetoing the Bank Bill, July 10, 1832. *Bartlett's Familiar Quotations*, 13th ed. (Boston: Little, Brown, 1955), p. 399.
13. Adlai Stevenson, campaign speech, September 6, 1952, Kasson, Minnesota. *Bartlett's Familiar Quotations*, 13th ed. (Boston: Little, Brown, 1955), p. 1086.

CHAPTER ONE

Culture: Should Elementary School Children Be Taught in Their Native Language?

■ Few concepts have had the longevity and significance in social science writing as has culture. Culture reflects our humanness; it differentiates us from other animals. But what do we mean by *culture*? Among the hundreds, and probably thousands, of definitions that have been put forth, American anthropologist Melville Herskovits defines culture in this general fashion: "Culture is essentially a construct that describes the total body of belief, behavior, knowledge, sanctions, values, and goals that mark the way of life of any people. That is, though a culture may be treated by the student as capable of objective description, in the final analysis it comprises the things that people have, the things they do, and what they think."[1]

This vastly broad definition suggests that culture is fluid. Within a society, it can include material artifacts (such as the flag or works of art), behaviors (hand-shaking or kissing), or social expectations (the norm of fairness). This last category has two important aspects: norms and values. *Norms* refer to rules that specify appropriate and inappropriate behavior, the *shared expectations* that people have of each other. *Values* refer to those *shared conceptions* that are used to evaluate the desirability or correctness of objects, acts, feelings, ideas, or events. In understanding norms and values, however, we should not assume that they are universally accepted, nor need they be consciously understood. According to interactionist theory, both values and norms are abstractions. People, say the interactionists, do not behave as they do because they are consciously or deliberately attempting to follow a set of rules, rather they do what seems best in the specific situation in which they find themselves. Although the concepts of values and norms are useful for social scientists who search for regularities in behavior (for instance, people behave *as if* these things exist), they may not tell us *why* people behave as they do.

Culture is not an innate part of human nature; it must be learned, even though it is made possible by our biological equipment. Socialization, the process of learning a society's culture, is critical to human development. From about age two to about age fourteen, a child is transformed from an egocentric savage into a responsible, civilized human being—a most remarkable change in only a dozen years.

Another remarkable aspect of culture is its diversity. Behaviors and norms that are appropriate in one society are inappropriate in others. Some societies venerate people who are obese; others give special treatment to those who are thin. In some societies the young are revered, in others the old are given deference. In some, twins are given a place of honor; other societies see twins as a curse. These marked differences between societies raise an important issue: Are there cultural traditions that are universally moral or are particular cultural traditions right for each particular society? This is the distinction between *cultural absolutism* and *cultural relativism*. Should we say that things like racism or infanticide are absolutely wrong, or should we refrain from making these judgments? If we cannot say that another culture is acting immorally, how can we set any standards for ourselves? If everything is right, then, by implication, nothing is wrong. Although most social scientists would grant that different societies can have different traditions, few deny all standards of moral propriety.

No aspect of culture is more important than language. One of the most tragic stories in the Bible is that of the Tower of Babel, in which the previously monolingual humanity was transformed into hundreds of groups of people who spoke mutually incomprehensible languages. Historically, we have had only modest success trying to understand each other.

The study of language suggests that it shapes the way in which people see the world. This approach to the social effects of language on thought and perception is known as the *linguistic relativity hypothesis*, or the *Sapir-Whorf hypothesis*, after the two American linguists who stated it the most emphatically.[2] Any group develops specialized vocabulary for those topics that are important to it. Here are some simple examples of how culture and language are related: While many outside the snow belt have a limited vocabulary for talking about "this white stuff," the Central Alaskan Yupik Eskimos have at least a dozen words for snow (or several dozen if one is liberal about what counts).[3] The Hanunoo people in the Philippines have names for ninety-two different varieties of rice. Even the color spectrum is viewed very differently by different groups.[4] Linguistic relativists suggest that people admit some things to their consciousness (they "see" them) while filtering out other things for which they do not have words. According to this theory, language is not only a basic means by which culture and information are communicated, but it also structures the way in which we experience the world.

■ Question:

Should Elementary School Children Be Taught in Their Native Language?

By the year 2000 it is expected that the largest minority group in the United States will be Hispanic[5]—Americans whose native language is not English but Spanish. Between 1986 and the year 2000, the Hispanic labor force is projected to increase by 74 percent! The 1990 census listed 22 million Hispanics; that figure may more than double to 47 million by 2020. Hispanic Americans, because of their numbers and the seeming unwillingness of many to give up their native culture and become "Americanized," pose special problems for American society. Although many Hispanics can be distinguished from "majority" Americans by their brown skins, perhaps their most distinctive feature as a minority group is language. Should they be encouraged to keep their first language as their primary language or should they be forced to make the transition to English?

The problem of linguistic unity in a nation is not unique to the United States. Canada provides an example of the tensions that a battle over language can produce. In nations such as Belgium and India, language has been a festering problem for years. Some nations (Switzerland, most notably) have several language groups that live in relative harmony, but this is more the exception than the rule. Many people believe that a crucial part of nationhood is a single national language; a common language reflects a common unity. Carll Tucker, editor of the New York-based opinion journal *Saturday Review*, frustrated by his polyglot neighbors, writes:

> If America does have a purpose, as our founders and most subsequent generations have heartily believed, then America has the right and obligation to demand certain contributions and sacrifices from its citizens beyond those that are required simply to maintain the peace and fund government operations. We have the right, for instance, to require a stint of government service, wartime or not. We have the right to require the teaching of American history, the pledging of allegiance, the observance of national holidays. And we have the right to require the learning of our national language in schools.[6]

As J. R. Joelson writes in *The Humanist*, "English is the language of our political freedom."[7]

The controversy of communicating with people who speak a different language and who share the same land is not new. One of the first books printed in the Massachusetts Bay Colony was a translation of the Bible into the Algonkian speech of local Indians. But by the mid-eighteenth century, Benjamin Franklin was so concerned about the influx of German speakers into Pennsylvania that he wrote: "Why should the [German] boors be suffered to swarm in our settlements and, by herding together, establish their language and manners to the exclusion of ours? Why should Pennsylvania, founded by the English, become a colony of *aliens*, who will shortly be so numerous as to germanize us instead of our anglifying them?"[8]

Americans' ambivalence toward incorporating foreigners was evident during the War of Independence when the Continental Congress sought support from German Americans by printing the articles of confederation in German.[9] The tension between those who wanted English adopted as the official language in the United States and those who were willing to grant the legal importance of other languages continued throughout the nineteenth century.[10] In 1840, for example, the state of Ohio explicitly sanctioned German-English schools. Minnesota printed its constitution in German, Swedish, Norwegian, and French; and, prior to the Civil War, Louisiana allowed the use of both French and English in its legislature and courts. Yet, the Congress, on several occasions, refused to publish important public documents in German during this period.

Although the roots of the movement began earlier with increases in immigration from southern and eastern Europe, World War I seems to be the point at which the opposition to second languages in America became more intense.[11] In 1917, former President Theodore Roosevelt drafted and circulated a statement, signed by prominent Americans of a variety of backgrounds, that reflects the sentiment at the time:

> We must have but one flag. We must also have but one language. This must be the language of the Declaration of Independence, of Washington's Farewell Address, of Lincoln's Gettysburg Speech and Second Inaugural. We cannot tolerate any attempt to oppose or supplant the language and culture that has come down to us from the builders of this republic with the language and culture of any European country. The greatness of this nation depends on the swift assimilation of the aliens she welcomes to her shores. Any force which attempts to retard that assimilative process is a force hostile to the highest interests of this country.[12]

At the same time that Americans were becoming more nationalistic and passing restrictive immigration laws, they were limiting education to English. Nebraska outlawed the use of foreign languages in elementary schools, while the town of Findlay, Ohio, imposed a fine of twenty-five dollars for using German on the street.[13] Throughout their history, Americans have been of two minds about the use of second languages in schools and political institutions.

After World War II, and particularly during the last three decades, the United States has accepted a large number of Hispanic immigrants. This immigration is posing challenges similar to the immigration of Germans that Benjamin Franklin worried about two centuries earlier. In parts of the

United States—southern Florida, southern Texas, New Mexico, and southern California—it is almost as likely for someone to hear a conversation in Spanish as in English. Miami, in fact, has become an international finance center for all of Latin America.

With the large influx of Spanish-speaking people by the 1960s, the pendulum began to swing back toward a greater acceptance of the value of teaching children in their native languages. In 1968 Congress passed Title VII of the Elementary and Secondary Education Act (also known as the Bilingual Education Act). This act provided funding for projects that would meet the special problems of children (mostly, but not exclusively, Hispanic) with limited English-speaking ability. Many people involved in implementing this act did not see the language children used at home as merely transitional, but rather the use of their first language was a way to promote linguistic and cultural pride by improving their cultural awareness and their native language skills.[14] This act was strengthened considerably by a 1974 Supreme Court decision in the case of *Lau* v. *Nichols*, which stated that communities had the constitutional requirement to provide students with appropriate education, despite English deficiencies. The Court, however, did not specify how this must be done. Since then the number of limited-English children has increased enormously to the point where 153 languages are represented in our nation's schoolrooms,[15] although blessedly not 153 separate bilingual programs.

There are several ways in which non-English-speaking children can learn English. First, as was once common, immigrant children could be thrown in an English language class and allowed to sink or swim. Many swam, of course, particularly when the community shared a cultural value that children should learn the language of their adopted land. But many suffered. A second approach is called English as a Second Language (ESL), in which the student is intensively trained in English without reliance on his or her native language. The child takes instruction in other subjects in English, but he or she has a special class in English-language skills. The third approach is bilingual education (sometimes called bilingual-bicultural education), which was defined by the director of the U.S. Commission on Civil Rights as "an instructional program in which two languages—English and the native tongue—are used as mediums of instruction and in which the cultural background of the students is incorporated into the curriculum."[16] This method teaches children in their native language, while slowly teaching them English.

One obvious question is which of these programs works best for the 3.5 million "limited-English" schoolchildren. Unfortunately, the answer is not equally obvious. Some bilingual education programs seem to work, whereas others do not.[17] One U.S. Office of Education study indicates that children deficient in English are not acquiring it through bilingual education and that many of the programs are in fact aimed at maintaining a separate language and culture.[18] A tabulation of studies by Christine Rossell finds that 71 percent of the studies show no benefits or actually demonstrate harms of bilingualism, although a 29 percent success rate is for some impressive.[19]

Perhaps not surprisingly, by the late 1970s and early 1980s something of a backlash against bilingualism occurred. In 1980 in Dade County, Florida, voters, by a 3 to 2 margin, repealed a statute that had established Spanish as the county's *official* second language. In 1981, then California senator S. I. Hayakawa introduced a constitutional amendment making English "the official language of the United States," which, if passed, would eliminate the possibility of official second languages. In the 1988 elections, the states of Florida, Arizona, and Colorado—all states with many Hispanic residents—decided that English would be the official language in those states. With these three states, there is a total of seventeen states that have adopted some version of the Hayakawa proposal.

The Conservative Point of View

Surely one cannot deny, argues the conservative, that success in America requires fluency in English. English is part of the tradition and heritage of the United States. America has always been a melting pot—an ethnic fondue—in which immigrants with widely different backgrounds were melted into Americans. Even black Americans have in all important regards left their African roots behind and are culturally Americans (even if they have a distinctive subculture). For the conservative, the existence of two competing languages is divisive and ultimately debilitating.

Nathan Glazer, a leading neo-conservative critic of bilingual-bicultural education, warns against cultural disunity. "Bilingual-bicultural education" comments Glazer, "prevents the development of a common culture, a common loyalty, a common allegiance. . . . It is the unity-divisiveness argument, the belief that this is a better country because people from many countries and with many languages were turned into people having loyalty to one country and speaking one language."[20] He is further worried about the new Hispanic immigrants who may have only a fleeting and uncertain attachment to this country. Glazer wonders if "undocumented aliens" really wish to become Americanized, or whether they hope to return to their country of birth at some later date.

The conservative suggests that belonging to a society does not diminish a person's sense of heritage or ethnic self-worth; indeed, it may have exactly the opposite result. Consider the comments of Mexican-

American writer Richard Rodriguez, who was forced to learn English in parochial school:

> Bilingual educators say today that children lose a degree of "individuality" by becoming assimilated into public society. . . . [They] do not realize that, while one suffers a diminished sense of private individuality by being assimilated into public society, such assimilation makes possible the achievement of public individuality. . . . Those middle-class ethnics who scorn assimilation seem to me filled with decadent self-pity, obsessed by the burden of public life. Dangerously, they romanticize public separateness and trivialize the dilemma of those who are truly socially disadvantaged.[21]

If someone cannot speak English, Rodriguez suggests, it is inevitable that most people will stereotype him or her as "just another Latino"; speaking the dominant language gives one the opportunity to participate meaningfully in public life—without requesting or demanding special treatment.[22] Conservative columnist George Will concurs: "Bilingualism, by suggesting that there is no duty to acquire the primary instrument of public discourse, further dilutes the idea of citizenship. . . . Americans should say diverse things, but in a language that allows universal participation in the discussion."[23]

The conservative also offers southern and eastern European immigrants as examples of groups that have been successfully "stewed" in the melting pot. The United States' public school system was great, according to this view, because it took all these "disadvantaged" children with conflicting cultures and, after twelve years, turned them into Americans. Conservatives note that although bilingualism might appear to help immigrants at first, eventually it prevents them from moving into the economic mainstream. "Learning English" says former senator Hayakawa, "has been the primary task of every immigrant group for two centuries. Participation in the common language has rapidly made available to each new group the political and economic benefits of American society. Those who have mastered English have overcome the major hurdle to full participation in our democracy."[24]

While conservatives may overly romanticize the experience of being an immigrant in the public school system, they are arguing against the curious proposal of those who support bilingualism—that we should maintain two separate school systems. Essentially, this calls for a segregation of people who speak a different language in a way that would be illegal if they were a different race. Conservatives recognize that Hispanics have real and significant problems, but they do not believe these people are unique, nor do their problems warrant the creation of a nation permanently divided by language.

The Social Democratic Point of View

Although many social democrats support bilingual education, others do not. Agreeing with some of the conservative arguments, some social democrats contend that bilingualism is harmful to the nation and to the individual child and is not a "liberal" issue.[25] Indeed, the large majority of Americans oppose bilingualism. In 1980, a Gallup Poll asked, "Many families who come from other countries have children who cannot speak English. Should or should not these children be required to learn English in special classes before they are enrolled in the public schools?" By a margin of 82 to 13 Americans responded that they should learn English first.[26] In 1988, Los Angeles teachers opposed bilingual education by a 78 to 22 margin.[27]

Yet, despite this vox populi, there are arguments in favor of bilingualism. It is clear that prior to the emergence of the bilingual movement, public schools were not training Hispanic youngsters well. Only 30 percent of the Hispanic students in the United States completed high school, and in urban ghetto areas, the dropout rate may have been as high as 85 percent.[28] Most of these students did not have the opportunity to participate in bilingual programs.

The leaders of the Hispanic community typically support bilingual education; some Hispanics feel that in many ways bilingual education is their "civil rights act." Social democrats see no harm in helping groups of people that have special problems, and bilingual education is such a case. Bilingual supporter Kenji Hakuta notes that "the most significant thing about bilingual education is not that it promotes bilingualism, but rather that it gives some measure of official public status to the political struggle of language minorities, primarily Hispanics." He argues that the cultural and political components are as important as the linguistic.[29]

Supporters of this program see the United States consumed by "lingui-chauvinism," an attitude, which in its own way, is as debilitating as racism. Carey McWilliams, the former editor of the liberal opinion journal *The Nation* writes:

> Whenever a majority has insisted on a rigid monolingualism, it has generally meant that language was being used as a strategy for keeping the minority in its place. The effect has often been to stimulate the nationalism of minorities. . . . If a majority wants to avoid . . . divisive movements, then it should opt for a policy of intelligent bilingualism as a means, first, of permitting the minority to preserve its cultural heritage and, second, of enabling it to make the best use of the official language as a means of improving its lot. Any attempt to suppress or discourage the minority's language is likely to stimulate separatist tendencies.[30]

Many social democrats feel that a multilingual society could be a culturally rich, free, and happy one. Social democrats question whether it is necessary to maintain cultural imperialism or impose uniformity on a nation; if there is mutual respect for all cultures, people can live in harmony and borrow the best from each culture.

The question is a good one: Why must we enforce cultural uniformity? Sanford Levinson, an instructor in politics at Princeton, lays open the question of whether a society can exist as a collection of dissimilar groups:

> It is obviously open to question whether it is legitimate to expect all American citizens to master English, especially if the numbers of Spanish speakers are large enough. . . . Does the government, whether state or Federal, have a duty to print its materials in Spanish as well as English? Does it deny equal protection of the laws by assuming that all American citizens are responsible for knowing English? . . . To accept the premises of strong bilingualism means accepting the fact that large numbers of one's fellow citizens simply have no desire (or ability) to communicate in the most effective manner possible—the speaking of a common language. It means an ultimate rejection of the premise that we are indeed a united nation in favor of the recognition that we are congeries of groups joined together, often uneasily, in a political alliance.[31]

This is a somewhat extreme position, but it is consistent with the view of the American Republic as a confederation of states. It assumes that each group should be given as much freedom as it needs to gain equality for itself and its members. For those who support interest-group politics, like social democrats, the fact that Hispanic leaders generally support bilingualism is a potent argument. The assumption that bilingual-bicultural education (even one that is less extreme and does teach English) protects a group's cultural heritage and self-respect matters to the social democrat; the minority group is the best judge of what is necessary to ensure its own equality.

The Libertarian Point of View

Extreme libertarians are suspicious about the role of public schools, so more government involvement in this area only serves to increase this basic suspicion. In theory, the libertarian has no objection to any particular form of private education (providing the student is willing to accept the consequences), and since private schools should be free to do as they wish bilingualism is acceptable. Many Hispanics do attend private Catholic schools that could offer bilingual programs if they wished. Others attend "for-profit" schools to learn English. Libertarians doubt the effectiveness of bilingualism since it removes Hispanics from the mainstream of American social and political life, but they believe that people can do what they wish, as long as it does not infringe on other people's rights.

Libertarians are particularly concerned that this program is a matter of political expediency with little accountability and critical evaluation. The program is seen by some as a sop thrown to Hispanic activists—a jobs program, rather than an educational one. Author Abigail Thernstrom agrees with this assertion. She writes that "support for bilingual instruction, particularly among Hispanic activists, has not lessened. And the reason is clear: the programs provide both employment and political opportunities, as schools are forced to hire Hispanics without regular teaching credentials, and as students are molded into an ethnically conscious constituency."[32] Luis Acle, Jr., director of Hispanics for English Language Proficiency, concurs, noting that "bilingual education is not an education program, it's an employment program. Schools get additional funding in direct proportion to the number of children in bilingual programs. So there's a built-in incentive to keep children there and an incentive to keep children from achieving English proficiency."[33] Although some defend the hiring of Hispanics on the grounds of providing needed role models for Latino children, particularly in the primary grades, this disturbs the libertarian who sees another large bureaucratic project without clear educational objectives, but with a Department of Education price tag of over a hundred million dollars each year.

Another concern for the libertarian is that a policy is being developed at the behest of one group (primarily Mexican Americans) and is being applied to everyone, whether or not they want it. They see some advocates insisting that children be forced into such programs. Nathan Glazer strongly condemns the idea of bilingualism for this reason.

> We suffer from the fact that these policies are being developed and imposed by national bureaucracies, applying their own rules, and by federal courts, and that important distinctions between groups and what they think is best for them will be ignored. One way of taking into account these differences between groups and within groups is to make these programs, in greater measure than they are, voluntary. In the case of the New York City consent judgement, there was an unsettling dispute in which the plaintiff lawyers . . . wanted to require students deemed to need bilingual education under the test developed to take it, despite the opposition of some Spanish-speaking parents. Fortunately Judge Marvin Frankel rejected this demand. A true voluntarism will permit each child or its parents to select what they think is best.[34]

If we do need school systems, libertarians believe they should be systems that permit as much freedom of choice as possible for the students.

Hispanic Education and Social Research

Many Hispanic youngsters do not do very well in school. Why? One explanation is to blame "them" for not having the same values that "we" have. Such a view is convenient—at least if you are one of "us" and not one of "them"—but it may overlook certain crucial pieces of information such as student perceptions.

How can we find out what these kids "really" think? One method is to spend time with them. This rather obvious technique of sociological investigation is known as *participant observation*. In using this technique, sociologists enter the community and attempt to join the activity they wish to study. They can either join by pretending to be a member of the group (such as getting hired on a construction job or joining a gang of pickpockets) or by informing the group that they wish to spend time with them. Although journalists sometimes observe people or groups, the sociological observer typically is interested in more than merely describing the setting to outsiders; he or she wants to discover sociological principles that transcend the observational setting.

Sociologists have been observing poor urban communities for many years. Originally, the concern was to examine what was patronizingly called "social disorganization," which suggested that these people or their communities were "disorganized." Actually, poor neighborhoods are as organized as suburbs; it is just that the organization is somewhat different. One of the best recent studies of the urban poor is Ruth Horowitz's *Honor and the American Dream*. Horowitz, as a young graduate student at the University of Chicago, spent several years observing the behavior of young Chicano men and women in one of the poorest areas of Chicago, a community that she calls 32nd Street. Horowitz explained to the members of the community that she was interested in the lives of the young people who lived in this area. Eventually, she was accepted as someone who could be told things in confidence—even by gang members.

One of the major themes of Horowitz's book is the ambivalence that these young men and women feel toward traditional American values. Horowitz demonstrates that while these Chicanos are *not* hostile toward American values, there are other local community and cultural values that prevent them from capitalizing on the American Dream. Consider this description of the junior high school graduation of some of the gang members:

> Wearing their caps and gowns, the more than four hundred eighth grade graduates arrived in yellow school buses at the new downtown auditorium. . . . All were dressed for the occasion, the graduates in new dresses or suits, the family members in their best clothes. Many of the parents took the day off from work. . . . After the speeches and award announcements each

student's name was called as everyone clapped. The loudest, and the most prolonged cheers were for each of the graduating Lions. Fifteen of the Lions attended the graduation wearing their gang sweaters. That evening they had a celebration in the park.[35]

Evidently education was valued and supported by these adolescents' peer culture. So how did this positive feeling toward education become a set of negative expectations, leading to a 70 percent dropout rate? While the answer is too complex to do justice to here, Horowitz identifies competing pressures that helped assure a high dropout rate among the Chicano youths she studied. First, many of the teachers came from very different cultural backgrounds and expected little from these youths. One teacher, for example, confided in Horowitz that it was her job to "tame the natives."[36] The schools required little homework, and many teachers were satisfied if the students were merely quiet. But the blame was not only placed on the teachers—the world of the streets spilled into the school corridors; guns were a frequent part of the school environment; knives were even more common. Some youths in the community did not respect schooling and charged the school atmosphere with tension and, occasionally, violence. Most young men felt that defending their "honor" took priority over other cultural values. And their lack of English-language skills posed a major problem. Finally, many students questioned whether it made economic sense to graduate from high school, particularly if they were only "average" students in a "below average" school. They knew that some high school graduates earned as little as some dropouts. The young women also wondered why they should complete high school if their real goal was matrimony.

Although Horowitz is not concerned with bilingual education as such, she effectively demonstrates some of the problems of students who are ambivalent about the basic values of American education. The Chicano values, which focus on honor and reputation, easily come into conflict with the traditional American value structure, which emphasizes the long-term benefits of education. Supporters of bilingualism are inclined to argue that these other cultural values must be taken into account in any successful educational program, whereas opponents of bilingual education suggest that success in education has always depended upon adopting the traditional values over and above one's own. Traditionalists have not had much success in converting these students because they ask them to reject the values in their community. However, bilingual educators have not been completely successful in demonstrating that they can merge the two value systems.

Horowitz's approach to sociology is basically interactionism. That is, she believes that individuals have a large role in shaping their own lives.

She also emphasizes that it is improper to lump all of the members of the community together:

> While the failure to finish school does place significant limits on job pos-
> sibilities, it does not mean that youths have given up completely their hopes
> of achieving the American dream of economic success. Nor does the school
> system's failure to provide the mechanisms to develop the competitive ethic
> mean that youths do not mature into competent and steady workers. The
> problem that many youths face is the constant gap between their desire to do
> well and the lack of opportunities. Some confront this problem, while others
> continue to hedge their bets.[37]

By singling out some as "confronting this problem" and others as "hedging their bets," she seems to emphasize individual freedom. Yet, it would be a mistake to see this "hands-off" approach as condemning any public involvement. Horowitz is critical of the educational system and makes it clear that she believes schooling can and should be improved, especially with input from the community. Horowitz sees what occurs in the school as very important for the adult lives these adolescents will lead. Policy decisions that affect the classroom also affect the streets.

Culture and Bilingualism

Can a society remain stable and free when it has more than one major cultural tradition? Most societies have many cultural strands, with one typically predominating. Most nations choose (consciously or implicitly) which symbols and language will represent them to each other and to the outside world. Countries and organizations that have attempted to be bilingual, such as Canada or the United Nations, have found that one language has dominated either in law or in practice, often causing tension for the whole system. Only a few small nations, most notably Switzerland, have shown that harmony can exist within a confederacy of different languages. Although all nations have within their borders a wide variety of ethnic, regional, economic, and occupational subcultures, there is usually a national "culture" in which most people participate. In the United States, such common cultural elements include the concept of America as a melting pot, Paul Revere's midnight ride, the fireworks on the Fourth of July, and the flag. These cultural traditions reflect how we see our nation. A nation's culture reflects its soul; bilingualism raises the question of whether the United States can remain the United States with two large language communities that cannot—or will not—communicate with each other.

Ultimately, bilingualism raises the question of social cohesion. Sociologists differ over how much consensus of values, beliefs, and culture is necessary in a happy, well-functioning society. Critics of bilingual education (especially when it threatens to produce two different language communities) claim that uniformity is healthy and functional, while conflict is by its nature dysfunctional. Conflict theorists (who tend to be oriented toward the social democratic point of view) see social differences and disagreements as potentially healthy because they prevent a society from becoming static. They much prefer the image of a stew pot to a melting pot.

Everyone agrees that true bilingualism is beneficial. If everyone could speak several languages, Americans would be able to communicate better with each other, and multilingualism would permit us to compete better in the world economic market. Although many Japanese businessmen speak English well, few Americans can speak Japanese.

But this chapter has not addressed true bilingualism. The real goal of today's bilingual education is not to permit most Americans to speak two languages, but rather to retain and develop the culture and language of an immigrant group. We are not attempting, in any significant way, to have Anglo children learn Spanish. America chooses to define itself as a nation with a single language and a dominant culture; second languages and cultures are welcome only so long as they realize they are second.

Questions

1. Should the public schools teach children in their native tongues?
2. Are Americans lingui-chauvinists?
3. Why are Hispanics so vehement about bilingual-bicultural education, whereas most other immigrant groups are not?
4. Why is the American public so opposed to bilingual education?
5. How important is learning English to being successful in the United States?
6. Should parents have the option of deciding if their children should be in bilingual classes or should it be on the basis of language test scores?
7. Is it important for an ethnic group to maintain a sense of its "roots"?
8. Can a multicultural, multilingual society survive and be stable?
9. Should the government have the obligation to provide an education for students who do not have the ability to speak English?

For Further Study

"Bilingualism: A Symposium." *The Nation* (March 17, 1979): 263–266.

Hakuta, Kenji. *Mirror of Language: The Debate on Bilingualism*. New York: Basic Books, 1986.

Porter, Rosalie Pedalino. *Forked Tongue: The Politics of Bilingual Education*. New York: Basic Books, 1990.

Rodriguez, Richard. "Aria: A Memoir of a Bilingual Childhood." *American Scholar* 50(Winter 1980–1981): 25–42.

Special Issue, "English Plus: Issues in Bilingual Education." *Annals of the American Academy of Political and Social Sciences*, 508 (March 1990).

Symposium on "The New Bilingualism." *Society* (November/December 1981): 29–62.

Thernstrom, Abigail M. "Bilingual Miseducation." *Commentary* (February 1990): 44–48.

Notes and References

1. Melville J. Herskovits, *Man and His Works* (New York: Knopf, 1948), p. 625.
2. See Edward Sapir, *Selected Writings in Language, Culture, and Personality* (Berkeley: University of California Press, 1949); Benjamin Whorf, *Language, Thought, and Reality* (Cambridge: MIT Press, 1956).
3. Geoffrey K. Pullum (*The Great Eskimo Vocabulary Hoax* [Chicago: University of Chicago Press, 1991], pp. 159–171) provides an amusing and provocative discussion of this claim. Whatever the precise number of "snow-related" words among the Inuit and Americans, there is no doubt that peoples who specialize tend to create more terms for what they specialize in.
4. Verne F. Ray, "Techniques and Problems in the Study of Human Color Perception." *Southwestern Journal of Anthropology* 8(Autumn 1952): 251–258.
5. Although there are a number of terms used to describe Spanish-speaking Americans, I will use the term *Hispanic* as the most general but least cumbersome term.
6. Carll Tucker, "English Spoken Here." *Saturday Review* (May 12, 1979): 56.
7. J. R. Joelson, "English: The Language of Liberty." *The Humanist* (July/August 1989): 35.
8. Stephen T. Wagner, "America's Non-English Heritage." *Society* (November/December 1981): 37.
9. Ibid., p. 37.
10. Ibid., pp. 36–40.
11. Ibid., p. 41.
12. Ibid., p. 41.
13. Ibid., p. 41.
14. Ibid., p. 43.
15. Rosalie Pedalino Porter, "Language Trap: No English, No Future." *The Washington Post* (April 22, 1990): B3.
16. Susan Gilbert Schneider, *Revolution, Reaction or Reform: The 1974 Bilingual Education Act* (New York: L. A. Publishing Company, 1976), p. 2.

17. Jim Cummings, "The Language and Culture Issue in the Education of Minority Language Children." *Interchange* 10(1979–1980): 72–88.
18. Abigail Thernstrom, "Bilingual Mis-education." *The New Republic* (April 18, 1981): 17.
19. Abigail Thernstrom, "Bilingual Miseducation." *Commentary* 89(February 1990): 44–48.
20. Nathan Glazer, "Pluralism and the New Immigrants." *Society* (November-December 1981): 34.
21. Richard Rodriguez, "Aria: A Memoir of a Bilingual Childhood." *The American Scholar* 50(Winter 1980–81): 34–35.
22. Ibid., pp. 29–30.
23. George Will, "In Defense of the Mother Tongue." *Newsweek* (July 8, 1985): 78.
24. *The Congressional Record* (April 27, 1981): S3998.
25. Thernstrom, 1981, "Bilingual Mis-education," p. 16.
26. "Crisis of Confidence in Public Schools Continues." *The Gallup Opinion Index*, No. 180 (August 1980): 13.
27. Porter, "Language Trap," p. B3.
28. Isabel Schon, "It is the Primary Job of American Schools to Teach Students the Language of their Country which is, after all, English: Con," *English Journal* 70 (February 1981): 9.
29. Porter, "Language Trap," p. B3; Kenji Hakuta and Eugene Garcia, "Bilingualism and Education," *American Psychologist* 44 (February 1989): 374–379.
30. Carey McWilliams, "Bilingualism: A Symposium." *The Nation* (March 17, 1979): 263.
31. Sanford Levinson, "Bilingualism: A Symposium." *The Nation* (March 17, 1979): 263–264.
32. Thernstrom, 1981, "Bilingual Mis-education," p. 16.
33. Luis Acle, Jr., "Bilingual Education," *Los Angeles Times* (March 3, 1991): M7.
34. Glazer, "Pluralism and the New Immigrants," p. 36.
35. Ruth Horowitz, *Honor and the American Dream: Culture and Identity in a Chicano Community* (New Brunswick, NJ: Rutgers University Press, 1983), p. 137.
36. Ibid., p. 146.
37. Ibid., p. 158.

CHAPTER TWO

Socialization: Should Parents Be Allowed to Hit Their Children However They Wish?

■ British folklorist Douglas Newton once remarked that "the worldwide fraternity of children is the greatest of savage tribes, and the only one which shows no signs of dying out."[1] Despite the affront to our vanity, Newton's point is crucial for understanding how sociologists view the process by which human beings mature. When we enter this complex and confusing world, we are nothing but a bundle of cute and complicated biological mechanisms; we are not social beings. We must be trained to live in a world in which we have been placed without our consent.

We are "uncivilized." Our guardians, especially our parents, are given the formidable challenge of making us into responsible Americans, Britons, Poles, Dominicans, Nigerians, or Vietnamese. Within these nationalities, we are taught to be Black Americans, Scots, Moslems, Hottentots, socialists, or upper class. Finally, but not least important, we must learn to fit into the culture of our family. Socialization is the process by which an infant human child is shaped into a responsible, mature adult. *Primary socialization* is the learning that occurs through the core institutions of society, most particularly the family, and occurs largely, although not entirely, during childhood. *Secondary socialization* typically refers to more specific, formal training, such as learning one's occupation or how to behave properly in some public association.

Socialization results from a combination of factors—biological and social. Often children are unable to learn a task or skill until they are biologically ready. Most parents at some time or another become frustrated in raising their children because the child seems unwilling to master something that the parents are sure the child "should" be able to do. Ask any parent about toilet training. Despite the parent's frustration, the child is probably not so much unwilling to learn as not ready to learn. Experts in child development look at this biological readiness in terms of a series of stages through which each child will pass. These stages involve not only such obviously biological factors such as bladder control, but intellectual skills as well. Swiss child psychologist Jean Piaget has argued that there is a series of intellectual or cognitive stages that a child will reach. For instance, until children reach approximately the age of seven, it is difficult to teach them that the larger of two objects need not be the heavier (a pound of feathers versus a pound of lead).[2] When they reach the appropriate stage (what Piaget terms the "concrete operational stage") such a connection becomes obvious.

At times children seem like information vacuum cleaners. Even a youngster who does not do well in school frequently picks up other kinds of knowledge and can become a street performance virtuoso or mechanical wizard. Learning is as natural as breathing, although what is learned is not always what parents wish to be learned. For this reason, parents strive to set up reward/cost systems so that it is in the child's interest to do what the parents want. The fact that children consider the consequences of their actions, and eventually internalize the rewards and punishments, supports a behavioristic (or Skinnerian) understanding of socialization. Many people believe reinforcement does change behavior. Parents are constantly orchestrating a dance of treats and punishments to direct the behavior of their offspring, including using physical force.

Through socialization children learn who they are. They become familiar with the core of personality: the self. The self is what people believe makes them special, different from everyone else, uniquely themselves. Development of the self-concept is too complicated to explain completely here, but some aspects should be mentioned. Perhaps most important from a sociological viewpoint is the recognition that the development of the self is a social process. American social psychologist Charles Horton Cooley recognized that we come to know ourselves after we know others. In other words, our self-concept is a function of the "reflection" of others. We discover how others view us and eventually we see our selves in the same or similar ways. If others see us as great beauties or unendurable prigs, we will use these attitudes to build our own self-concept. Cooley refers to this as *the looking-glass self*.[3] George Herbert Mead,[4] a prominent American philosopher and social psychologist, extended this by emphasizing the importance of role taking. This is the process by which children come to internalize the expectations that others have of them. By understanding how others see them, children can shape their behavior to be perceived in a favorable light. Later children expand their role taking to include the expectations of large groups or of the entire society; Mead called this skill "taking the role of the generalized other."[5] The acquisition of these skills helps people to "present" themselves in desirable ways—a technique that sociologist Erving Goffman has labeled "impression management."[6] This skill is largely mastered by the time a child reaches adolescence, although it has roots much earlier, stretching back to infancy.

■ Question:

Should Parents Be Allowed to Hit Their Children However They Wish?

All studies of American child-rearing practices indicate that corporal punishment has been and remains a common form of discipline. In these studies (particularly studies of younger children), three quarters or more of those who answer admit to punishing their child physically. A recent survey finds that 65 percent of American adults approve of spanking children as a form of discipline.[7] The parent who claims *never* to have hit his or her child is either a saint or, more likely, a liar, and is certainly a deviant.[8] Hitting children is part of the American way of life, and, yet, consider one mother's account of what happens when this "normal" behavior gets out of control: "I started abusing my boy because he was an accident and a screamer. When he was four months old, I hit him so hard my engagement ring carved a deep bloody furrow across his soft face. His screams shattered my heart. I sank to the floor with self-loathing. Then I held him tightly in my arms, so tight he turned blue. I told him he had to do his share. Why didn't he stop screaming? Deep down, I knew he couldn't understand. But I also thought he was doing it on purpose."[9] This account could make you want to cry for and to strangle this woman all at once. The publicity accorded to the sadistic death of six-year-old Lisa Steinberg in a filthy apartment in a fashionable New York City neighborhood by a father who was an attorney and a mother who was a children's book editor reminds us that child abuse is not limited to the impoverished.

As anyone who reads the newspaper knows, there seems to be an epidemic of child abuse in the United States. Statistics on its extent vary so widely that we do not know how widespread the problem is nor do we know if it has increased in recent years. Figures for the number of abused children each year range from 650,000 to a million to six million. We learn that 2.2 million cases of child abuse were reported in 1986, but we do not know how many of these cases were unfounded and how many cases were missed. We simply do not have very good ways of measuring the problem, nor do we have an agreement on the definition of "child abuse." Some researchers include any form of corporal punishment as family violence, which would probably label all of us as abusers; others allow welts and bruises as part of normal, strict parental discipline. Of course, if even one child dies because of the neglect or abuse of a parent (and, according to the

National Committee of Child Abuse, the figure was 1,300 in 1986),[10] this is cause for alarm.

Many sociological studies that attempt to measure child abuse or violence in the family use broad definitions that include any kind of physical action, including slapping and shoving. This broad definition, while alerting us to the possibility of serious abuse in families, equivalent to legal definitions of assault, also suggests to some that the figures on child abuse are so inflated as to be meaningless. Although much remains to be studied, there are some things we know about family violence. First, there is a cycle of violence; those who had violent and abusive childhoods have an increased probability of being violent and abusive as parents and engaging in violent crimes. Second, family violence is directly related to the amount of stress on a family and to the extent of its social isolation. Although both strict discipline and child abuse are found in all economic classes, both are relatively more common among poor families.[11] Finally, there is some evidence that a philosophy of strict and humiliating corporal punishment is moving out of favor and is being replaced by a philosophy that emphasizes permissiveness and the control of anger.[12] Nevertheless, we face a cruel paradox. As civilized people, we react with disgust when we hear of some atrocity, violent or sexual, that has been perpetrated on a child. And probably we can all agree with Sergeant Dick Ramon, head of the sex-crimes division of the Seattle police department, when he says, "Child abuse is the ultimate crime, the ultimate betrayal."[13] Yet most Americans do hit their offspring and were hit themselves by their parents, and many people believe corporal punishment is valuable in teaching children right from wrong, even if there is no definitive scientific evidence to support our commonsensical view and considerable research that suggests the opposite. Most of us accept that there is a hazy, wobbly line that divides guidance from villainy.

Americans agree that child abuse is a crime. The question is how far should the law go? Should it go as far as the Swedish law, passed in 1979, that says: "The child should not be subjected to corporal punishment or other humiliating treatment."[14] Or should it restrict as much as possible the intrusion of the state into what some feel is family decision making? Where shall we draw the line, and on what grounds shall the line be drawn?

The Social Democratic Point of View

The social democrat wishes to insure that the rights of all groups are protected, particularly groups, such as children, that cannot easily protect themselves. When a social democrat hears of a problem, he or she is likely to suggest that the government should step in and do something. Even if the action infringes on the "rights" of individuals and families, government intrusion may be necessary to protect a greater right—that of not allowing a child to be beaten. Irene Barth, an editor for *Newsday*, writes:

> Recently, the public has been treated to accounts of a 5-year-old snuffed out by means of a plastic bag placed over her head, a 3-year-old boy beaten to a pulp with a bat and a 2-year-old shaken into the hereafter with bare hands. Another 3-year-old, a girl, according to police, was shredded with a belt because she showed too little interest in arithmetic flash cards. . . . Because of increased public awareness, the number of tips [to social service agencies] is up. Now comes a suit charging that social workers caused $6.5 million worth of "anguish and humiliation" to a family by looking into an unfounded allegation of child abuse. Richard and Dee-Ann Marrone complain that they were asked personal questions and that their children were undressed by a child-welfare worker looking for bruises. The family doctor, friends and school officials are said to have been told of the investigation. . . . Even if the plaintiffs are the tenderest of parents and the accusation against them was malicious, their suit has terrifying implications. . . . What is worse than the anguish visited upon innocent parents is the anguish visited upon the innocent children of guilty parents. . . . In an ideal world, all parents would receive thoughtful instruction in child-rearing and all homes housing young children would be visited at least once or twice by family experts. . . . Children's rights to protection from cruel and unusual punishment should outweigh adults' right to secure their houses against searches.[15]

Barth makes a strong and coherent argument in favor of the social democratic position. She believes the rights of a group of vulnerable individuals take priority over the property and privacy rights of parents. That individual parents might be hurt is more than offset by the fact that children are not abused. Of course, there is no certain way of knowing how many parents will be hurt by this intervention and how many children will be spared pain.

Barth is explicit about her "ideal world." Parents would be thoughtfully trained in child rearing (presumably by the government), and every home would be visited by "family experts." Recently, the U.S. Advisory Board on Child Abuse and Neglect supported this view, proposing in a government report that health-care workers should visit new parents, instructing them in child care.[16] This, however, is not everyone's idea of utopia. Conservatives and libertarians would react with horror to this army of bureaucratic intruders. Some might see thoughtful child-rearing instruction as ideological manipulation of youngsters by an all-powerful state. While these proponents are obviously sincere about the beneficial role of a helpful government, it would be a living hell for critics.

One social democrat, former Philadelphia judge Lois Foner, believes that we have gone too far in our attempts to "preserve the family," and writes:

I suggest that it is time for us to demand that government provide permanent, well-run orphanages for the more that 2 million abused children who are de facto orphans. . . . Public institutions are answerable to the public. They can be inspected regularly by public officials.[17]

Foner implies that the government is ultimately a parent for its citizens, a form of the legal doctrine of *parens patriae* ("the parenthood of the state").

Which position you adopt may relate to the faith you have in families and governments. If you see individual parents as ignorant, apathetic, or primitive, you are likely to be more willing to grant that there is a place for the thoughtful, altruistic government official. The cases rhetorically presented by the advocates of large-scale government intervention attempt to paint this picture: What kind of a world do we live in when a father could "shred" his three-year-old daughter with a belt for not caring about mathematics? On the other hand, there are an equal number of horror stories of bumbling, incompetent bureaucrats. Do-gooders may intrude on your family espousing their own narrow ideology or following government regulations to the letter. Each position has its own fantasies associated with it.

To understand where this government concern with the health and well-being of young children might lead, let us turn to Sweden. In 1979, this progressive Scandinavian nation passed a law that outlawed spanking, slapping, locking a child in a closet, or in general humiliating the child. This law added to strong Swedish laws that provide stiff punishment for child abuse. The law was not primarily designed to be punitive but rather educational. As a Swedish Ministry of Justice spokesman put it: "We hope to use the law to change attitudes. If we launched a big campaign on the subject, it probably would be forgotten in a year. But the law stays, and it enters the public consciousness."[18] In the first decade since it was enacted, only one Swede was taken to court.[19] Still, even if it is unlikely to send parents who swat their kids to jail, the proposal does have the force of law.

The Swedish politicians who passed this legislation believed that it is a legitimate role of the state to insure "proper" child-rearing practices. The majority were convinced that children who are hit or threatened do not respond positively, and being convinced of this, they acted.

Of course this social democratic legislation has been subject to heated attacks and ridicule by those with a more conservative bent. Jim Klobuchar, a popular Minneapolis newspaper columnist, imagines satirically the length to which government interference might go:

My cousin [from Sweden] said the family had torsk the other day, or whatever the Swedes call cod, and the kid refused. The wife tried all the gentle, loving approaches and when that didn't work, the guy ordered the kid to eat the torsk. The kid angrily refused. He said he was studying to be a vegetarian and the old man was intruding on his right of choice. When the predictable impasse developed, the old man said Ingemar couldn't go outside to play. The kid then went into his room and came out with a banner four feet high, which he put in the picture window, announcing: "This house practices grounding and other methods first used by the Spanish Inquisition." The guy might go to jail.[20]

As silly as this scenario might be, the social democrat does believe the government has a place in the home. The family is not seen as a sacred institution, but the government and its laws are. Government can right the wrongs caused by others. The social democrat believes that people can be made more moral and happier through legislation. When they see child abuse or any social wrong, they have no difficulty in correcting the problem by the most direct and universal solution—a law.

The Conservative Point of View

No conservative enjoys being beaten. Yet, we are more likely to find a conservative approving of corporal punishment than a member of the other two groups. Conservatives believe that those tried and true methods of discipline are best. They believe, along with the Bible, that "he that spareth his rod hateth his son: but he that loveth him chasteneth him early" (Proverbs 13:24). They believe like Odin, the Norse God of War and Wisdom, that "he who goes without corporal punishment will go lawless and die without honor." The conservative is far less likely to agree that reason is the guiding force of child development. A child must learn to accept and obey legitimate authority. Physical discipline is a forceful (if perhaps not totally effective) means of impressing the power differential between child and adult on the former in an emotional, rather than rational, way. A nineteenth-century minister put it this way:

> [Corporal punishment] must be viewed not as simply the pain produced, but pain as the expression of disapprobation of a moral governor; and the dread of it, or the appeal made to fear, must be on account of the association it recalls of the displeasure of the beloved parent. To fear such displeasure is a proof of affection; and the appeal made to such a feeling, even by means of external infliction, has no tendency to produce or cherish slavish submission. . . . the family is a monarchy, though not a despotism; the father and mother, considered as one, are invested with patriarchal authority: and we carry out our idea still further; for we say that a holy family is in a sense a Theocracy.[21]

The authority of the family is central to conservatives, who would agree with philosopher Herbert Fingarette's claim:

In terms of child abuse, [critics of corporal punishment] include the notion that it is wrong for the parent to use, or even to have authority to use, any kind of disciplinary action that involves what we call corporal punishment, which means laying a hand on the child. Now, if that is child abuse, then it is something which many people over the ages, and many people today . . . are well-convinced is a perfectly reasonable way to run a family. [When] you deal with the family, you are dealing with an institution . . . that is the one fundamental opportunity for intimacy in a little community, a kind of peculiar, special intimacy, one which is rooted in aeons of traditions. We don't know what we are fiddling with when we fiddle with that. It is an enormously valuable thing that a family should have a certain kind of intimacy.[22]

Of course, one should not caricature this position by pushing it too far. As conservative columnist William F. Buckley writes, "It is sometimes difficult to draw the line, but a line simply can and must be drawn between domestic discipline and domestic savagery."[23]

Fingarette is particularly concerned about the possibility of legislation damaging the integrity of the family. Rather than emphasizing the problem of child abuse, he sees a totally different problem: that of preserving and strengthening the family. The strength of the traditional family is considered one of the foundations of western society, but now conservatives believe the family is being attacked from all quarters: delinquency, feminism, sex education, divorce, and premarital intercourse. Of course, when conservatives speak of the family, they are likely to refer to the traditional nuclear family (two parents and their offspring). This structure has never been as common as its staunchest defenders have implied. Throughout history, numerous family forms have existed: extended, single-parent, communal, and the like. The conservative, then, is protecting an ideal, rather than a universal reality.

This moral privileging of the family makes little sense to the extreme libertarian or social democrat. They view the family as a contract between consenting individuals. Admittedly, children do not consent to this contract at birth and must be slowly given rights; still, they see nothing particularly sacred about the nuclear family structure. It may be efficient, but not *specially* moral, and so does not deserve to be specially protected by tradition or by law. The rights of individuals or protected classes are more relevant. One critic of Professor Fingarette has reminded him that the same argument he makes about parents and children might be made about plantation owners and slaves.[24] A conservative would counter this by saying the family has a special status that did not apply to antebellum cotton plantations.

Whereas the social democrat is concerned with the "epidemic" of child abuse, the conservative is equally concerned with the "epidemic" of permissiveness. Conservatives attribute the "moral decline" of America to the permissive child-rearing techniques of the past few decades and to the shunning of the basic and traditional values of society. The list of troubles is long and depressing: divorce, unwed mothers, public homosexuality, recreational drug use, and the decline in religiosity, to name but a few. Some Americans (particularly some libertarians) do not see these problems as problems but simply as the diverse flowering of a free and open society that should be allowed to flourish, rather than be repressed. (Of course, some conservative concerns such as an increase in violent crime worry everyone, regardless of their philosophy.)

Despite this focus on moral laxity, conservatives do not support harsh discipline for its own sake. No one argues that children should be hit as an end in itself. Conservatives emphasize that pain and love should be mixed and that corporal punishment is only a last resort and a sign of parental concern. It is a sad commentary on the chasm between attitudes and behaviors that many parents who share these reasonable beliefs find themselves engaging in unloving, brutal behavior.

The Libertarian Point of View

The debate over the issue of whether parents should be allowed to hit their children is primarily between social democrats and conservatives. For libertarians, the debate pits two undesirable consequences against each other. Corporal punishment seems, in general, alien to the spirit of libertarian child rearing, which attempts to maximize the freedom and dignity of the child. Many child-rearing books of the post-war era are more or less congruent with the libertarian emphasis on the child as an individual worthy of respect and responsibility. One libertarian child-rearing manual advises parents that "children are rational and logical within the context of their limited experience. Making allowances for their lack of experience, we should treat children exactly as we treat adults."[25] To hit an adult is assault; should it be any different when done to a child? Bernice Weissbourd, president of a Chicago area agency that provides drop-in centers for parents of young children, suggests that "a child learns many lessons from being spanked, but responsibility is not necessarily one of them. He learns that there are forces in his world to be feared. . . . He learns that the bigger and stronger you are, the more power you have. He learns that hitting is a way to express feelings and solve problems."[26] Libertarians consider such lessons harmful because they undermine the personal respect and rationality that is necessary in a free society. Likewise, corporal punishment demeans the parent. From a libertarian position, it really does "hurt me, more than it does you." Lillian Katz, a professor of early childhood education, warns of the dangers of spanking. "Overall, spanking can best be thought of as something we use against our better judgment. It is something we do in 'hot' (as opposed to 'cold') blood. To spank in the heat of the moment is not recommended; but, once in a while, it is inevitable and forgivable. But to spank in cold blood, as a matter of deliberate, premeditated policy, is sadistic."[27] Violence is outside the pale of libertarian thought because it denies the validity of a society based on rationality.

Libertarians also fret about the intervention of government in child rearing. A tenet of their philosophy is the right of privacy. Consider the comments of John Maher, the founder of San Francisco's Delancy Street Foundation, a self-help foundation for drug addicts and criminals:

> Children's rights seems like something I would like to be in favor of. On the other hand . . . my fear of intervention in my family by the kind of clowns I find in our juvenile justice system would increase the possibility of violence in our culture. I would be outraged. On the other hand, the concept of children's rights sounds like something I should support. But I can't get my teeth in it. Does this mean we simply add rights for children to the Constitution, or do we create intervention agencies that we must then deal with?[28]

Unlike for the true conservative, the idea of children's rights is not offensive to libertarians; the problem is rather the government's enforcement of these rights. The libertarian rejects the legal doctrine of *parens patriae*—the belief that the state is a parent to its citizens, and spins fantasies of state control, as in an article titled "Family Abuse":

> The police often strike at night. Your children are seized and taken to a secret location. They are placed in the hands of state doctors who strip them down and give them thorough examinations, focusing attention on their genitalia. Meanwhile, you are hauled into court to face an inquisitorial hearing into your character. . . . Your guilt is essentially assumed. . . . Even among those who, against all odds, manage to prove their innocence and recover their children, many escape only by agreeing to state-directed psychological counseling, where therapists work to restructure one's mind and values.[29]

The images used by the libertarians could not be more different that those used by the social democrats.

As is true for conservatives, most libertarians will grit their teeth and agree that the government has a right to be involved in cases of extreme child abuse; one legitimate role of any government is protecting its citizens from harm. This does not imply that the libertarian will be happy with the government's involvement in personal relations. Even though the family does not have the same sacredness for the libertarian that it does for the conservative, government intervention provokes the same concern.

Child Abuse and Social Research

There is little consensus on the effects of physical punishment on children. While we can say with considerable conviction that "child abuse" is morally wrong and ineffective because it produces parents who will abuse their own children, the boundaries of child abuse are not entirely clear. Despite the fact that spanking is unfashionable among experts in child development, it is widely practiced. Many Americans feel they are what they are because of child-rearing practices that included corporal punishment. Punishment can either be a horrible crime or a necessary evil, depending on its motive and its extent.

What can sociologists contribute to the understanding of child abuse? How can they, as social scientists, integrate their personal concerns as citizens with a desire to understand an objective reality? Richard J. Gelles, one of the most influential scholars in this area, was the first to conduct a national survey on parental violence toward children. In early 1976, Gelles interviewed 1,146 parents of children ages three to seventeen as part of a larger study of family violence. All of these parents (about half mothers and half fathers) were living in two-parent households. Parents were asked whether they had ever engaged in physical actions toward one of their children (the child used as the subject of the interview was randomly selected). The participants were given a series of possible actions: slapping or spanking; pushing, grabbing, or shoving; kicking, biting, or hitting with one's fist; "beating up"; threatening with a knife or gun; or using a knife or gun.

Before discussing Gelles's findings, note that he considers *all* of these behaviors as indicators of family violence. Gelles comments:

> For the purposes of this study, violence is nominally defined as "an act carried out with the intention, or perceived intention, of physically injuring another person." The injury can range from slight pain, as in a slap, to murder. . . . We chose a broad definition of violence (which includes spanking as violent behavior) because we want to draw attention to the issue of family members hitting each other; we have defined this behavior as "violent" in order to raise controversy and call the behavior into question. . . . Indeed, one thing that influenced our final choice of a concept was that acts parents carry out on their children in the name of corporal punishment or acceptable force could, if done to strangers or adults, be considered criminal assault.[30]

Gelles' concept of "violence toward children" provides a legitimation of government intervention and creation of a social policy. If the study was on "parental discipline," it would not have the same implications, despite identical findings. The way in which a sociologist describes his or her study will direct the public's attention. While Gelles is not *wrong* to describe his study as he does, he has made a choice that is based on his view of the world.

Gelles sees his findings as supporting his assumption that there is a great deal of violence within the American family. For example, 71 percent of the sample of parents admitted to having slapped or spanked their children, with 58 percent saying they had done so within the previous year; 46 percent of the parents had pushed or shoved their child, with 32 percent saying they had done so within the previous year. As for using a gun or knife, only one father admitted he had done so recently, and only 2.9 percent said that this had occurred at least once in the child's life.

Does this represent an extraordinary amount of violence or normal home life? It depends. If we choose to consider spanking, slapping, pushing, and shoving as acceptable parental behavior, the figures seem less daunting. Relatively few parents admit to going beyond this. Even with regard to the more troubling use of knives or guns, we don't really know what this statistic means:[31] horrible brutality or protection from a violent teenager, throwing a butter knife or slashing a child with a switchblade, murdering a child in cold blood or frightening him or her with an unloaded pistol. Gelles admits that a weakness of the study is a lack of information on the consequences of these behaviors. Yet, public policy will be based on the imagined consequences of these actions.

The choice of conducting interviews with a random sample of the adult population also affects the conclusions that Gelles can draw. First, he can claim that the survey is representative of the American people because the results could approximately be duplicated if additional surveys were conducted. Second, Gelles can estimate the actual number of instances based on his sample. He found 2.9 percent of the sample of 1,146 parents used a gun or knife on their children. By extending this percentage to the total number of children in the United States, Gelles can estimate that from 900,000 to 1,800,000 have experienced such brutality.[32] (This technique is called *extrapolating from data*.) Finally, because this is self-reported data (that is, what parents said they had done), Gelles can argue that the "real" figures of family violence are much higher since some parents would probably choose to make themselves look good by claiming to be less violent than they actually are.

This research can be used by partisans in several ways to emphasize or minimize the significance of the problem. Gelles wants to emphasize the seriousness of family violence in our society and to suggest that action needs to be taken; by implication, he would fall closest to the social democratic point of view. While it would distort his position to claim that he is a conflict theorist, he does criticize American family behavior and the social norms, such as traditional gender roles, that stand behind them.

Spanking and the Socialization Process

The type of discipline parents select is a major factor in how their children develop. Parents are the primary role models for children. Children are likely to define their morals by what they see their parents do. If a child is spanked by a loving parent, he or she could feel that, in some circumstances, inflicting pain is morally right. If parents insist that children obey them, this may lead children to have respect for authority. If children receive love from their parents or guardians, they will probably be accepting of others and contented with the justice of the social order.

Children see their reflection as adults in their parents. Interactionists explain that parents are the primary "looking-glass self" in our culture, serving to allow the child to "create" his or her own identity through that of the parents. The faults children resent in their parents their children will likely resent in them. Those things children most admire about their parents their children will admire in them. Children, in other words, are the products of the parents who socialize them. This is the reason why family violence is so troubling. One of the strongest predictors of child abuse is whether the adult was abused as a child. Child abuse is not only a social problem but a self-perpetuating one.

Yet, a completely undisciplined child poses problems as well. Children are, alas, not "naturally" obedient; so parents must, somehow, impress their will on their offspring. Perhaps the discipline used in the home will also reflect itself in society's courts of law and prisons. The question this chapter has raised involves whether the choice of child-rearing discipline is best left up to parents or to the community.

Social democrats believe that there is a moral imperative to protect the vulnerable members of society—the children. The government in some sense serves as an advocate for the child. The libertarian, on the other hand, is more willing to let children fend for themselves in the rough and tumble of family life. The power of the government to decide for the child is as abhorrent as the tyranny of the family. For the conservative, there is no contest; the family is a "natural" institution whose autonomy must be protected. The family, rather than the government, prevents society from breaking down. These views are reflected in the source of socialization of the three philosophies; while the conservative looks to the family and the social democrat to the society, the libertarian stresses the autonomy of the children, mothers, and fathers.

Questions

1. Do you believe that under some circumstances parents should spank their children?

2. What lessons do children learn from being spanked?

3. What does the term *child abuse* mean?

4. What is the appropriate punishment for a parent convicted of child abuse?

5. Should doctors and teachers be forced to report all suspected cases of child abuse?

6. Should welfare agencies interview friends and neighbors of a family suspected of child abuse before it has been proven?

7. Is Sweden's law forbidding all corporal punishment a proper use of government power?

8. Should the government be involved in family discipline?

9. Since people who are abused as children are prone to become child abusers, should they be forbidden to have children?

10. Is it a good idea for every home to be visited by a government child care expert once a year?

For Further Study

Erlanger, Howard. "Social Class and Corporal Punishment in Childrearing: A Reassessment." *American Sociological Review* 39(1974):68–85.

Gelles, Richard. *Family Violence.* Beverly Hills, CA: Sage, 1979.

Gil, David. *Violence Against Children.* Cambridge: Harvard University Press, 1970.

Greven, Philip. *Spare the Child: The Religious Roots of Physical Punishment and the Psychological Impact of Physical Abuse.* New York: Knopf, 1990.

Hewlett, Sylvia Ann. *When the Bough Breaks: The Cost of Neglecting Our Children.* New York: Basic Books, 1991.

Pfohl, Steven J. "The Discovery of Child Abuse." *Social Problems* 24(1977): 310–323.

"Violence Toward Youth in Families" (special issue). *Journal of Social Issues* 35(1979): 1–176.

Strauss, Murray A. "Discipline and Deviance: Physical Punishment of Children and Violence and Other Crime in Adulthood." *Social Problems* 38(1991): 133–154.

Strauss, Murray A., Richard J. Gelles, and Suzanne K. Steinmetz. *Behind Closed Doors: Violence in the American Family.* New York: Doubleday, 1980.

Notes and References

1. Quoted in Iona Opie and Peter Opie, *The Lore and Language of Schoolchildren* (London: Oxford University Press, 1959), p. 2.
2. Jean Piaget, *The Origins of Intelligence in Children* (New York: International Universities Press, 1952).
3. Charles Horton Cooley, *Human Nature and Social Order* (New York: Schocken, 1964), p. 184.
4. George Herbert Mead, *Mind, Self, and Society* (Chicago: University of Chicago Press, 1934), pp. 150–152.
5. Ibid., pp. 152–163.
6. Erving Goffman, *Presentation of Self in Everyday Life* (New York: Anchor, 1959), pp. 208–237.
7. George Gallup, Jr., *The Gallup Poll: Public Opinion 1990.* Wilmington, DE: *Scholarly Resources*, 1991, p. 59; see also, E. S., "Spare the Rod in School, but Not at Home," *Psychology Today* (December 1989): 10; Murray Strauss, "Discipline and Deviance," *Social Problems* 38(May 1991): 331, 333.
8. Barbara Carson, "Parents Who Don't Spank: Deviation in the Legitimation of Physical Force." Doctoral dissertation (Sociology), University of New Hampshire, 1986.
9. Ed Magnuson, "Child Abuse: The Ultimate Betrayal," *Time* (September 5, 1983): 20.
10. Cited in Lois G. Foner, "For Children's Sake, Bring Back the Orphanage," *Star/Tribune* (Minneapolis), (November 21, 1988): 9A.
11. Howard Erlanger, "Social Class and Corporal Punishment in Childrearing: A Reassessment," *American Sociological Review* 39(1974): 68–85; Richard J. Gelles, "Violence in the Family: A Review of Research in the Seventies," *Journal of Marriage and the Family* 42 (November 1980): 878–879.
12. Herbert Costner, *The Changing Folkways of Parenthood: A Content Analysis* (New York: Arno Press, 1980); Peter Stearns, "The Problem of Change in Emotions Research: New Standards for Anger in Twentieth-Century American Childrearing," *Symbolic Interaction*, 10 (1987): 85–99.
13. Magnuson, "Child Abuse: The Ultimate Betrayal," p. 22.
14. Amelia Adamo, "New Rights for Children and Parents in Sweden," *Children Today* (November–December 1981): 15.
15. Irene Barth, "Bruising a Parent's Image to Protect a Battered Child," *Minneapolis Star and Tribune* (September 13, 1983): 13A.
16. "U.S. Seems Powerless on Child Abuse," *Atlanta Journal/Constitution* (September 15, 1991): A20.
17. Lois G. Foner, "For Children's Sake," p. 9A.
18. John Vinocur, "Swedes Shun Norse Adage, Ban Spanking," *The New York Times* (April 4, 1979): A7.
19. Similar laws have been passed in Austria, Finland, Norway, and Denmark. See Claire Sanders, "Smack Habits," *New Statesman* (July 14, 1989): 25.
20. Jim Klobuchar, "Will Kindergarten Kids Caucus?" *Minneapolis Star* (April 11, 1979): 1B.

21. D. Newell, "A Holy Family—Parental Government and Discipline," *Christian Family Magazine* (1842): 123–124.

22. Quoted in "Family Discipline, Intimacy, and Children's Rights," *Center Magazine* (November-December, 1981): 36–37.

23. William F. Buckley, "The Child Beaters and Their Critics," *National Review* (April 16, 1982): 449.

24. Quoted in "Family Discipline, Intimacy, and Children's Rights," p. 39.

25. Frances Kendall, *Super Parents, Super Children* (Johannesburg: Delta, 1983), p. 20.

26. Bernice Weissbourd, "A Good Spanking: A Bad Idea," *Parents* (September, 1981): 100.

27. Lillian G. Katz, "Spank or Speak?" *Parents* (February, 1980): 84.

28. Quoted in "Family Discipline, Intimacy, and Children's Rights," p. 39.

29. Allan C. Carlson, "Family Abuse," *Reason* (May 1986): 34.

30. Richard J. Gelles, *Family Violence* (Beverly Hills, CA: Sage, 1979), pp. 78–79.

31. Ibid., p. 89.

32. Ibid., p. 82.

CHAPTER THREE

Deviance and Social Control: Should Drug Use Be Legalized?

■ Sometimes society seems to be a minuet between forces of social control and forces that attempt to evade that control. Whatever is ordered, some resist. Indeed, the enforcement of norms and values may be necessary because the actions that are being controlled are those we "really" would choose. If we were not unconsciously interested in such behavior, no need would exist for such control. Freud claimed that the strength of our taboos against incest was that this represents our fondest, though most socially destructive, wish.

Perhaps no arena of social life has been as closely examined by sociologists as the relationship between deviance and social control. Sociological studies date back well into the nineteenth century and include the classic empirical study by Emile Durkheim, *Suicide* (1897). The question of why deviance occurs is as central to the discipline as the question of how social order is possible. Indeed, the two questions demand each other. In orderly societies, human beings establish various institutions to enforce social control. Some social scientists distinguish between the forces of ideological social control and those of direct social control.[1]

Ideological social control refers to attempts to shape people's perceptions so they are willing to accept the status quo and the legitimacy of social institutions. The family, the church, one's peer group, the schools one attends, and the mass media each contribute to the belief that the dominant view of the world is the correct one. Of course, these institutions are not in complete agreement, nor do they work sufficiently well to enforce a total ideology; yet, most people adopt the world view of these institutions. It takes either a person with a very strong (or perverse) sense of self or a person in a strong subculture to reject the dominant view of how life should be lived.

In order to deal with major deviations, society maintains a collection of institutions to force a person into appropriate patterns of behavior or to remove someone from society. Direct social control involves the attempt to punish, change, or isolate those who do not "fit in," including the mentally ill, criminals, and extreme political dissidents. Even institutions that, on their face, have a humanitarian goal can indirectly serve to enforce social control. For example, some argue that public welfare programs function in times of recession to defuse social unrest.[2] The main elements of direct social control are the police force, the courts, the prison system, and mental hospitals. Controversy about mental institutions had been particularly dramatic in light of charges that the totalitarian Soviet Union used mental institutions to detain political dissidents.

Although it would be nice to believe that such institutions treat all individuals who come before them equitably and without regard to class or race, many sociological research studies show that, sadly, such is not the case. African Americans and the poor, in particular, are given less leniency than others not similarly damned. Even the bumper sticker on your car may affect the number of traffic citations you will receive.[3] (Stock up on "Support Your Local Police" stickers.) Rich white kids do sometimes get into trouble, but there is a presumption that their "crimes" are just a phase, rather than the beginning of a career of crime—and this may be right, since other forms of social control push them into moral lives and they never get labeled with their youthful sins. Still, that is little comfort for those not afforded similar mercy.

These engines of social control are designed to prevent or limit deviant behavior. Simply put, *deviance* is behavior that is thought to be improper by large numbers of people in a society and that violates their social expectations. Deviance is not only behaving in a distinct manner from most people (becoming a surgeon would qualify under that criterion); rather, deviance is negatively valued behavior. Few behaviors are inherently deviant; what is considered deviant is socially determined and differs from one culture to another.

In explaining deviance, some researchers examine the characteristics of those who break the rules. One approach contends that criminals are not like "normal" people. They have, perhaps, a genetic anomaly (an extra male chromosome), special physiques, brain malfunctions, or hereditary factors based on race or ethnicity. Such biological theories have not been shown to be valid. To be taken seriously, they will have to be more sophisticated and complex than they currently are.

Others examine the psychological characteristics of deviants and suggest they lacked affection in childhood, had psychosexual traumas, or never developed proper attachment to adults or other children. In theory, it should be possible to predict which children will "get into trouble" and then give them appropriate conditioning or training to prevent this. Yet, at our current stage of knowledge, such prediction is far from exact and, in any event, raises questions of civil liberties.

Another approach to explaining the behavior of deviants is to look at their environment. Certainly, the fact that most deviant behavior occurs in urban areas is of more than passing interest, and some claim that there are psychological and social features of living in cities that contribute to this behavior.[4] A second argument is that the sort of people a person associates with determines his or her behavior: Deviants associate with different individuals than nondeviants. This approach is termed *differential association*.[5] Current arguments along this line attempt to explain the behavior of the "underclass" by virtue of its social isolation from those with more socially approved life-styles. A third view examines the goals and values of potential criminals and argues that they do not follow socially approved means to achieve socially desired ends, mostly because they find these approved means closed to them.[6] Other studies focus on the distinctive subculture of the lower class—the so-called *culture of poverty*. Many values of this group run directly counter to the culture of the larger society and are more congruent with deviant behavior.[7] Again, social isolation and de facto segregation help to reinforce these values. There is, of course, little agreement among social scientists as to which, if any, of these approaches best explains deviant behavior.

Other sociologists do not examine the deviants themselves but rather the society they feel makes them so. According to these theorists, society "blames the victim."[8] The leading approach of this type is *labeling theory*. According to this argument, almost everyone has been deviant, but not everyone is so labeled. Whether a person gets labeled depends on who he or she is and whether he or she has been fortunate enough to avoid an official stigma. In the case of drugs, since most young adults have tried marijuana, presumably more than half the youthful population could be labeled as drug offenders, yet relatively few have had this misfortune. Once labeled, people find themselves treated specially: Their behavior is evaluated differently (and with closer scrutiny), and there is less tolerance for future offenses. Because of these constraints, *secondary deviance* occurs, that is, deviance that is the result of the labeling process. Being denied rewards and being shunned by those not labeled encourages further deviant behavior. Other deviants may be the only friends one can make; the underground economy may become one's only job market. How a person is labeled is, from this interactionist perspective, a consequence of the person's relations with others.

As in most things, functionalists and conflict theorists disagree about the nature of deviance. The functionalist believes deviance is illegitimate but has some positive effects. The labeling of some people as deviant brings the nondeviant members of society together and emphasizes their similarities in contrast to the behavior of the deviant. The functionalist sees deviance as ultimately caused by the failure of a social system to socialize its members properly. Conflict theorists, on the other hand, stress the social and political components of deviance. For the conflict theorist, deviance, in many cases, is necessary because it sends a message about the injustices of society. To eliminate deviance, people must radically restructure their social system, altering the social conditions that cause the deviance and the class system that permits some people the luxury to define others as deviant.

■ Question:

Should Drug Use Be Legalized?

A quarter of a century ago, Bob Dylan sang, "Everybody must get stoned."[9] With the double meaning of "stoned," this lyric has great resonance for the continuing drug debate in U.S. society. If we include alcohol and nicotine among drugs, almost everyone has gotten "stoned," yet relatively few have been "stoned" by the legal system.

The National Commission on Marijuana and Drug Abuse defines a drug as any chemical that affects the structure or function of a living organism.[10] Such a definition covers a lot: marijuana, cocaine, heroin, LSD, alcohol, nicotine, caffeine, and perhaps salt, sugar, and beef fat. Nevertheless, most people agree on what is meant by "chemical abuse," "substance abuse," or "drug abuse." Alcohol, which by all reasonable definitions is a "drug," and a potentially harmful one at that, is legal (though regulated), whereas marijuana, which seems to be harmful when used continually, but less clearly so than alcohol, is not legal in the United States.[11] Tobacco, more deadly than either marijuana or alcohol, is not typically discussed in terms of drug abuse, and so will not be examined here.

Alcohol is the drug of preference for most Americans, due to its easy availability and relatively mild consequences when used in moderation. According to the National Institute on Drug Abuse, over 92 percent of all eighteen- to twenty-five-year-olds have used alcohol, with over 55 percent of those twelve to seventeen having had a drink at least once. Seventy-two percent of young adults now use alcohol, as compared to 32 percent of teenagers. The equivalent figures for marijuana are that 61 percent of young adults and 24 percent of teens have tried it, and 22 percent and 12 percent are current users. The figures for other drugs are much lower, but still over 25 percent of young adults have tried cocaine; 1.2 percent of this group have tried heroin.[12] Despite legal constraints, Americans are willing to pay the price of using a wide variety of mind-altering substances.

Much of the discussion of the legalization of drugs has dealt with how harmful they are. This is a complicated area about which we are learning more each year. It is fair to say that drugs are not harmless, but neither are they as harmful as a bullet from a revolver.[13] The specific amount of damage they do is not crucial to the issues I describe. After all, knowing the evidence about cigarette smoking has not caused our society to outlaw cigarettes, and some high schools even provide rooms in which students can smoke at their leisure. The first federal law aimed at controlling the use of drugs was the 1914 Harrison Act, which was designed to regulate, license, and tax the distribution of narcotic drugs. Perhaps unexpectedly, the Narcotics Division of the Treasury Department, given the responsibility to enforce the law, criminalized the use of these drugs, turning users into "criminals." The first law regulating marijuana was the 1937 Marijuana Tax Act, which provided severe penalties for the use of the drug—as much as twenty years imprisonment for mere possession. Some state laws were even tougher, providing for life imprisonment. Louisiana and Missouri permitted the death penalty for drug sales to minors.

By the late 1960s and 1970s, sentiment slowly began to change toward control of marijuana, a consequence of the drug's widespread popularity and perhaps the use of the drug by the children of leading politicians. Although no state has legalized marijuana, eleven states from Mississippi to Minnesota, Maine to Oregon, decriminalized the use of small amounts of it. In 1970 the federal government sharply reduced the penalties for "crimes" involving marijuana. During this period, politicians from Barry Goldwater to Jimmy Carter supported its decriminalization. From 1969 to 1977, the number of Americans who supported the legalization of marijuana increased from 12 to 28 percent. It seemed, by the late 1970s, that marijuana would soon be legalized. Since 1978, however, no new states have decriminalized marijuana and some have recriminalized its use. By the late 1980s and into the 1990s, there was a greater concern among parents and politicians about the use of all drugs (with only 14 percent supporting drug legalization).[14] Evidence of the health risks of various drugs has perhaps also affected people's attitudes; by 1988 there were approximately 6,000 deaths from illegal drugs—about half of these from cocaine.[15] Drug use seems to be decreasing in general, although in some communities it is still a major problem. It now appears that no public policy changes are likely. In fact, attitudes toward "drugs" have changed dramatically in the 1980s, with marijuana being almost forgotten in the process of making cocaine "a folk devil." Although a few brave politicians, like Baltimore mayor Kurt Schmoke and former secretary of state George Shultz, have called for decriminalizing cocaine, the rush is on to increase penalties for those caught using and, especially, selling cocaine and its potent form, crack. "Just Say No!" may be the most symptomatic phrase of the Reagan-Bush era; the "War on Drugs" may be the most revealing metaphor of the period. Drug testing in the workplace and for hiring is becoming increasingly common.

In 1988 the retail value of the marijuana grown in America was approximately $33 billion, making it, according to one source, the largest cash crop grown in the United States.[16] Marijuana represents a significant portion of the U.S. economy. It is estimated that marijuana provides $7 billion to organized crime, and cocaine provides nearly twice that.[17] Cocaine plays a role in our unfavorable balance-of-trade picture with other nations. It has been estimated that drug use cost over $60 billion in medical care, law enforcement, drug treatment, and absenteeism. In the words of Harvard economist Robert Reich, "Narcotics is one of America's major industries, right up there with consumer electronics, automobiles and steel."[18]

The Conservative Point of View

Most, though not all conservatives, are opposed to legalizing drugs, and public opinion clearly supports them. Drugs, with their mind-altering properties, give people pleasure, and this private pleasure separates them from those social institutions that should be most important; they separate the individual from the community, and they reflect and cause the rejection of social mores, a major threat to order. This view is reflected in the extreme rhetoric of California's former state superintendent of public instruction, Max Rafferty. "What to do about the dope syndrome, Mom and Pop?" asks Rafferty. "First, recognize it for what it is. Just one more symptom of the nation's unraveling moral fiber. A sign of our times. Then resolve to combat it in your own family, mercilessly, with no holds barred. Remember that souls are the things actually at stake in the war you're declaring, and fight accordingly."[19] Ronald Reagan claimed that drug sellers are "killing America and terrorizing it with slow but sure chemical destruction."[20] One New York City councilman responded to this threat by sugggesting that we chain addicts to trees so that people could spit on them.[21] Some claim that drug users display an "amotivational syndrome" that deprives the society of these citizens' work in its behalf. In other words, they remove themselves from the community to which they should be contributing. Consider the remarks of columnist Carl Rowan:

> As surely as if they were nuclear bombs from a dreaded enemy, the tons of heroin from Asia, the mountains of cocaine from Bolivia and Peru, the endless supply of marijuana, Quaaludes and other illicit drugs from Columbia—and from American farms and laboratories—are wrecking this society. . . . Illegal drugs are playing havoc with our business communities, with sales of marijuana, heroin and cocaine commonplace on Wall Street. Drug abuse has become the scourge of professional athletics, the curse of our entertainment world from Hollywood to Broadway, a shame of Congress. It is a tragedy that touches every type of family in this land.[22]

The real threat of drugs for the conservative is the danger they pose to social order. In particular, conservatives are concerned about the effects of drug use on children. If children are not properly socialized, the continuation of an orderly society is hopeless. The fact that the young are likely to indulge makes drugs a particular menace for the conservative. Richard Vigilante, an editorial writer for the *Charleston Daily Mail*, recognizes this, commenting: "The special dangers for young users and the prospect of 10 to 15 percent of the adolescent population being too doped up to mature normally or get an education certainly justify, in theory, state intervention."[23] As former drug czar William Bennett noted pungently, "Why, in God's name, should we foster the use of a drug that makes you stupid?"[24] While conservatives do not like government interference, they do believe that government action is necessary when there is a substantial danger to the fabric or structure of society. Conservatives accept the basic right of government to intervene to protect "core values." Ultimately, it is harm to people that justifies action, even though there may be a reduction in drug-related crime if drugs were widely available. Judianne Densen-Gerber, founder of Odyssey House, an experimental program for young drug abusers, is concerned that "the major value question brought into focus is whether society values its property more than its people. The legalization of all narcotic substances, particularly heroin, would lessen the amount of crime, especially crimes against property. But such legalization would increase the number of the afflicted and the severity of the disease in each individual addict. As an example, during Prohibition, although millions of people violated the law by drinking, the number of alcoholics markedly decreased."[25] The conservative contends that taking drugs is not a "victimless crime." The drug user does not live in isolation but is part of a family, a church, a community, and a society, and society has an obligation to uphold moral standards. As political scientist James Q. Wilson notes:

> Society is not and could never be a collection of autonomous individuals. We all have a stake in ensuring that each of us displays a minimal level of dignity, responsibility, and empathy. We cannot, of course, coerce people into goodness, but we can and should insist that some standards must be met if society itself—on which the very existence of the human personality depends—is to persist. Drawing the line that defines those standards is difficult and contentious, but if crack and heroin use do not fall below it, what does?[26]

Taking drugs signals that one refuses to take responsibilities as a citizen. In this way, drugs are a threat to the continuation of social order.

The Libertarian Point of View

As usual, the extreme libertarian is entirely consistent. The 1992 Libertarian Party platform advocated the repeal of all laws that prohibit the production, sale, possession, or use of drugs. In the midst of the public outcry to increase penalties on drug use, the libertarian journal, *Reason*, devoted a special section of its October 1988 issue to drug legalization. For the libertarian, drug use is a personal matter in which the state has no business. This position was stated eloquently by the radical psychiatrist, Thomas Szasz. Szasz writes, "Every individual is capable of injuring or killing himself. This potentiality is a fundamental expression of human freedom. . . . I believe that just as we regard freedom of speech and religion as fundamental rights, so we should also regard freedom of self-medication as a fundamental right."[27] Szasz, like most libertarians, believes strongly in individual free will. The choice of individuals to do well or do ill, to help themselves or harm themselves, is ultimately a personal choice. Szasz even goes so far as to argue that drugs can be likened to ideas. "Although I recognize that some drugs—notably heroin, the amphetamines, and LSD, among those now in vogue—may have undesirable or dangerous consequences, I favor free trade in drugs for the same reason the Founding Fathers favored free trade in ideas. In an open society, it is none of the government's business what idea a man puts into his mind; likewise it should be none of the government's business what drug he puts into his body."[28] This right to control one's body is similar to the argument that pro-choice feminists make about their right to have abortions. Szasz makes an interesting point in generalizing his argument by noting that most medicines are available only with a doctor's prescription. If you wished to give yourself insulin or penicillin, you would need a doctor's signature (and pay her or him for that signature), rather than just purchasing it for yourself. Szasz sees this control as being as wrong as restrictive laws on drug use.

For some, the issue is the right to privacy, for others it is the right to freedom of choice, and for still others it is the right to pursue happiness. After all, according to Michael Aldrich, drug use is enjoyable: "Marijuana should be legalized because it's fun. Social use of *cannabis* [marijuana] depends primarily on the fact that altering one's perception is pleasurable; if the mental changes produced by smoking, eating, or drinking marijuana are not pleasurable, use will not normally be continued."[29] This assumes that the drug will not control the individual, but that the individual will have sufficient power of thought to decide about his or her own drug use. The debate over the "addictive" properties of cocaine deals with this issue. There are many things that we strongly enjoy consuming and consume regularly, even against "our own" better judgment (for example, coffee or chocolate), but does this mean that we are physiologically addicted? There is no single definition of what "addiction" means. Just as our society (imperfectly) socializes people to the use of alcohol and regulates its use, so libertarians suggest that we can do that with drugs.[30]

Libertarians believe the drug "problem" is created by drug laws, rather than by the drugs themselves. Prohibition turns otherwise honest citizens into criminals. Further, making drugs illegal may increase drug impurities and may make the drugs stronger.[31] (Consider the increased potency of "crack" and the decreased potency of "lite beer.") The libertarian disputes the conservative's claim that drug use is not a victimless crime, saying that although some may be indirectly hurt or offended by drug use and relationships may change, coercion is not involved. Indeed, laws against drug use cost the society enormous sums in law enforcement (estimates are as high as $10 billion per year) and thousands of lives in drug-sale-related murders and crimes committed in order to get money for drugs, priced artificially high because they are illegal.

Libertarians perceive a serious problem in that drug laws give the government additional powers. An editorial in *Reason* entitled, "Making War on Americans," articulates this point:

> What the New Right and their allies want is nothing less than an all-out mobilization, enlisting the Army, the Navy, the Air Force, the IRS, the Justice Department, and the State Department in an all-out war on drug producers and consumers. The price we would pay for all this: the loss of more of our dwindling freedoms. . . . [W]ar is the health of the State . . . the main result of the war on drugs will be to build an ever more powerful and oppressive American State.[32]

Drug laws (particularly those in force in the 1960s) gave the police extensive powers to search homes, cars, and people—powers that libertarians feel are far more deadly than an occasional toke or even a snort of cocaine. As theologian Walter Wink notes, arguing for legalization, "When we oppose evil with the same weapons that evil employs, we commit the same atrocities, violate the same civil liberties and break the same laws as do those whom we oppose. We become what we hate."[33] The war on drugs has us as casualties.

The Social Democratic Point of View

Social democrats are of several minds about regulating drug use. They realize that drugs often harm the most vulnerable groups in society—minorities and the young; yet, they also recognize that drug enforcement has typically come down hardest on these groups.

The social democrat points out that for most of our history, drugs have not been regulated. Why did this change? The answer: racial and ethnic prejudice. David Richards, in his book *Sex, Drugs, Death, and the Law*, writes that "the use of liquor in the United States was identified with the Catholic immigrants and their subversive (non-Protestant) values; when heroin came under attack, it was identified with Chinese influences from which

America, it was said, must be protected; marijuana was associated with undesirable Hispanic influences on American values, and cocaine with black influences."[34] President William Howard Taft, for example, linked cocaine to rape by southern blacks.[35] More recently, the attack on drugs has been seen by some to be an attack on young people. Significantly, one of the states with the most liberal drug laws is Utah, a state with a homogeneous population.[36]

Class bias is evident in who gets arrested for drug abuse and who does not. Typically, middle-class citizens are not affected by drug laws, whereas the poor, the young, and nonwhites receive the brunt of the enforcement. For some on the left, such as Michael Rossman, a San Francisco political activist, this presents a cruel paradox: While the government attacks the young, it ignores other "criminal elements." "As for the government, I think it should keep its bloody hands off the young and its sacraments . . . and turn its attention towards cleansing our society of its dreadful ugliness and violence, instead of helping industry turn the sky black for a buck, exploit man as badly as nature, and play at genocide here and there."[37]

Ultimately, the drug problem becomes, for social democrats, an economic problem, connected to societal racism. Ira Glasser, executive director of the American Civil Liberties Union, notes that drug dealing occurs because of a lack of economic justice: "Drug dealing is the major economic opportunity this country provides ghetto youth. How do we tell kids with no realistic economic opportunity, 'just say no' to $300 or more a day? The money, not the drug, attracts many ambitious young people into a life of violence."[38] Pushing drugs is one of the few means of escaping poverty.

Social democrats are not calling for government inaction, but, rather, for government to act in other areas, such as fighting discrimination and pollution. With regard to drug use, social democrats do not call for a free market in drugs, as do libertarians; they want a regulated market. Some, such as *Consumer Reports*, speak of drugs (especially marijuana) as a hazardous product that should be regulated. Implicit in the social democrat's view is the extensive government regulation of the quality of drugs. This would require the Food and Drug Administration or the Consumer Product Safety Commission to ensure the purity and quality of the drugs and to tax or even sell them. Columnist Charles Krauthammer satirizes where this might lead:

> You come in and browse at a government-run store that prices and sells the stuff. After checking out competing brands of hashish, heroin, crack, and PCP, you pay for what you want and take the lot home. But . . . you are not permitted to buy a lethal dose unless you have a doctor's prescription. . . . *The Economist* . . . weighs in with the helpful suggestion that it should be distributed by the . . . "post office, which has perfected the art of driving customers away."[39]

Ultimately, this social democratic approach makes the "problem" of drug "abuse" a medical problem, rather than a legal one.

There is, however, another side to the social democratic argument—a position that is not as lenient toward legalized drug use. Social democrats who oppose drug legalization are concerned about the effects of the legalization of drugs on African Americans and Hispanics. In 1970, the Board of the American Civil Liberties Union refused to support a proposal to allow the freedom to use and purchase heroin because of what it might do to minorities.[40] Since social democrats believe in a benevolently paternalistic (or maternalistic) government, such thinking makes sense. Their approach criticizes the "ideology of tolerance." Ronald Bayer, an expert on attitudes toward heroin, sees heroin decriminalization as repressive.

> The ideology of tolerance, present as a critical force in the service of freeing those caught in the web of contemporary social control, actually tends to serve a profoundly repressive function. . . . Instead of assisting in the struggle against human misery those concepts provide the justification for choosing human misery. Because the ideology of tolerance tends to conceal the extent to which certain forms of deviance are reactions to deprivations rooted in the social order—indeed, can be considered as determined by that order—and because it seeks to integrate behavior that should serve as the starting point for a critique of society, it serves to neutralize the possibility of opposition.[41]

This view denies some of the drug user's autonomy, but it does so because the proponents believe these individuals do not understand the structural reasons for their drug habit. These users do not recognize that drug use prevents them from asserting their rights and gaining economic and social equality. Physical addiction and a profit-driven economic system reinforce each other in destroying the human potential of these young people. Such an understanding puts decision making where, some suggest, it rightfully belongs—in the hands of the sociologist.

Marijuana and Social Research

For many students, marijuana seems almost as much a part of college life as multiple-choice tests. It was not always so. Prior to the mid-1960s, "blowing smoke" or "sipping tea" was something that "good" people did not do. Marijuana was found in various deviant subsocieties: jazz musicians, beat poets, and prostitutes. It was partly for this reason that Howard S. Becker's article, "Becoming a Marijuana User," had such a dramatic impact when it was published in the prestigious *American Journal of Sociology* in 1953.[42] Not only did Becker present the thoughts and actions of marijuana users in their own words, but he did not treat them as criminals! He did not ask where these people went wrong.

The problem for Becker, a prominent symbolic interactionist, was, How does a person learn to smoke marijuana properly, how does he or she define the effects of the drug, and how does he or she decide these effects are pleasurable? In order to answer these questions, Becker (and his colleagues Harold Finestone and Solomon Kobrin) conducted in-depth interviews with fifty marijuana users to learn about their experiences with the drug—how they became socialized to marijuana use.

Unlike the in-depth interview study of transracial adopted parents to be discussed in Chapter Eight, Becker is not particularly concerned with the *people* he interviewed but, rather, with the *process* of becoming a marijuana user or the *natural history* of drug use. Becker does not agree with those who suggest that marijuana use is related to some trait in the individual user—a point of view that we can now largely discard since a majority of American youth has tried the drug. Instead Becker asks, What must someone *do* to "get high"?

Choosing to rely on in-depth interviews, Becker is, in some sense, at the mercy of the users for his information and, thus, must rely on their perceptions. By treating a "deviant" as a normal person, this research technique leans toward the libertarian attitude of refusing to condemn this behavior on the basis of societal attitudes. To accept the informants' accounts as accurate implies (although does not insist) that someone must see this behavior as an acceptable choice of rational, reasonable people—or why else trust them? While conducting the interviews, Becker moonlighted as a professional jazz musician, so we might suppose that he had some familiarity with this subculture. This permitted him to check his interview findings with information gained elsewhere.

Have you smoked marijuana? If you have, recall the first time you tried it. Did you try to smoke the reefer as if it were a cigarette? Did you wonder what all the fuss was about? One of Becker's conclusions is that knowing how to smoke dope does not come naturally. Just as we must learn our multiplication tables, so we must learn how to inhale—deeply and long. If you do not draw the marijuana smoke into your lungs, nothing much happens. Without learning the proper technique to get high—often taught by a friend—you are not likely to continue to smoke.

Becker also suggests that you must learn what being "high" feels like. Specifically, you must "feel" the effects caused by marijuana and then must connect them with the use of the drug. At first, you may not be sure how you will react, and you search for clues. You get high "with a little help from [your] friends." One user explains, "I heard little remarks that were made by other people. Somebody said, 'My legs are rubbery,' and I can't remember all the remarks that were made because I was very attentively listening for all these cues for what I was supposed to feel like."[43] Becker argues that it is crucial to label feelings in such a way that you know you are high. Because the user is focusing so hard on what he or she is feeling, possibly part of being "high" the first time is simply becoming aware of those things that are always present but that are never noticed.

Finally, to continue to use marijuana you must decide that the feelings are pleasant. For some people (usually former users), the experience may be decidedly unpleasant. You could, for example, feel like you are losing your mind. Distortion of spatial relationships and sounds, violent hunger and thirst, and panic are not always fun. Unless you can label your physical reactions as enjoyable, marijuana use will stop. Thus, Becker places great emphasis on the definitions that users have of their experience and on the fact that these experiences are not only chemical but are also social. Your fellow users have a large impact in determining the nature of your experiences but, ultimately, it is a personal decision whether to continue to smoke.

> It is quite common for experienced users suddenly to have an unpleasant or frightening experience, which they cannot define as pleasurable, either because they have used a larger amount of marijuana than usual or because it turns out to be a higher-quality marijuana than they expected. . . . [He] may make this the occasion for a rethinking of his attitude toward the drug and decide that it no longer can give him pleasure. When this occurs and is not followed by a redefinition of the drug as capable of producing pleasure, use will cease.[44]

Note that Becker discusses drug use as a voluntary decision of the user. People have free will in their marijuana consumption. Since marijuana is not overtly harmful and does not harm others, Becker's conclusions are consistent with the libertarian approach to social order. Why should society prevent rational, reasonable people from doing what they wish? If some people do not find marijuana pleasant, they are not forced to smoke it. Like the libertarian, Becker, accepting the word of those he interviewed, appears to advocate personal decision making, rather than government control of citizens. Marijuana is a "recreational" drug, so this line of reasoning goes, and it would be a highly intrusive government that would limit personal "recreation."

Social Control, Deviance, and Drug Use

What should the role of the state be in dealing with deviance? How tolerant should we be in dealing with behavior that is different from our own? No one wishes to live in a society in which everyone must march in lock-step, but how much diversity is too much? Libertarians have the simplest answer to this problem. If it feels good, do it—just as long as it does not physically coerce others. They see the ability to be deviant as a sign that freedom exists. Perhaps the most frightening aspect of George Orwell's *1984* is not the various tortures and murders practiced by the government, but the horrifying sameness of the people, the drabness of their lives and world. For the libertarian, youthful rebellion is not something to be feared but is simply the attempt of the new generation to demonstrate that it is free. Only to the extent that young people choose to behave like their peers is there danger of deviance actually being subcultural conformity.

The social democrat sees each act of deviance in its own context. Who is doing what to whom, and how does it conform to the ideals of equality and justice? Painting swastikas on Jewish synagogues is deviant, but it is not the sort of deviance that a government should tolerate. On the other hand, dress styles that express ethnic or subcultural values might be seen by the social democrat as an indication of a healthy multicultural state.

A critical issue for the social democrat is the structural conditions of society that gave impetus to the deviant display. Some deviance, crime, for example, is due as much (or more) to the social condition in which the criminal finds himself or herself, than it is to any free will of the criminal. For the social democrat, who generally accepts conflict theory, deviance indicates structural inequalities that need to be corrected by changing the priorities of society. What the powerful do is often considered "normal," but similar behaviors by the powerless are labeled criminal or mentally ill. The powerful have greater access to the means of defining behavior and more control over those who enforce that behavior. Drugs favored by the rich are legal, or not very illegal, whereas the drug preferences of the poor have long prison terms attached to them.

The conservative, of course, sees the issue of deviance in quite a different light. There is within any society an absolute moral order; as a result, there should be little tolerance for behavior that attacks the core values of that order. Drugs, pornography, homosexuality, and abortion fly in the face of what most American conservatives believe is morally proper behavior. These behaviors are defined as undermining the family and the work ethic. If we permit behavior that undercuts these fundamental institutions, little will hold us together as a society. Although conservatives do not wish to enforce a rigid uniformity, they are much more willing to draw lines beyond which we must not pass under penalty of law. Because conservatives value order and, thus, a stable functional interrelationship within social systems, the smaller the diversity on important value questions, the stronger will a society be. Drug *use* poses the same bogey for the conservative that drug *laws* pose for the libertarian.

Questions

1. Should marijuana be legalized? If it is legalized, should it be regulated by the government?
2. Should cocaine be legalized? If it is legalized, should it be regulated by the government?
3. Should marijuana possession be decriminalized?
4. Are certain drugs still illegal because of the characteristics of their users?
5. Should there be a free market in drugs?
6. Does drug use undermine the "fabric" of society?
7. Should young people under eighteen be allowed to use drugs if they wish?
8. Does the "ideology of tolerance" actually serve a repressive function in society?
9. Should society welcome deviance or try to outlaw it? Is diversity healthy for society?

For Further Study

Adler, Patricia. *Wheeling and Dealing: An Ethnography of an Upper-Level Drug Dealing and Smuggling Community*. New York: Columbia University Press, 1985.

Bayer, Ronald. "Heroin Decriminalization and the Ideology of Tolerance: A Critical View." *Law and Society* 12(1978): 301–318.

Benjamin, Daniel, and Roger Leroy Miller. *Undoing Drugs: Beyond Legalization*. New York: Basic Books, 1992.

Becker, Howard. *Outsiders*. New York: Free Press, 1963. (This work includes "Becoming a Marijuana User.")

Galliher, John F. *Morals Legislation Without Morality: The Case of Nevada*. New Brunswick, NJ: Rutgers University Press, 1983.

Hart, Harold W., ed. *Drugs: For & Against*. New York: Hart, 1970.

Nadelmann, Ethan A., "U.S. Drug Policy: A Bad Export." *Foreign Policy* 70(Spring 1988): 83–108.

Szasz, Thomas. *Ceremonial Chemistry: The Ritual Persecution of Drugs, Addicts, and Pushers*. New York: Anchor, 1975.

Wilson, James Q. "Against the Legalization of Drugs." *Commentary* 89 (February 1990): 21–28.

Notes and References

1. D. Stanley Eitzen, *In Conflict and Order: Understanding Society*, 2nd ed. (Boston: Allyn and Bacon, 1982), pp. 180–199.
2. Frances Fox Piven and Richard Cloward, *Regulating the Poor: The Function of Public Welfare* (New York: Random House, 1971).
3. Frances K. Heussenstamm, "Bumper Stickers and Cops." *Transaction* (February 1971): 32–33.
4. Louis Wirth, "Urbanism as a Way of Life," *American Journal of Sociology* 44(July 1983): 1–24.
5. Edwin H. Sutherland and Donald R. Cressey, *Principles of Criminology*, 7th ed. (Philadelphia: J. B. Lippincott, 1966), pp. 81–82.
6. Robert K. Merton, *Social Theory and Social Structure*, enlarged ed. (New York: Free Press, 1968), pp. 185–214.
7. Walter B. Miller, "Lower Class Culture as a Generating Milieu of Gang Delinquency," *Journal of Social Issues* 14:3 (1958): 5–19.
8. William Ryan, *Blaming the Victim* (New York: Vintage, 1972).
9. Bob Dylan, "Rainy Day Woman #12 and 35," *Blonde on Blonde*, Columbia Records, 1966.
10. National Commission on Marijuana and Drug Abuse, *Drug Use in America: Problem in Perspective* (Washington, D.C.: U.S. Government Printing Office, 1973), p. 9.
11. Lester Grinspoon, *Marijuana Reconsidered* (Cambridge: Harvard University Press, 1977).
12. National Institute on Drug Abuse, *The National Survey on Drug Abuse: Main Findings*, 1985, reported in the U.S. Bureau of the Census, *Statistical Abstract of the United States* (Washington, D.C.: U.S. Government Printing Office, 1988), p. 112.
13. One former government official noted that marijuana contains "dioxin." Allegedly it contains dioxin because of government spraying. Abbie Hoffman, "Reefer Madness," *Nation* 245(November 27, 1987), p. 580.
14. Gallup Poll, December 4–7, 1990, Survey #GO 922001.
15. Walter Wink, "Biting the Bullet: The Case for Legalizing Drugs," *Christian Century* 107(August 8–15, 1990): 738.
16. Marvin C. Miller, "Why Prohibition Has Failed," *High Times* (January 1989): 33.
17. Ethan A. Nadelmann, "U.S. Drug Policy: A Bad Export," *Foreign Policy* 70(Spring 1988): 100.
18. Rae Corelli, "A New War of Words," *Maclean's* (January 22, 1990): 39.
19. Max Rafferty in Harold H. Hart, ed., *Drugs: For & Against* (New York: Hart, 1970), p. 28.
20. Quoted in Tom Morganthau, "Drug Fever in Washington," *Newsweek* 108(September 22, 1986): 39.
21. Wink, "Biting the Bullet," p. 736.
22. Carl T. Rowan, "The Drug Scourge Must Be Stopped," *Readers' Digest* (August 1983): 135.
23. Richard Vigilante, "Pot-talk: Is Decriminalization Advisable: No," *National Review* (April 29, 1983): 489.

24. William J. Bennett, "Drug Policy and the Intellectuals," *The Police Chief* (May 1990): 31.
25. Judianne Densen-Gerber in Hart, *Drugs: For & Against*, p. 113.
26. James Q. Wilson, "Against the Legalization of Drugs," *Commentary* 89(February 1990): 24.
27. Thomas S. Szasz, "The Ethics of Addiction," *Harper's* (April 1972) 75, 77.
28. Ibid., p. 75.
29. Michael Aldrich, in Hart, *Drugs: For & Against.*, p. 77.
30. Charles Paul Freund, "Legalize Everything," *Reason* (October 1988) 29.
31. David Boaz, "The Corner Drugstore," *Reason* (October 1988): 23; Michael Aldrich, "Legalize the Lesser to Minimize the Greater: Modern Applications of Ancient Wisdom," *Journal of Drug Issues*, 20(4): 543.
32. Robert Poole, Jr., "Making War on Americans," *Reason* (October 1981): 6.
33. Wink, "Biting the Bullet," p. 736.
34. David A. J. Richards, *Sex, Drugs, Death and the Law* (Totowa, NJ: Rowman and Littlefield, 1982), p. 179.
35. Michael C. Monson, "The Dirty Little Secret Behind Our Drug Laws," *Reason* (November 1980): 49.
36. John F. Galliher and Linda Basilick, "Utah's Liberal Drug Laws: Structural Foundations and Triggering Events," *Social Problems* 26(1979): 284–297.
37. Michael Rossman, in Hart, *Drugs: For & Against*, p. 180.
38. Ira Glasser, "Now for a Drug Policy That Doesn't Do Harm," *The New York Times*, (December 18, 1990): A24.
39. Charles Krauthammer, "Mistakes of the Legalizers . . .," *The Washington Post* (April 13, 1990): A25.
40. Ronald Bayer, "Heroin Decriminalization and the Ideology of Tolerance: A Critical View," *Law and Society* 12(1978): 307.
41. Ibid., p. 314.
42. Howard S. Becker, "Becoming a Marijuana User," *American Journal of Sociology* 59(1953): 235–242.
43. Ibid., p. 238.
44. Ibid., p. 241.

CHAPTER FOUR

Human Sexuality: Should Adolescents Engage in Premarital Sexual Intercourse? Should Contraceptives Be Distributed in High Schools?

> When two people are under the influence of the most violent, most insane, most delusive, and most transient of passions, they are required to swear that they will remain in that excited, abnormal, and exhausting condition continuously until death do them part.
> —George Bernard Shaw, Preface to *Getting Married*

■ Passion is the most prickly of our social relations. By controlling it, we *almost* destroy it. This control is perhaps what makes us distinctively human. Unlike other animals, we *can* redirect or repress our sexual desires in the name of social order. Human beings can sublimate passion.

Even though there are biological components of human sexuality, the form that sexual behavior takes is learned, rather than innate. Men and women are socialized to their places in the sexual order. Cross-cultural studies of sexual behavior[1] show a wide variation in what is acceptable. Homosexuality, for example, is treated quite differently among cultures—from being required to being punishable by death. The positions in which men and women practice sexual intercourse reveal how incredibly plastic human anatomy can be. The "missionary position," which our society defines as "normal," is not universal, and much sexual satisfaction occurs from other angles.

Research on sexuality has not had a long history, partially as a result of our "Puritan" or "Victorian" belief (until recently) that it is not a fit subject for study. Nearly a half-century ago, Alfred Kinsey and his colleagues at the Institute for Sex Research at Indiana University undertook the first major studies of human sexuality. Kinsey, a zoologist by training, published lengthy volumes on male and female sexual behavior (in 1948 and 1953, respectively).[2] These volumes, based on large, if biased, samples, demonstrated that there was a much greater variety of sexual behavior in the United States than many people had imagined. For example, Kinsey uncovered that nearly 40 percent of all adult males had engaged in homosexual behavior, nearly 70 percent had visited a prostitute, 60 percent had had oral sex, about 25 percent of the married women had committed adultery, and so forth. Based on his figures, Kinsey could claim that "a call for a cleanup of sex offenders in the community is, in effect, a proposal that 5 percent of the population should support the other 95 percent in penal institutions."[3] While Kinsey's exact figures cannot be trusted because of the difficulties in obtaining honest responses, his data are reliable enough to demonstrate that there is considerable diversity of sexual behavior in the U.S. population. Recent studies have partially overcome Kinsey's problem of validity.

Although people speak glibly of the "sexual revolution," what appears to have changed most dramatically in the last thirty years is *attitudes*. Attitudes are becoming increasingly liberalized to conform to more liberal behavior. The *double standard*, which required different sets of behavior for men and women and suggested that women could not enjoy sex, has diminished considerably. Likewise, the moral outrage that many people at one time reserved for homosexuals has been curtailed, although not eliminated entirely. It would have been unthinkable three decades ago for a publicly admitted homosexual to run for public office, much less to win. It would have been unthinkable for a law to prohibit discrimination against homosexuals. Today, there are even marriage manuals for devout, evangelical Christians that suggest that sexual intercourse (inside marriage, of course) can be fun and not simply for procreation. Television movies gain large ratings by dealing with topics such as incest, prostitution, and adultery—words that could not be *mentioned* on the airwaves a few decades ago. American society has become sexualized, and the real losers of the sexual revolution are those people for whom sexuality is not that important. Today, however, values may be changing again. The publicity accorded to the herpes epidemic has only intensified given the AIDS pandemic. Sex must now be "safe." For many, the danger of sex had been its lure. It is not clear how this will affect sexual behavior in the heterosexual community, but the changes among homosexual males have been dramatic. The promiscuity of the 1970s has changed dramatically to emphasize intimacy with fewer partners and avoiding the "exchange of bodily fluids." As the death toll continues to mount, other changes in our attitudes toward sexuality and our intimate behaviors are likely.

In a diverse society such as our own, we should expect differences in sexual ideology. Ira Reiss, a prominent sex researcher, describes two major ideologies[4] that he claims characterize American society. The first he defines as the *traditional-romantic ideology* and characterizes it by the following tenets:

> 1. Gender roles should be distinct and interdependent, with the male gender role as dominant. . . . 2. Body-centered sexuality is to be avoided by females. . . . 3. Sexuality is a very powerful emotion and one that should be particularly feared by females. . . . 4. The major goal of sexuality is heterosexual coitus and that is where the man's focus should be placed. . . . 5. Love redeems sexuality from its guilt, particularly for females.[5]

This sharply contrasts with the *modern-naturalistic* perspective, which currently seems more dominant. Its tenets consist of the following:

> 1. Gender roles should be similar for males and females and should promote equalitarian participation in the society. 2. Body-centered sexuality is of less worth than person-centered sexuality, but it still has a positive value for both genders. 3. One's sexual emotions are strong but manageable, by both males and females, in the same way as other basic emotions. 4. The major goals of sexuality are physical pleasure and psychological intimacy in a variety of sexual acts and this is so [for] both genders. 5. A wide range of sexuality should be accepted without guilt by both genders providing it does not involve force or fraud.[6]

Of course, it is altogether possible to accept a stance that merges these two perspectives. An egalitarian view of sexuality might be coupled with certain traditional themes such as the importance of love and marriage. Reiss's ideologies stress two different functional properties of sexuality, procreation and intimacy. Since the two perspectives are typically held by different groups, the conflict between them is not only ideological, but social as well (for instance, religious people versus nonreligious people; or less educated Americans versus those with more schooling). Approaches to sexuality are based on attitudes toward human nature (it is good or tainted by selfishness or original sin) and toward social order (it should be open to a wide range of possible behavior or needs to be controlled by social institutions). Nowhere is the dispute over human sexuality more evident than in discussions of teenage sexuality.

■ Questions:

*Should Adolescents Engage in Premarital Sexual
Intercourse? Should Contraceptives Be Distributed in
High Schools?*

An eighth-grader once asked a sex counselor, "Why, if God did not
want teenagers to have sex, did He make it possible?" She might also have
asked why did He make it so much fun? While data on the extent of
premarital teenage sexuality are not entirely to be trusted, most studies find
that approximately half of America's teenagers have engaged in premarital
intercourse at least once, with the figures somewhat higher for boys than
for girls.[7] By the time young adults leave college, a substantial majority of
them are no longer virgins. Whether or not this is a problem is a matter of
opinion. But the number of teenage pregnancies is a major social problem.
One study estimates that 1,000,000 adolescents become pregnant each year,
but only one-third are married.[8] Ira Reiss reports that 240,000 children are
born each year to unmarried teenagers.[9] While the numbers change, these
findings do indicate that teenage sexuality is a cause for concern.

This sexual activity occurs within a social context. As mentioned
previously, attitudes toward sexuality have changed. One study found that
83 percent of college students approved of premarital sex if the couple was
engaged or in love.[10] As might be expected, adults are less likely to approve
of premarital sex than young people, but even here more adults now accept
premarital sex than reject it. A 1986 survey found that only 27 percent of
adults felt that premarital sex was "always wrong," while 39 percent felt that
it was not wrong at all; the rest of the sample fell between these extremes.[11]
Many states now permit consenting adults to do what they wish in the
privacy of their own bedrooms. Likewise, many states have changed their
statutory rape laws. Previous laws criminalized a girl's sexual intercourse
below a certain age. That a girl was willing and that the boy was her peer
were typically not considered. These laws assumed a young girl could never
freely choose to have intercourse and that the sexual act was always forced
upon her. This is one way in which the double standard worked to the
detriment of males. Changes in these rarely enforced laws have made them
sex blind and have lowered the age for consent to make them more realistic.
Laws are slowly changing, reflecting and, according to some, *encouraging*
the present sexual behavior and creating the increase in teenage pregnancies.

Like any significant portion of the social fabric, a change in something
as basic as sex will affect many aspects of social life. Psychologist Albert Ellis,
in his book *The American Sexual Tragedy*, explains how this chain of events
could occur:

Just suppose, for example, that a group of social scientists made an intensive study of the problem of premarital sex relations, and finally recommended that such relations be encouraged and legalized, and that effective birth control and prophylactic measures be taught to all school children. Concomitant with such an acceptance of fornication, the entire meaning of marriage might be radically altered, population statistics might begin to be seriously affected, the vocational plans of millions of young people might have to undergo considerable change, present-day concepts of individualism versus social living might undergo drastic revision, enormous socio-economic changes might be brought about, religious practices and theory might have to alter greatly, and numerous other profound changes in American ways of living might well occur.[12]

The point that Ellis is making is crucial for sociologists. Sex is not simply the pleasant friction produced by two bodies; rather, sexuality has social meaning, and changes in it are not independent of other social changes. For this reason, if for no other, there is a considerable public policy interest in adolescent sexuality.

Ellis was more prescient than he might have imagined in raising the issue of providing birth control information to children. In 1970, in response to the increasing number of teenage births, Congress added Title X to the Public Health Service Act. This law provided federal funds to clinics that offered contraceptives to women under eighteen. Now a girl could receive birth control devices, including the "pill," without her parents' approval—free, if she could not afford to pay. The federal government was helping girls to engage in behavior that was illegal under the statutory rape laws. Still, such a provision struck many people as a sensible solution to the growing number of teenage pregnancies. Despite the claims of supporters that this provision would decrease the number of pregnancies and cut down on venereal disease, the incidence of both increased dramatically—although possibly by not as much as they would have if contraceptives had not been made available. One study suggests that 400,000 pregnancies were averted by these family planning clinics.[13] Whatever their effect, by the 1980s these clinics had mushroomed and were heavily used. By the 1980s, the government spent $162 million on approximately 5,000 family planning clinics that treated 1,300,000 adolescents and gave out half a million prescriptions for birth control pills.[14] Inner-city high schools have increasingly established health clinics, which as one of their services, dispense or prescribe contraceptives.

But the pill is not a perfect solution for the contraceptive needs of teenagers. Putting aside the health risks, for a teenage girl to remember to take her pill on a daily basis is a considerable triumph of willpower. Further, being on "the pill" serves as an indicator to many that intercourse is "planned," rather than spontaneous. Finally, and perhaps most consequential, "the pill" doesn't protect the couple from AIDS and other sexually transmitted diseases. The pill might prevent a life, but it can't save one.

The "hot" contraceptive in the 1980s has been the condom, which is inexpensive, user-friendly, prevents disease, and requires little forethought. With the increase in public support for sex education in schools (87 percent now support it with the majority saying that it should begin by sixth grade)[15] and a willingness to see advertisements for condoms on television (70 percent supported them in 1991),[16] some believe that the distribution of condoms in public high schools is an effective and appropriate means for preventing the spread of AIDS and preventing teenage pregnancies. School boards, such those in San Francisco, Philadelphia, and New York, that have considered making contraceptives available in schools have often found themselves at the center of intense controversy. The public is divided on whether schools should provide contraceptives. According to one poll in 1986, 36 percent approve and 53 percent disapprove.[17] The issue raises an interesting debate on how teenage sexuality should be handled. Should it be subsidized or squashed?

The Conservative Point of View

The conservative has sometimes been pictured as the Scrooge of the Bedroom. It is not so much that conservatives do not enjoy sex, but rather they are more concerned about its effects on society. For the conservative, sexual behavior is potentially dangerous because if left unchecked it could subvert the social order. It needs to be explicitly regulated. David Carlin, Jr., writing in *Commonweal* magazine, explains the tie between sex and the social order:

> Though sexual activity might be *performed* in private, it was not really a private act. Others—family, friends, neighbors, potential spouses, and society generally—felt that they had interests which might be jeopardized by one's sexual activity; hence social regulation of that activity was warranted. The traditional rule that sex should be confined within marriage meant that one was not free to act sexually in one's capacity as a mere private or natural individual; instead, one acted in virtue of a kind of public office—husband or wife—that society had artificially created and inducted one into.... Since even our genitalia were not available for free private use, society must have powerful claims, indeed, on the use to which we put our hands and brains. Though this lesson was aimed at everyone, its special target was adolescents; if they could be taught to regard so fascinating a business as sex as subject to societal discipline, there was hope they might appreciate the need for social control and social solidarity generally.[18]

The important sociological issue is individual control versus social control. The reason that conservatives want to control sexuality is not because they feel that the physical act is sinful, but because its effects may undermine the social order. Some conservatives use religious dicta—particularly in the New Testament—to support the view that this is God's will. This goes only so far since others can point to joyously erotic passages in the Song of Solomon and other parts of the Old Testament. Nevertheless, the religious rationale serves as a convenient means of enforcing the social order that conservatives feel is vital to a stable society.

Once a girl under eighteen who lost her virginity was a rebel; today she is a conformist. A teenager must have a strong will to be chaste in the face of peer pressure. Author Joyce Maynard relates the agony that some teenagers must go through if they resist this pressure: "I—the one who slept alone, the one whose only pills were vitamins and aspirin—I was the embarrassed one. How has it happened, what have we come to, that the scarlet letter these days isn't A, but V? ... Virginity has become not a flower or a jewel, a precious treasure for Prince Charming or a lively, prized and guarded gift, but a dusty relic—an anachronism. Most of all, it's an embarrassment."[19] Today most adults, even those who do not like the change in public values, believe there is little they can do about teenage sexuality; so, rather than trying to convince teenagers not to "do it," they try to teach them to use birth control. The attitude seems to be "If you can't be good, at least be careful!"

The conservative believes that the availability of birth control devices to adolescents creates an atmosphere that tells the child that recreational premarital sex is acceptable, normal, and expected. Boston's Cardinal Bernard Law argued that distributing birth control devices in schools would "place the Boston public schools in the position of implicitly condoning or encouraging sexual activity among students."[20] Boston University president John Silber sees this as part of "the decadence of [our] time."[21] While others suggest that the choice is between providing birth control or having pregnancies, the conservative offers a third option: the less fashionable one of abstinence. Just as mores have changed to permit open sexuality, they can revert back.

Ultimately, the issue is the conservative's belief that the state has the obligation to legislate for morality, rather than legislate against it; allowing adolescents access to the techniques of sexual experimentation weakens what the conservative sees as the glue of moral order, and in the process weakens family relationships by taking contraceptive decisions away from parental control. Some conservatives hoped that the Age of AIDS would usher in an age of abstinence, not a safe-sex scene.

The Social Democratic Point of View

The social democrat tends to take a pragmatic attitude toward sexuality; so long as it does not disrupt the social fabric it should be left alone. To the extent it causes a social problem—such as unwanted pregnancies and disease—it should be dealt with as a health and welfare problem. Since primary social institutions, such as the family and the church, do not have special standing in the eyes of the social democrat, enforcing the chosen morality of these institutions is not a governmental requirement. Indeed, the support of "traditional morality" (in the conservative's sense) may well direct us away from considering those real social problems that cause inequality and injustice in a society. Writing in 1931, Robert Briffault makes this point in strong terms:

> The grotesque incongruity which, in the current usage of Western culture, assigns the appellation of "morality" to sexual restrictions exclusively, ignoring as appertaining to a lower plane of ethical obligations, justice, intellectual and social honesty, charity, and every moral demand on the conduct of human beings in their social relations, is not only grotesque, but grossly immoral. . . . Western morality is quick at suppressing literature, but slow at suppressing war; zealous in the abolition of obscene postcards, but lukewarm in the abolition of obscene slums; active in putting down white slavery, but apathetic in putting down wage-slavery; alert in preventing vice, but slothful in putting down starvation; shocked at clothing insufficient for purposes of modesty, but indifferent to clothing insufficient for purposes of warmth. It spares no effort to secure a perfectly pure world, but is ready to tolerate a perfectly iniquitous one.[22]

These same charges might equally apply to contemporary conservative Republicans. They might object, however, by saying that concern about morality does not exclude concern about social inequality. Yet for social democrats, control of sexual behavior takes second place to the concerns of economic equality.

When social democrats consider providing contraceptives in high schools, their primary concern is with its effects, rather than with its morality. School Chancellor Joseph Fernandez denies that there is a moral overtone to his desire to make condoms available in New York City public schools. He claims that "this is not an issue of morality. It is a matter of life and death."[23] While we cannot be certain how many teenagers would have gotten pregnant or ill because they did not get contraceptives at a school clinic, we can be reasonably certain that the availability of contraception prevents some disease and some pregnancy. One study found that sex education courses do not work well in promoting birth control unless they are combined with ready access to a health clinic.[24] For example, one early school clinic program in St. Paul, Minnesota, cut the pregnancy rate by half.[25] The social democrat assumes that teenagers will remain sexually active, and so the choice is between preventive medicine or cleaning up a mess afterward. Social democrats distinguish between enforcing an economic morality that decreases group prejudice and interfering with personal morality.

Ironically (and controversially) one of the groups that has underlined this pragmatic approach has been the National Conference of Catholic Bishops in a draft of their 1987 report, "The Many Faces of AIDS: A Gospel Response." The bishops wrote:

> Because we live in a pluralistic society, we acknowledge that some will not agree with our understanding of human sexuality. We recognize that public educational programs addressed to a wide audience will reflect the fact that some people will not act as they can and should. . . . In such situations, educational efforts, if grounded in [a] broader moral vision . . . could include accurate information about prophylactic devices proposed by some medical experts.[26]

This document did not specifically address the issues of contraceptives in school, but the same argument applies. The response from other church leaders, such as Cardinal O'Connor of New York, was one of outrage, arguing in conservative fashion that this was an invitation to promiscuity. The question comes down to whether we believe that people can and will change their sexual behaviors and how we should respond if they don't.

A final issue raised by social democrats is that those children who most need contraceptives are inner-city minorities. While girls in the best suburbs get pregnant and both boys and girls get AIDS, the statistical bulk of the problem is in poor and minority neighborhoods, and this is where most clinics are located. These programs are needed for the health of those the government has a particular responsibility to protect. As high school clinic coordinator Mary Hennrich noted of those who protested her clinic, "They think all kids are from ideal families in the suburbs and that all parents can talk openly with the kids about sex. It's not at all like that out there."[27] Yet some African-American ministers see these clinics as an effort to further destroy the black family, rather than to save black adolescents. Whenever we attempt to provide something for someone's own "best good," the questions of ulterior motives and stereotypes are raised.

The Libertarian Point of View

Libertarians are likely to be more permissive about sexual activity than either conservatives or social democrats. As long as the act is between two responsible individuals, then the government should not be involved. Unlike the conservative, the libertarian does not see society as having a vested interest in the pleasure two people give to each other. David Carlin, Jr., writes:

> Contemporary sexual morality . . . considers sex to be a strictly private concern. As for pre-marital sex, it regards as absurd the notion that one should be held answerable to others—even, or perhaps especially, to one's ultimate spouse who, according to old-fashioned ideas, was thought to have the right to resent one's early sexual activities with other persons. . . . [A]dolescent sex, at least when practiced with contraception and backstopped by abortion, is essentially unobjectionable.[28]

Libertarians consider sex natural and fun. They believe no one has the right to tell another person what his or her sexual values should be. This goes for teenagers as well as adults. Each teenager should make a personal decision. Birth control counselors, therefore, should help young men and women implement whatever decision they have made, but not help them make it. They should provide technical assistance, not morality. Libertarians, however, are often vague on the age at which this right of decision making begins.

The problem of sex is not sex itself, but the laws and repressive values related to it. This attitude of "Do your own thing, providing it doesn't hurt others" is sometimes called the Playboy Philosophy after a series of articles written by *Playboy* editor Hugh Hefner in 1962–1965, well before the era of AIDS. In these articles, Hefner proclaims that "sex can be one of the most profound and rewarding elements in the adventure of living; if we recognize it as not necessarily limited to procreation then we should also acknowledge openly that it is not necessarily limited to love either. Sex exists—with and without love—and in both forms it does far more good than harm. The attempts at its suppression, however, are almost universally harmful, both to the individuals involved and to society as a whole."[29] This is not to say that libertarians do not have values, but rather that their values emphasize maximizing pleasure. They define sexual freedom as equally important as political freedom. State control is offensive whether it is in the boardroom or in the bedroom, and in this they sharply disagree with social democrats. Remember that libertarians are not necessarily arguing for promiscuity or for "free sex." Instead, they suggest that these are personal issues on which reasonable people can differ.

The debate over distributing contraceptives in school health clinics is a curious one for libertarians. They believe the government has no place in subsidizing birth control devices for teenagers nor does it have any business spending taxpayers' monies preventing teens from getting pregnant or ill. Yet, the government is heavily involved in the "sex education" business.

Planned Parenthood receives one-quarter of a billion dollars each year from the government for its various programs.[30] Libertarians see no reason why adolescents should receive free contraceptives from the state. After all, with only modest embarrassment and a few dollars, any teen can walk into a drugstore and purchase a package of condoms. What is the state doing providing these easily available goods?[31]

Further, state control of health clinics often involves enforcing a "government morality." Libertarian psychiatrist Thomas Szasz notes that there is a moral struggle over what is taught in the public school: "You can see a pattern . . . when one group imposes its values on the schools, everyone else feels mugged."[32] Hence, the libertarian goal is that the long arm of the state should not extend to health clinics and, *ultimately*, that schools should be privatized.

Premarital Sex and Social Research

Sex is a topic, like religion, where there is an abundance of opinions, but a minimum of hard facts. Only recently has our society become sufficiently open to allow research on sexual subjects to be conducted. Several decades ago a national survey of the sexual behavior of teenage girls would have been impossible. In 1971 and then again in 1976, three sociological demographers, Melvin Zelnik, John F. Kantner, and Kathleen Ford, interviewed several thousand young women between the ages of fifteen and nineteen in their homes to learn about their premarital sexual activity, their use of contraceptives, and the frequency with which they became pregnant.[33] The value of this study rests particularly on the fact that it represents a random, representative sample of young American women. To the extent we can trust their responses (which the authors claim we can), these studies provide an accurate cross-section of American female adolescent behavior at two points in time.

By choosing an activity, in this case premarital sex, that is typically considered outside the bounds of "decent society" and treating those involved in an objective and nonjudgmental way, the study may be read by some as implicitly legitimating that behavior, and for this reason many conservatives object to research on sexual attitudes and behaviors. Although survey methodology seems congruent with either conflict theory or functionalism, the topic of these two surveys leans more heavily toward a more critical view of conventional morality. This suggestion, however, should not be pressed too far; clearly the researchers do not believe that the pregnancy of unmarried women is desirable.

Zelnik, Kantner, and Ford find that most young women see sexual intercourse prior to marriage as permissible, particularly if the two parties are planning to marry. In all age and racial groups, the majority of young women believe that premarital sex is acceptable—with over 80 percent of African-American females over the age of eighteen agreeing.[34] These statistics, however, are not matched by actual behavior. In the 1976 sample, for example, 41 percent of the interviewees were no longer virgins: 18 percent of the fifteen-year-olds and 60 percent of the nineteen-year-olds. Interestingly, of those young women who were married at the time of the survey, over 80 percent had had intercourse prior to their nuptials—indicating that the virgin bride is a rarity indeed. Furthermore, the likelihood of premarital intercourse was considerably higher among those women who did not have high educational aspirations. Of those women who intended to graduate from college, more than two-thirds were virgins, whereas of those who did not intend to complete high school or who had already dropped out, under 30 percent were still virgins.[35] Other factors that are associated with premarital intercourse include religiosity (the less religious, the more likely will premarital intercourse occur, with those who claim to lack religion being the most likely to engage in sexual intercourse), social class (the higher, the less sex), and the age at first menstruation (the younger, the more likely to have had sexual experience).[36] Similar variables explain the age of first intercourse. There seem to be both biological and social factors that influence a young woman's decision to have intercourse.

Most American adolescent girls (about 60 percent) have their first sexual experience "unprotected." According to the survey, only about 30 percent of all sexually active adolescent girls regularly use contraceptives; this includes girls who hope boys will withdraw before ejaculation.[37] Most rely on a wing and a prayer. Apparently part of the problem of using contraception is that the *idea* of contraception is contrary to the meaning of intercourse. If intercourse is a spontaneous dance of passion, then only a premeditating schemer would prepare. Many young women apparently find it difficult to reconcile the meaning of sexual intimacy with the meaning of contraception. Only by making sex rational and routine does contraception become possible—a choice that for some people removes the charm of the act. Perhaps not surprisingly, those girls of higher social class, those from more stable families, and those who are older at first intercourse are more likely to use contraception.[38]

Like many scientific surveys, this one is not focused on policy considerations. Instead, its primary goal is to provide factual information for others to make a decision. Yet in their conclusions, the authors hew to a social democratic perspective. They suggest that premarital sex is inevitable and that government services can help the situation. Specifically, Zelnik, Kantner, and Ford argue

> that some [young women] do become pregnant is hardly sufficient to argue for the elimination of contraceptive service programs. . . . The inability of young people to obtain contraceptive services is unlikely to have a negative

effect on the prevalence of pregnancy or of intercourse. . . . It seems likely that to reduce premarital intercourse in the United States would require far more governmental intrusion than now exists, and at a cost of personal rights that many would be unwilling to accept. Thus, teenage sexuality might recede if we could bring ourselves to accept greater censorship of movies, television, books and magazines, including the advertising therein, combined with regulations to discourage the participation of more than one parent in the labor force at any one point in time, combined with greater restrictions on the daily movements of teenagers and on their finances, combined with greater surveillance of their "trysting places"—whether motels or open fields—combined with a drastic reduction in unchaperoned social activities for teenagers and an increase in "family" activities, combined with restrictions to prevent young people from leaving home for either work or school, combined with social sanctions against open displays of affection by young people, combined with the imposition of punishment in some form for those who stray from clearly marked "paths of righteousness." . . . For ourselves, we prefer to cope with the consequences of early sex as an aspect of an emancipated society, rather than pay the social costs its elimination would exact.[39]

A position that combines a belief that government contraceptive programs provide a valuable service with the desire not to take drastic steps to curb premarital sexuality is the hallmark of the social democratic approach to adolescent sexuality.

Human Sexuality, Adolescents, and Society

Human nature is sexual nature. Our conception of human nature, whether it is essentially good or evil, colors our opinion about how people should behave sexually. The libertarian, who believes in the potential of rational behavior, sees little danger in the grand emotion of sexuality, provided that biological dangers are heeded. Sexuality is merely pleasurable and has little effect on social intercourse. Sex is a *natural* function that connects human beings with their primate forbears.

The conservatives see sexual passion bubbling beneath human behavior, and while sex is good, unrestrained passion may be destructive. People are continually struggling against their baser, animal instincts; sex provides a case in which those instincts win. Conservatives do not wish to eliminate sexuality entirely, but they do believe it needs to be controlled, like a leopard in a cage. Sexuality can undermine the moral order of a fragile social structure. The family, the home of sexuality, is also the police force to suppress its excesses with support from the government. The state should exercise its influence to maintain the family as the bastion of morality and one of the primary institutions of society.

The social democrat feels less strongly about sexuality than either the libertarian or the conservative. Sexuality is not a primary concern of government unless its effects influence the economic order. Thus, teenage *pregnancy* is a concern, whereas teenage *sex* is not. Discrimination on the basis of age or gender is a proper place for government intervention, whereas family or church concerns should be handled by those institutions. It is not that social democrats wish to encourage sexual promiscuity, it is just that they dislike the effects of unwanted pregnancy more.

The broad underlying question in the debate over teenage sexuality is who should be allowed the freedom to experiment sexually? Specifically, should adolescents be given the rights and privileges of adults? If the age of sexual maturity were also the age of marriage and if, prior to marriage, there were no strong desires to experiment sexually, we would have few problems. This biological utopia obviously does not exist. Two trends exacerbate the problem. First, young people are waiting longer to get married, leaving more time to fulfill their sexual desires. Second, and more surprising, the age at which young people become sexually mature is decreasing. On average, menstruation begins at age twelve-and-a-half today as opposed to thirteen-and-a-half in 1940, presumably because of better nutrition and health care. Thus, there is more time in which young people can test the sexual waters, and thus more opportunities for them to conceive children out of wedlock. The "epidemic" of teenage pregnancies may not entirely be due to "moral decay," but to these social and biological changes.[40] Society can suggest to adolescents that they remain sexually abstinent, but many, if not most, of them would find this advice more relevant in theory than in practice. It is a case of young men fighting old men's wars.

The libertarian and the social democrat are united in thinking that the call for teenage chastity is bound to fail. The libertarian believes it should fail, while the social democrat sees failure as inevitable. Although the conservative can point to historical instances in which large numbers of people did remain chaste, this solution cannot be effective when contradictory messages fill the media and peer-group gossip. Sexuality represents a social reward, and the debate over teenage sexuality is one of who should receive the reward. It is not self-evident that all rewards should freely go to all people. Are teenagers full-fledged members of society? If they are not old enough to drink and vote, are they really old enough to make whoopee?

Questions

1. Is sex a purely private act, or does it affect society?
2. Is there any justification for the "double standard"?

3. Should unmarried adolescents engage in sexual intercourse?

4. Are teenagers psychologically prepared for sexual intimacy?

5. Should adolescents be allowed to set their own moral codes?

6. Can laws prevent adolescents from engaging in sexual intercourse?

7. What are the best ways to prevent teenage pregnancies?

8. Should the government subsidize contraceptives for adolescents?

9. Should contraceptives be available in high schools?

10. Should condoms be given to all teenage boys "just in case"?

For Further Study

Davis, Murray S. *Smut: Erotic Reality/Obscene Ideology.* Chicago: University of Chicago Press, 1983.

Ellis, Albert. *The American Sexual Tragedy,* 2nd ed. New York: Lyle Stuart, 1962.

Greenberg, David. *The Construction of Homosexuality.* Chicago: University of Chicago Press, 1988.

Furstenberg, Frank F., Jr., Richard Lincoln, and Jane Menken, eds. *Teenage Sexuality, Pregnancy, and Childbearing.* Philadelphia: University of Pennsylvania Press, 1981.

Reiss, Ira L. "Some Observations on Ideology and Sexuality in America." *Journal of Marriage and the Family* 43(1981): 271–283.

Shilts, Randy. *And the Band Played On: Politics, People and the AIDS Epidemic.* New York: St. Martin's, 1987.

Zelnik, Melvin, John F. Kantner, and Kathleen Ford. *Sex and Pregnancy in Adolescence.* Beverly Hills, CA: Sage, 1981.

Notes and References

1. David Greenberg, *The Construction of Homosexuality* (Chicago: University of Chicago Press, 1988).

2. Alfred Kinsey et al., *Sexual Behavior in the Human Male* (Philadelphia: W. B. Saunders, 1948); Alfred Kinsey et al., *Sexual Behavior in the Human Female* (Philadelphia: W. B. Saunders, 1953).

3. Quoted in Ian Robertson, *Sociology,* 2nd ed. (New York: Worth, 1981), p. 215.

4. Murray Davis divides sexual ideologies into three categories: the Jehovanist (traditional), the Naturalist (the modern *Playboy* philosophy), and the Gnostic (á la Marquis de Sade). See Murray Davis, *Smut: Erotic Reality/Obscene Ideology* (Chicago: University of Chicago Press, 1983).

5. Ira Reiss, "Some Observations on Ideology and Sexuality in America," *Journal of Marriage and the Family*43 (1981): 279–280.
6. Ibid., p. 280.
7. Center for Disease Control study conducted by Lloyd J. Kolbe, reported by Jan Gehorsam, "Most Sexually Active Teens Don't Use Condoms," *Atlanta Journal/Constitution* (January 4, 1992): p. A1.
8. Beth Brophy, "A Hard Pill to Swallow?" *Forbes* (May 10, 1982): p. 99.
9. Ira Reiss, *Family Systems in America*, 3rd ed. (New York: Holt, Rinehart and Winston, 1980), p. 209.
10. Jane Burgess-Kohn, *Straight Talk About Love and Sex for Teenagers* (Boston: Beacon Press, 1979), p. 24.
11. *Index of International Public Opinion, NORC Survey 1986–1987*. (New York: Greenwood Press, 1987): p. 534.
12. Albert Ellis, *The American Sexual Tragedy*, 2nd ed. (New York: Lyle Stuart, 1962), pp. 295–296.
13. Editorial, *Denver Post*, January 21, 1982, printed in *Editorials on File* 13 (March 1–15, 1982): 296.
14. Brophy, "A Hard Pill to Swallow?" p. 99.
15. Jean Seligmann, "Condoms in the Classroom," *Newsweek* (December 9, 1991): 61.
16. Gallup Poll, November 14–17, 1991.
17. John Leo, "Sex and Schools," *Time* 128(November 24, 1986): 59.
18. David Carlin, Jr., "The 'Squeal Rule' and 'Lolita Rights,'" *Commonweal* (September 9, 1983): 465–466.
19. Joyce Maynard, *Looking Back* (New York: Avon, 1974), pp. 137, 139.
20. Quoted in Barbara Kantrowitz, "Kids and Contraceptives," *Newsweek* (February 16, 1987): 58.
21. Quoted in Seligmann, "Condoms in the Classroom," p. 61.
22. Robert Briffault, *Sin and Sex* (New York: Macaulay, 1931), pp. 192–193.
23. Quoted in Seligmann, "Condoms in the Classroom," p. 61.
24. Leo, "Sex and Schools," p. 56.
25. Kantrowitz, "Kids and Contraceptives," p. 57.
26. Quoted in Robert E. Burns, "The Catholic Bishops and AIDS," *Christian Century* 105(January 27, 1988): 77.
27. Quoted in Kantrowitz, "Kids and Contraceptives," p. 57.
28. Carlin, "The 'Squeal Rule' and 'Lolita Rights,'" pp. 465–466.
29. Hugh Hefner, "The Playboy Philosophy," *Playboy* (July 1963): 48.
30. Kenneth Kantzer, "Planned Parenthood Attacks a Parent's Need to Know," *Christianity Today* (May 20, 1983): 11.
31. Jacob Sullum, "Prophylactic Measure," *Reason* (December 1991): 6.
32. Leo, "Sex and Schools," p. 61.
33. Melvin Zelnik, John F. Kantner, and Kathleen Ford, *Sex and Pregnancy in Adolescence* (Beverly Hills: Sage, 1981).
34. Ibid., p. 46.
35. Ibid., p. 65.
36. Ibid., p. 70.
37. Ibid., p. 95.
38. Ibid., pp. 98, 103.

39. Ibid., pp. 181–182.
40. Phillips Cutright, "The Teenage Sexual Revolution and the Myth of an Abstinent Past," *Family Planning Perspectives* (January 1972): 24–31.

CHAPTER FIVE

Economy and Stratification: Should the Government Regulate Businesses to Protect Endangered Species?

■ Throughout most of the twentieth century, Americans were convinced that they were destined to be the most prosperous people that the world had ever seen. Because of U.S. economic growth and military power, this has been labeled "The American Century." With the increased competition from Europe and the Pacific Rim, with the structural problems in U.S. industry, and with the potential for massive development in Eastern European and Third World economies, many Americans are uncertain about how the next century will be labeled.

When sociologists speak of the economy they refer to a social institution that organizes the production and exchange of goods and services. Within the economy are many subsidiary institutions and organizations, including businesses, industries, corporations, markets, labor unions, government agencies, and banks. In a modern western capitalist system, this economic system is highly complex and not easily subject to control, as economic swings from recession to inflation demonstrate. Capitalist economies operate on the fundamental assumption that the "market" is self-regulating and that massive government involvement is unnecessary and undesirable, even though the "business cycle" may produce severe swings from prosperity to depression. Libertarians and some conservatives hold to this position. This is to be contrasted with those economic systems—socialist, communist, fascist—that rely more on centralized planning. The dissolution of the Soviet Union and the failure of the nations of Eastern Europe have caused many to doubt the effectiveness of government-controlled economies that do not take account of consumer demand.

Western nations fall somewhere between a true free market, a capitalist economy, and a planned, socialist one. They represent what are labeled "mixed economies." Such systems include some measure of a "welfare-state" mentality in which the government is expected to play a significant role in protecting people from the "excesses" of the free market. Scandinavian nations are often put forward as representing how this model should work. This is the approach of the social democrats and is generally accepted by moderate conservatives as well. Social democrats and some conservatives fret about what has been called "the deindustrialization of America."[1] Many formerly important industries such as steel, automobiles, clothing, and electronics are less dominated by U.S. firms, with a loss of well-paying, skilled "blue-collar" jobs. This change may contribute to the growth of an urban underclass, the need for dual-career families, the weakening of labor unions, and a decline in middle- and working-class standards of living.

Libertarians suggest that we need to let market forces take their course, permitting consumers to purchase the best products at the lowest prices, no matter where they are made. Others argue for protectionist legislation, either having the government subsidize American products (for example, through farm subsidies) or taxing foreign products that compete with U.S. industries (through tariffs). Still others argue that the U.S. government should own and operate critical industries, providing jobs for our workers. The U.S. economy is in the process of changing rapidly. Most new work opportunities are either low-wage service jobs or white-collar professional or clerical jobs.

The fate of the economy is tied to the various statuses of workers. Former President Jimmy Carter once reminded us: "Life is not fair." In this he recognized a profound sociological truth. People are not treated equally, and how they are treated is not entirely a result of their actions. Indeed, one justification for a free-enterprise economic system is that it distributes resources *unequally*, and people are therefore motivated to work hard. A society without a "work ethic" is not likely to be productive, or at least not very affluent. The American system of rewards depends not only on hard work, but on the "accident of birth." For better and worse, we do not have complete equality of opportunity and certainly not equality of outcome.

Social stratification refers to the hierarchial inequality of groups. Some of this inequality relates to the reality that groups near the top of the hierarchy have greater access to rewards than those toward the bottom. This stratification differs in kind and degree from society to society. In the most extreme case, a society is divided into castes. In this system, as was once true of India and is still largely characteristic of the Republic of South Africa, status (or socially defined position) is given at birth, with little opportunity for social mobility among the castes or for intermarriage. A second model of stratification, and one that characterizes the United States, is a class system. In a class system, individuals are ranked hierarchically, but this position is a function of their economic rank; even though a person's family affects his or her class position, there is opportunity for mobility between classes, and marriage is not so restricted. Some societies, such as those labeled socialist, have attempted to eliminate the class system and claim to provide for everyone according to their needs. Furthermore, people's expectations are supposedly based on their ability, not their social position. Because people need to make hierarchical distinctions, they need economic motivation to inspire them to work, or because those at the top are corrupt, no postindustrial society can truly be considered classless. In his book *Animal Farm*, George Orwell provides this cynical bon mot about class structure: "All animals are equal but some animals are more equal than others." Access to economic resources divides us.

Sociologists distinguish between two types of statuses: those that are ascribed and those that are achieved. *Ascribed status* refers to forms of social status that result from a category over which you have no control. For example, you didn't choose to be female, Latino, or nineteen years old, nor did you select your parents because they were wealthy. Yet each colors how others see you. By contrast, *achieved status* refers to positions achieved at least partially by your own efforts. If you complete your education, your status as college graduate will be achieved. Likewise, your occupation is an achieved status. This does not mean that the fact that you graduated from college had nothing to do with external forces (the fact that your parents saved for years), but only that a substantial share of your achievement can be attributed to your own efforts. The greater the extent to which a society relies on achieved characteristics to determine status, the more that society has open social mobility—people, in other words, can slip and climb through social hierarchies.

The dimensions of the class system can be conceptualized in several ways. Two of the most widely used are those postulated by Karl Marx and Max Weber. Marx believed that economic factors were decisive in determining status. Those who own and control the means of production are dominant. Those who are employed by those who own the means of production are the proletariat or working class. For Weber, determining status was not as simple. He divided the idea of class into three closely related factors: power, wealth, and prestige. While these factors often go hand in hand, some people have power without wealth (some politicians), others have wealth without prestige (certain nouveau riche millionaires), and others have prestige but little power (clergymen, for example).

Any observant person will recognize that the United States is a stratified society. We do not have the excesses of wealth of Saudi Arabia nor the depths of poverty of India, but we do have many millionaires and many more poor people. Even if few people starve, many fall beneath the "poverty line."

In a society in which all individuals were nearly equal, we would expect the 20 percent with the least income to make nearly as much as the

20 percent who make the most. Actually, as of March 1990 the lowest 20 percent made only 4.6 percent of the total income of the United States, whereas the top 20 percent made 44.6 percent.[2] These percentages have not changed much in the past twenty years, which suggests that U.S. society is becoming neither more nor less stratified. If we examine wealth—that is, assets, including property, stocks, savings, and other capital—we find that it is distributed even less equally. The richest 20 percent of all Americans owns 76 percent of the country's wealth, whereas the bottom 20 percent owns only 0.2 percent of the wealth.[3]

To some it is not enough to be wealthy; they must also *seem* wealthy. For these people—all of us in some ways—the symbols of success are important. We wear designer jeans, drive expensive cars, or insist on alligators on our shirts. Sociologist Thorstein Veblen[4] termed this *conspicuous consumption*, or the desire for others to know and appreciate how much wealth, power, or prestige a person has. We attempt to shape the impressions that others have of us and our position through material symbols of the self.

■ Question:

Should the Government Regulate Businesses to Protect Endangered Species?

It is hard not to love a bunny. What about a Northern Spotted Owl? Now that cosmetic companies have found other means of testing their products, no longer putting them in rabbit eyes, bunnies seem relatively secure. But the fate of the Northern Spotted Owl hangs very much in the balance. There is currently a heated battle over the responsibility of the government to protect this nocturnal bird, perhaps significantly curtailing the amount of logging in "old-growth" forests in the Pacific Northwest, and in the process putting tens of thousands of loggers out of work.

How did we reach such a point where we had to balance the rights of owls and humans? One can trace public concern to the first Earth Day, held in April 1970. This event, which was supposed to celebrate our planet and raise concerns about the threats to the environment, had an enormous effect in raising the nation's consciousness. Along with some important books published in the previous decade, such as Rachel Carson's *Silent Spring* about the dangers of pesticides, Earth Day persuaded many Americans that our Earth was fragile. The threats to the environment were often depicted as threats that arose from economic growth, business greed, and consumerism.

As one consequence of this environmental awareness, in December 1973 Congress passed and President Nixon signed the Endangered Species

Act. This law called upon the U.S. Fish and Wildlife Service to create a list of species that were "endangered" (that is, in immediate danger of becoming extinct) or "threatened" (likely to face extinction in the near future). While the act was designed to protect "charismatic megafauna"[5] (bald eagles, condors, whooping cranes, or elk), it does not distinguish among species. Under the law—at least in theory—insects, molds, bacteria, and viruses are covered. More than listing these species, the act also calls for them to be protected no matter the economic cost. Biodiversity is given legal precedence over economic development. Species are assumed to be "priceless." Since approximately 4,000 species are estimated at risk, the cost and the effects could be significant.[6]

The first major controversy involving this law involved the construction of a dam by the Tennessee Valley Authority. This dam had the potential of eliminating the only known colony of the snail darter, a three-inch-long fish, recently discovered by biologists, which inconveniently happened to make its home in the Little Tennessee River. After much political wrangling, Congress established a cabinet-level committee that could convene in exceptional circumstances to balance the rights of a species to exist with the economic effects of that decision. It was labeled the "God Committee."

Eventually, the Tellico Dam was built and subsequently it was learned that the fish wasn't as rare and the dam not as necessary as thought. Since then, butterflies and rats have been protected, using taxpayer dollars and restricting the choices of property owners.

The current controversy surrounds a small nocturnal bird, the Northern Spotted Owl (*Strix occidentalis caurina*). It is estimated (imagine how challenging it is to count a nocturnal bird) that there are only about 1,700 pairs of owls, less than half the number of two hundred years ago.[7] These birds are not being protected for themselves alone, but because they are "indicator species." As owls go, so goes their forests.[8] Thus, those who wish the federal government to protect the owls are concerned about more than the birds themselves (although this would be sufficient for the law), but about the forests.

The forests at issue are labeled "old-growth," "ancient," or "virgin" forests,[9] and are found in the Pacific Northwest on the west side of the Cascade Mountains. The definition of these woods apparently is complex, as there is considerable variety in what constitutes "old growth." Most have large numbers of Douglas fir or Sitka spruce with some hemlock, alder, and cedar. *Science* magazine comments:

> It is relatively easy to identify . . . 'classic old growth,' or the green Cathedrals printed on the postcards and in the nature magazines. These forests are older than 250 years, with big trees, big downed logs, and big standing snags. Some trees survive 1000 years or longer, and reach heights of 300 feet and diameters of 6 feet.[10]

These forests have a layered forest canopy and an abundance of ferns and moss. However, these are the classic forests. Others don't fit this pattern. Some are temperate rain forests, while others are drier. Thus, there is little agreement on how much "old growth" there is: The forest service claims that in six national forests there are 2.5 million acres. The Wilderness Society finds only 1.1 million acres. All agree that many old-growth forests have been cut—perhaps only 15 percent remain from before logging[11]— and some suggest that in thirty years there may be no "old-growth" forest outside protected wilderness areas.[12]

In June 1990 the Fish and Wildlife Service formally declared the Northern Spotted Owl a threatened species, entitled to government protection. This protection put the owl squarely in conflict with the loggers and lumber industry in the Pacific Northwest. If the Bureau of Land Management and the Forest Service did not permit lumber companies to cut down trees in government-owned forests (setting aside up to 3 million acres of forest) and if these corporations were restricted from using their own land, the economy of the region would be crippled. Some estimates suggested that 30,000 jobs might be lost permanently. In May 1992, the federal government's God Committee met and agreed on a compromise—approximately 17,000 acres of protected owl habitat could now be logged. This was far more than what environmentalists wanted and far less than what the timber industry had hoped for. Both sides will try to change this compromise. Time will tell if mills will close and communities that depended on the forest industries will become ghost towns. One surely sympathizes with local residents sporting caps reading, "Save a Logger, Kill an Owl." What is good for owls, seems, in the short run, bad for people, and vice versa.

The Social Democratic Point of View

In Oregon's Umpqua National Forest, a lumberjack presses his snarling chain saw into the flesh of a Douglas fir that has held its place against wind and fire, rockslide and flood, for 200 years. The white pulpy fiber scatters in a plume beside him, and in 90 seconds, 4 ft. of searing steel have ripped through the thick bark, the thin film of living tissue and the growth rings spanning ages.[13]

This passage reads like ecological pornography—green smut; here is the "rape of nature." While social democrats are sympathetic to economic suffering, ecological activists tend to fall within the social democratic orbit in their desire to have the government intervene to *protect* the environment, which cannot otherwise protect itself. The "enemies" are greedy, unfeeling businesses that have no concern for the future in their rush to maximize immediate profits at the expense of those who cannot defend themselves, and loggers, who are apes who like to wreck the forest.[14]

It is fashionable to speak of the "rights" of nature, an extension of "animal rights." Ecological historian Roderick Nash notes that some contemporary ecologists

> see the green world (nature, environment, land, or earth) oppressed by the same exploitative, hierarchical values and institutions that once denied rights to slaves and continue to oppress many women, racial minorities, and laborers of all colors. Nature in their eyes is just the latest minority deserving a place in the sun of the American liberal tradition.[15]

This leads to the position, known as the Noah Principle (after the Ark's captain), that all species have a *right* to exist:

> The smallest grub has the same right to exist as the biggest whale; so does every species of cockroach, every species of stinging nettle . . . and even the microorganisms that cause malaria and syphilis. . . . All are precious, and human beings have a moral responsibility to each and every one.[16]

Imagine the pickle we could find ourselves in if the AIDS virus were given civil rights! Of course, it is unfair to caricature this position, but the dividing line is thin. Environmental activist Andy Kerr explicitly links the movement to defend the owl with the civil rights movement, declaiming that "asking the Oregon congressional delegation in 1990 to deal rationally with the end of ancient-forest cutting is like asking the Mississippi delegation in 1960 to deal rationally with the end of segregation."[17]

For many, the argument revolves less around rights of viruses than around the pragmatic goal of protecting *human* life. From this perspective, we are all part of a "web" of existence—a web that we did not create, but one over which we humans have stewardship. We need to be good stewards because it is impossible to know from where the next miracle drug might come. Wiping out a mold might destroy a new penicillin, although critics might note that it might equally likely eliminate the next killer disease.

One group of those who wish to preserve the forests suggest that what is needed is a massive change in human life-styles. Edward O. Wilson and Paul Ehrlich write that we should stop "developing" undisturbed land as a start, and that "the indisputable strategy for saving our fellow living creatures and ourselves in the long run is . . . to reduce the scale of human activities."[18] Indisputable? What would you give up for the Stephen's kangaroo rat, the Oregon silverspot butterfly, or the California gnat catcher?

The other approach, growing out of social democratic thought, is to suggest that government involvement is critical. Some suggest that to preserve the owl, we must restrict the export of raw logs to Japan (forget the trade deficit). Democratic congressman Peter DeFazio declaims: "We're allowing a few giant corporations to ship the future of our forests overseas. I've appealed to their hearts and minds and patriotism, to no avail. It's stupid, it's bad public policy and its got to stop."[19] His solution is to impose an export tax. Others suggest that the federal government must help retrain loggers and millworkers and provide communities with grants to increase economic diversity.[20] Finally, some such as Senator Albert Gore of Tennessee call for a "Global Marshall Plan" for the environment, in which wealthy nations help protect the planet's biodiversity.[21] A similar plan was discussed at the 1992 Environmental Summit in Brazil. This costs money and assumes government intrusion in private economic choices; yet, for the social democrat such a choice makes sense in an interdependent world.

The Libertarian Point of View

At first glance it appears that environmental concerns are the Achilles heel of the libertarian, who elevates economic rights to the pinnacle of concern. Yet, libertarians contend that they are equally troubled by the threats to the environment—they would simply handle these threats differently—and that forced, collective action (that is, governmental action) is not necessary. They contend that environmentalism is compatible with economic freedom.[22]

Finally, libertarians suggest that many environmental problems are caused directly or indirectly by government intrusions in the market. Consider the government's attempt to support the salmon population in Montana:

> The state introduced mysis shrimp into rivers to feed the salmon which flourished there. However, the tiny shrimp soon consumed large amounts of plankton, which is a major food source for the salmon. As a result, the number of salmon spawning in Lake McDonald in Glacier National Park fell from 100,000 to a mere 200. Moreover, bald eagles, which were attracted to the park by the fish, now bypass it. From a peak of 639 in 1981, only 13 bald eagles were last counted in the park. . . . The park thus no longer attracts so many visitors, whose trips to the area to view the eagles greatly contributed to the local economy.[23]

In fact, some argue that governmental mistakes have led to the threatened extinction of some species, such as the black-footed ferret.[24] However, the problems are not only a function of government miscalculation. Libertarians note that the federal government subsidizes the timber companies that are destroying the habitat of the Northern Spotted Owl.

After all, most of the land that is at issue is federal land. Liberal Democratic senator Albert Gore notes:

> In national forests throughout the country, logging roads are being built [by government] in order to facilitate the more rapid logging, even clear-cutting, of public lands under contracts that require the sale of trees at rates far below market prices. This enormous taxpayer subsidy for the deforestation of public land contributes to both the budget deficit and an ecological tragedy.[25]

Government subsidies to destroy the environment are outrageous, says the libertarian. Indeed, the 1992 Libertarian Party platform contends that federally held lands should be returned to private citizens. Since environmentalists tend to be well educated and many are well-to-do, they, as a private group, can purchase land and keep that land forever wild if they so choose. If there are enough people who are willing to pay, the environment will be protected. With a change in our understanding of air and water rights, pollution can be curbed since it affects the property rights of other individuals. Whether a large society such as ours can organize itself privately to do this remains an open question.

The libertarian believes that much environmental legislation involves *income redistribution*; those with little concern about the environment are forced to support those who care. For the libertarian, taxes always involve coercion. Environmentalism can be costly. For instance, a 1990 report from the Office of the Inspector General estimated that the recovery costs for all species currently listed as endangered or threatened would be $4.6 billion over ten years.[26]

Along with the expense comes the control of individual life that libertarians find abhorrent. Soil scientist Edward Krug speaks of the growth of what he calls sarcastically "the Environmental Party," alleging that their party line is that

> government must regulate all human activity. The masses must obey the environmental bureaucracy—it knows what is "best." Sacrifice must be made for the "just cause." There are only 5 to 10 years before it is too late to save the planet from the masses who inhabit it.[27]

He suggests that this powerful group manufactures environmental crises to persuade citizens to give up their rights to government and argues that, in many instances, such as acid rain, there simply is no crisis. Recently, a group of people often associated with industry, called the "wise use movement," has organized to fight what its members see as the excesses of "environmental radicals."

Ultimately, libertarians are concerned with government "takings" of private property rights.[28] The Takings Clause of the Fifth Amendment in the Bill of Rights says that "private property [shall not] be taken for public use, without just compensation." Economic rights for the libertarian are just as heartfelt as any of the rights listed in the First Amendment and more heartfelt than the rights of owls. The government constantly "takes" property—if not through confiscation then by altering what one can do with it. For instance:

> A man paid $975,000 for two beachfront lots in South Carolina. Before he could put up houses, the state rezoned the lots to forbid building. The lots are now worthless. The man argues, with some justice, that he is no better off than if the state had simply taken the land away—in which case the Constitution would have required that he be paid.[29]

Individual logging company owners are now suing the government because they claim that the overly restrictive guidelines prevent them from earning a living without just compensation. They never sue, of course, when their land has been made *more* valuable. Still, at times, individual dreams are being destroyed in the name of nature.

The Conservative Point of View

As in most things economic, conservatives and libertarians are allied in opposition to social democrats. While many conservatives do love "nature" and wish to "conserve" it, they mistrust a philosophy that attempts to shackle business, growth, and progress. While the libertarian tends to worry about government involvement per se and about the rights of individual property owners, conservatives speak about the desirability of growth and worry less about the health and well-being of obscure species.

This view is evident in the frustration that is expressed by bumper stickers reading: "I love spotted owls—fried!" Timber is seen as a crop like others—who would weep for wheat? As one Oregonian put it, "We survived without the dinosaur. What's the big deal about the owl!?"[30] Logger Bill Haire puts it this way:

> If it comes down to my family or that bird, that bird's going to suffer. Where would we be right now if everything that lived on the earth still survived—the saber-toothed tiger, the woolly mammoth? Things adapt or they become extinct.[31]

These loggers believe that it is not the owl that is endangered but an industry and a human way of life—a way of life that is being sacrificed to preserve wildlife. T. S. Ary, the head of the U.S. Bureau of Mines, told a conference of miners, loggers, ranchers, farmers, and developers that they are the real endangered species—endangered by environmental "nuts" whose goals are to prevent progress and protect resources, such as timber, at the expense of jobs.[32] As Charles Mann and Mark Plummer describe, "People who care little about the endangered species frequently invoke them as an excuse to stop projects; the science used to justify one side or another is often rushed. . . and can be so incomplete that it verges on the fraudulent."[33] The forestry industry, already under pressure from shrinking timber supplies, suggests that the Northern Spotted Owl is but a front for their real agenda: to limit development. These critics wish to impinge the integrity of their opponents.

Many conservatives see these environmentalists, like animal rights activists, as fundamentally *antihuman*. This movement is simply an outgrowth of a kamikaze attack on traditional American culture with the purpose of destroying capitalism and working-class communities. Oregonian Tom Hirons, owner of Mad Creek Timber, feels persecuted by the environmentalists. He claims that "the perservationists' campaign to lock up [the forests] is a brand of mental terrorism that has cast a great cloud of fear over our communities."[34] For the "wine and cheese crowd"[35] to blithely talk of promoting leisure industries, replacing well-paying ($15/hour) with minimum-wage tourist jobs, suggests to some an insensitivity to real economic needs. Of course, to others limiting human activity will preserve the planet.

This conflict is made dramatic when the issue is not economic welfare, but human life itself. Scientists believe that an extract (taxol) of the bark of the Pacific yew tree may be a potent anticancer drug, particularly in fighting ovarian cancer, which annually kills 12,000 American women. Alas, the yew shares the forest with the spotted owl. Is preserving the Pacific yew worth the price, particularly when one must cut three 100-year-old yews to get enough taxol for a single patient? An environmental group, the Save the Yaak Committee, protests the government's intention to harvest these trees for experimental treatments, fearing that the yew might become "endangered." Yet as Sally Thane Christensen, a federal attorney representing the Forest Service and a woman living with ovarian cancer, complains:

> I have news for the Save the Yaak Committee. I am endangered, too. . . . I've had the conventional chemotherapy for ovarian cancer, and it didn't work. . . . Taxol may be my last hope. . . . The yew may be prime habitat for spotted owls. It may be esthetically appealing. But certainly its most critical property is its ability to treat a fatal disease. Given a choice between trees or people, people must prevail. No resource can be more valuable or more important than a human life. Ask my husband. Ask my two sons. Ask me.[36]

Yet, sympathetic as we might be to Ms. Christensen's plight, environmentalists would suggest that the elimination of the species may ultimately have consequences that are far worse than the loss of a human life. Manage resources, but don't eliminate them. Had the yew become extinct last year, what hope would there have been for Ms. Christensen?

Sparrows and Social Research

Respecting the rights of all animals is not always easy. Even the most fervent believer in animal rights is sorely tempted to make an exception for mosquitos. All animals are created equal, but some are more equal than others. Despite the affection that bird watchers have for their winged friends, some birds are beloved, while others are scorned. Why are some species despised?

In a recent article that I published with Lazaros Christoforides,[37] we examined a curious historical dispute that ornithologists label the "Great English Sparrow War." This dispute reached its peak in the 1870s and 1880s and concerned the rapid spread and economic effects of the English sparrow (now labeled the "house sparrow" or *Passer domesticus*).

Since no one is alive who could shed light on this dispute, we had to rely on *archival records* and *published documents*. We were fortunate that the American Ornithological Union archives were available, and we had access to governmental reports and microfilm of newspapers of the period. As a result, we were able to construct a reasonably adequate picture of the dispute. This methodological choice to rely on historical artifacts is becoming increasingly common as sociologists extend the range of situations and events from which they can generalize. In this research, we can gain access to major portions of the public record from over a century ago. While these are not detailed records, they present the policies and rhetoric of the period. This technique has the advantage of permitting us to examine the development of a social problem that, although never "solved," is no longer considered to be a concern.

Perhaps outside your window this morning you were awakened to the squawk of a sparrow, for many an annoying sound. The sparrow has been described as "the rat of birds," and it is one of the few songbirds not covered by federal conservation legislation. The English (house) sparrow is the Rodney Dangerfield of birds: It gets no respect.

Despite this reputation, at one time it was thought that this bird might help U.S. cities decrease the infestation of caterpillars and cutworms. For nearly two decades, U.S. cities imported these birds from Europe, and the birds flourished and spread. Yet, what was originally imported to *solve* a problem later was defined as causing one. We label this process the *chaining of social problems*: The solution to one problem is said to cause another. A more recent example is the way that deinstitutionalizing mental patients may have led, in part, to the problem of the homeless.

Our particular concern was to examine how the rhetoric of the sparrow "problem" was linked to other social and economic problems in American life in the last half of the nineteenth century. Specifically, we were interested in the *metaphorical linkage* between the sparrow problem and the "problems" of increased immigration and the boundaries of the American community in the aftermath of the Civil War.

The objective concern about the sparrows involved the fact that, some claimed, these birds ate large quantities of grain and fruit, rather than the insects they were imported to control. Yet, the economic effect of this consumption was never demonstrated, although some farmers did complain. There were some economic consequences, but these paled compared to the "moral" threat of these birds. The peak of the debate occurred in the fifteen years from 1874 to 1889. By about 1880, the critics of the sparrow won the day and calls to exterminate these birds were common; some states even paid a bounty for dead sparrows. After 1890, the concern about sparrows died away as it became evident that there was little that could be done, sanitation in the city improved, which controlled some sparrow food sources, and we learned that other economic threats were more significant.

The rhetoric about sparrows was colored with purple prose. Specifically, we found four major themes in the attacks of sparrows: (1) they were seen as "immigrants," (2) they attacked native ("American") birds, (3) their character (lack of cleanliness, noise, sexual habits) was seen as disreputable, and (4) they needed to be controlled like any foreign enemy.

Sparrows were spoken of as "foreign vulgarians," living in "avian ghettos." Thomas Gentry, a leading ornithologist, made the issue of nationalism central in his objections to sparrows:

> Our smaller native species, the only rightful tenants of the soil, which have always been adequate to every emergency that has arisen . . . are vigorously assailed and forced to flee before these irascible creatures.[38]

Perhaps most dramatic was the text of a children's book, *Citizen Bird*, which attempted to introduce young people to the major species of birds by personifying them. The authors had this to say about the sparrow:

> [English sparrows] increased very fast and spread everywhere, quarrelling with and driving out the good citizens who belong to the regular Birdland guilds, taking their homes and making themselves nuisances. . . . Now it is decided that these Sparrows are bad Citizens and criminals; so they are condemned by everyone. . . . This disreputable tramp not only does no work for his taxes—he hates honest work, like all vagrants—but destroys the buds of trees and plants, devours our grain crops, and drives away the industrious native birds who are good Citizens.[39]

One cannot help but be impressed that such a small bird can arouse such large emotions. But as was clear earlier in the chapter, animals and plants are linked to a web of metaphors. Our desire to save the bald eagle is as much a role of its central symbolic role in our nation as it is a concern with its survival per se. "Charismatic megafauna" carry a moral stature that other living things cannot match.

The dispute over the English sparrow occurred at a point in history in which Americans were concerned about the boundaries of the American community. The Civil War had just ended and we were in the midst of Reconstruction, attempting to reincorporate the southern states. This period also witnessed the beginnings of a huge wave of immigration from eastern and southern Europe and East Asia, a "new immigration" that would change the face of the U.S. population. It represented the large-scale growth of basic industry with its demands for cheap labor, which these groups filled. They were economically valuable and socially worthless. New workers and the freed slaves posed both an economic and status threat to Anglo-Americans, and their presence was profoundly unsettling and a source of public controversy, as some nativist groups believed that the nation would eventually be composed of mongrels, rather than "pure" Americans. In this environment, it made emotional sense for the sparrow to be linked to these outsiders and seen in metaphorical terms as a similar threat.

Our approach, emphasizing the created meaning of sparrows, falls within the interactionist orbit. Indeed, the article was published in the journal of the Society for the Study of Symbolic Interaction. While we do not draw any policy conclusions, implicitly we suggest that the hostility to immigrants is as questionable as the concern about sparrows. Permitting the free flow of peoples and questioning nationalism are linked to a libertarian approach that questions governmental restrictions. Both birds and immigrants have a simple agenda: They want to live their lives without trouble from those with more power than they.

Environmentalism and the Economy

The web of life is incredibly complex. Decisions and choices have effects that reverberate through social life, often producing changes that few would have suspected. Unintended changes may be more powerful than those planned for. Who would have guessed that the pesticide DDT, aimed at controlling insects, would decimate the population of bald eagles and affect human reproduction. The conservative is right in being concerned with the outcomes of change. In this sense, perhaps, environmentalists are heirs to the conservative mantle, even though in political terms, they are affiliated with social democrats.

It is evident that the choices we make about a life-style and our world are choices that affect our economy. Libertarians believe that by letting the "market" have control all will be well. When left alone, the economy will generate what people want. If we wish forests to be preserved, then individuals or groups will buy these forests, because the worth of the undisturbed forest will be worth their cost. If there are no takers, then trees will be cut. This assumes that individual actions when combined together will produce optimal outcomes. Society may be too complex for that. Individual freedom may, suggest critics, permit some people to become very wealthy, and others, through no fault of their own, to be impoverished.

The social democrat is more concerned about providing for those less fortunate. In the case of protecting species, the social democrat typically focuses on the constraints necessary on the large lumber companies. If there is any economic dislocation for poor workers, the federal government can help out through unemployment compensation, welfare, and job retraining. In other words, whatever pain the government causes, the government can solve: That is its role. The social democrat is less concerned by the fact that small lumber companies may be the means by which some citizens are able to better themselves and change their class status.

The conservative is more than a little disturbed by the antibusiness attacks of the social democrat and the blithe disregard of those citizens who wish to maintain their *traditional* life-style. Who do these social engineers think they are anyway, manipulating human decisions? The industries social democrats wish to constrain have been cornerstones of the U.S. economy and should not be crippled by those with other agendas. Corporate profits from this perspective inevitably "trickle down" to workers and to the communities in which they reside. While nature is nice for the conservative, and while the government does have some responsibilities in this domain, it should not be at the expense of productive businesses and workers. After all, the Judeo-Christian ethic that conservatives so revere has been, for better or worse, a human-centered ethic in which the environment has played a secondary role.

Ultimately, economic decisions are connected to the demands of various status groups in society. In this case, environmental activists—the chablis and brie crowd—have different status and different culture than either the loggers or the corporate executives. Their status positions imply different values. The loggers and their bosses profit off the forests and the destruction of the owls, despite genuine love for the forests. In turn, most environmental activists don't live in those small towns of the Pacific Northwest that are slowly being starved to death by those who live in elite urban and suburban communities and love the forest as an idea, not as a neighborhood. Environmental protection may be crucial, but its effects are felt most keenly by others.

Questions

1. Should the federal government attempt to protect endangered species?
2. Should the effect on jobs and the economy be taken into account in protecting endangered species?
3. Should the government own forest land or should the land be sold to private individuals?
4. Do environmentalists care about economic well-being? Should they?
5. Do industrialists care about the environment? Should they?
6. Do all species have a *right* to exist?
7. Should we protect species from extinction because of the possible use we can make of them in the future?
8. Should the government subsidize timber production by building roads?
9. Should the Northern Spotted Owl be protected at all costs, should we let the owl become extinct, preserving jobs, or should some compromise be found that would completely protect neither owls or jobs?
10. Is the market the best model for economic order or should the government play a major role?

For Further Study

Anderson, Terry L., and Donald R. Leal. *Free Market Environmentalism.* Boulder, CO: Westview Press, 1991.

Chase, Alston. *Playing God in Yellowstone: The Destruction of America's First National Park.* San Diego: Harcourt, Brace, Jovanovich, 1987.

Efron, Edith. *The Apocalyptics.* New York: Simon & Schuster, 1984.

Epstein, Richard. *Takings.* Cambridge: Harvard University Press, 1985.

Gore, Albert. *Earth in the Balance: Ecology and the Human Spirit.* Boston: Houghton Mifflin, 1992.

Mann, Charles, and Mark L. Plummer. "The Butterfly Problem." *Atlantic Monthly* (January 1992): 47–70.

McKibben, Bill. *The End of Nature.* New York: Random House, 1989.

Nash, Roderick F. *The Rights of Nature.* Madison: University of Wisconsin Press, 1989.

Stone, Christopher D. *Should Trees Have Standing: Toward Legal Rights for Natural Objects.* Los Altos, CA: William Kauffman, 1974.

Notes and References

1. Barry Bluestone and Bennett Harrison, *The Deindustrialization of America* (New York: Basic Books, 1982).
2. U.S. Bureau of the Census, *Current Population Reports*, series P-60, reported in U.S. Department of Commerce, *Statistical Abstracts of the United States 1991* (Washington, D.C.: U.S. Department of Commerce, 1991), p. 428.
3. Executive Office of the President, Office of Management and the Budget, *Social Indicators 1973* (Washington, D.C.: U.S. Government Printing Office 1973), p. 182.
4. Thorstein Veblen, *The Theory of the Leisure Class* (New York: Macmillan, 1899).
5. Charles C. Mann and Mark L. Plummer, "The Butterfly Problem," *Atlantic Monthly* (January 1992): 49.
6. Ibid., p. 50.
7. "Environment's Little Big Bird," *Time* (April 16, 1990): 21. If it is difficult to determine the number of owls today, guessing at the number of owls 200 years ago must be nearly impossible. One would be wise to remain skeptical.
8. "Owlmageddon," *The Economist* (May 4, 1991): 27; Lisa Tuttle, "End of the Old-Growth Canopy," *National Parks* (May/June 1987): 16.
9. Ironically, these ecosystems are not so old—younger than 6,000 years. As Len Ruggiero, director of the old-growth wildlife program at the U.S. Forest Service notes: "They're ecological toddlers." See William Booth, "New Thinking About Old Growth," *Science* 244 (April 14, 1989): 142.
10. Ibid.
11. Michael Lemonick, "Showdown in the Treetops," *Time* (August 28, 1989): 58.
12. Ted Gup, "Owl vs. Man," *Time* (June 25, 1990): 58.
13. Ibid., p. 56.
14. "The Sound of Rage from the Forest," *U.S. News and World Report* (June 25, 1990): 29.
15. Roderick Frazier Nash, *The Rights of Nature* (Madison: University of Wisconsin Press, 1989) p. 212.
16. Mann and Plummer, "The Butterfly Problem," p. 51.
17. Quoted in David Seidman, "Terrorist in a White Collar," *Time* (June 25, 1990): 60.
18. Quoted in Mann and Plummer, "The Butterfly Problem," p. 51.
19. Quoted in Michael Satchell, "The Endangered Logger," *U.S. News and World Report* (June 25, 1990): p. 27.
20. Gup, "Owl vs. Man," p. 65.
21. Albert Gore, *Earth in the Balance* (Boston: Houghton Mifflin, 1992) pp. 295–360.
22. For a detailed treatment of the libertarian approach to environmentalistm, you should read Terry L. Anderson and Donald R. Leal, *Free Market Environmentalistm* (Boulder, CO: Westview Press, 1991).
23. James A. Maccaro, "Of Skunks and Salmon," *The Freeman* 42 (February 1992): 75.
24. Tim Clark and Ron Westrum, "Paradigms and Ferrets," *Social Studies of Science* 17 (1987): 3–33.
25. Gore, *Earth in the Balance*, p. 121.
26. Mann and Plummer, "The Butterfly Problem," p. 51.

27. Edward C. Krug, "Save the Planet, Sacrifice the People: The Environmental Party's Bid for Power." *Imprimis* 20 (July 1991): 2.
28. Richard Epstein, *Takings* (Cambridge: Harvard University Press, 1985).
29. Michael Kinsley, "Taking Exception," *The New Republic* (January 6 and 13, 1992): 6.
30. Gup, "Owl vs. Man," p. 60.
31. Ibid.
32. "Interior Official Chides Environmental 'Nuts.'" *The New York Times* (March 23, 1991): L6.
33. Mann and Plummer, "The Butterfly Problem," p. 52.
34. Quoted in Jordan Bonfante, "Showdown in the Treetops," *Time* (August 28, 1989): 59.
35. George Hager, "Small Owl Incites Big Battle Over Environment, Jobs," *Congressional Quarterly* (September 9, 1989): 2309.
36. Sally Thane Christensen, "Is a Tree Worth a Life?" *Newsweek* (August 5, 1991): 11.
37. Gary Alan Fine and Lazaros Christoforides, "Dirty Birds, Filthy Immigrants, and the English Sparrow War: Metaphorical Linkage in Constructing Social Problems," *Symbolic Interaction* 14(1991): 375–393.
38. Thomas G. Gentry, *The House Sparrow at Home and Abroad* (Philadelphia: Claxton, Bemsen, and Haffelfinger, 1878), p. 110.
39. Mabel Osgood Wright and Elliott Coues, *Citizen Bird*. (New York: Macmillan, 1897), pp. 204, 182.

CHAPTER SIX

Gender Roles and Sexual Stratification: Should Women Be Permitted to Serve in Military Combat?

■ Sigmund Freud once asked, somewhat plaintively perhaps, "What does a woman want?"[1] Although probably not meant in the same way, this question continues to haunt many, if not most, men. The problem seems to be that women are both very different from and very similar to men. It is this similarity but difference that makes figuring out what is fair and just so challenging. Even today it takes some effort not to treat women as subtly inferior to men, as in the preceding sentences in which women were being compared *to* men—as if masculinity represented some kind of standard by which all humankind is to be judged. What the role of women should be is hotly disputed, even within contemporary feminism. Some argue that women should have the characteristics of men, others maintain that women should remain distinctively feminine, and still others propose androgyny for both sexes, that is, having some characteristics of men and women.[2]

In U.S. society, as in many others, there are distinctively different expectations of women and men. Indeed, how could it be otherwise? Expectations must capitulate to biology. Anatomy is destiny—so said Freud. Only women can become mothers, although both sexes can "mother." Recognizing the limits of our physique and our hormonal equipment, the potential range of human action is broad. Both sexes can carry out the activities necessary to make a living, yet, in most societies, there is a sexual division of labor with some tasks defined as "female" and others as "male." Some of the tasks that are predominantly male in one culture are predominantly female in another.[3] But a division of labor based on physical prowess seems no longer necessary, particularly in western societies where work is becoming increasingly technological and where women have freedom from pregnancy through birth control measures.

The weight of scholarly evidence is that most sex-linked behavior typical of men and women is socially, rather than biologically, determined. Although this conclusion may change as we learn more about the subtle effect of genes and hormones, most sociologists feel that the traditional learned patterns of behavior, or *gender roles*, for men and women are not inevitable.

Numerous institutions direct individuals into what are considered proper gender roles. Women and men are socialized separately through families, the mass media, peers, schools, religion, and even the English language. "Man" still indicates all of humankind, and so girls learn, at least implicitly, that they are a subclass of "man." While linguists debate whether we need a whole new vocabulary, including neutered pronouns, it is difficult to dispute their basic point that our language communicates important features of society's world view. Most people still feel more comfortable in a world in which men and women are brought up and act differently. A world of people, rather than one of men and women, would be shocking to anyone who has grown up in this one.

Women still earn wages that are considerably below those earned by men, but despite women's lower wages, one cannot deny that during the 1970s and 1980s women have made large strides in entering the social, political, and economic mainstream of the United States. There is a greater tolerance for seeing women in a wide variety of jobs; indeed, by 1990 86 percent of all Americans claimed to be willing to vote for a woman for president.[4] Sociologists Andrew Cherlin and Pamela Walters have found that there are now relatively few differences between males and females in their attitudes toward gender equality.[5] Clearly a major change has taken place in U.S. society in terms of women's occupational and political rights even though it will take longer to gauge its full effects and forms of discrimination still exist.

The social side of the "women's revolution" is more difficult to evaluate. As divorce rates rose throughout the 1970s, many Americans began to worry that the family was falling apart and that this was due to the women's movement. People noticed other social trends that emerged at about the same time as the growth of women's rights, such as open homosexuality, increased premarital cohabitation, the decline of religion, and rising abortion rates. Although the causes of these trends are difficult to determine, they were facilitated, whether for good or ill, by some of the same changes in values that encouraged the women's movement.

Are traditional sex roles functional for society? Sociologists differ on this point. Functionalists argue that the division of labor between the sexes makes sense (or did once) because men are physically stronger and thus better suited to be providers. Women, on the other hand, bear children and are thus better suited to child rearing and family nurturance. The man has the instrumental role in the family and focuses on dealing with the external world and obtaining resources. The woman carries out an "expressive" role and focuses on relationships within the family and keeping it functioning smoothly by distributing support and love.[6]

Conflict theorists see the same facts in a different light. Rather than being functional for all of society, gender roles are beneficial to some (men), while exploitative of others (women). Men, because of their strength, are able to dominate women and make them work at low-paying, demeaning jobs. Women are, in this view, similar to every other oppressed minority group and must revolt to become free.

■ Question:

Should Women Be Permitted to Serve in Military Combat?

The greatest change that has come about in the United States forces in the time that I've been in the military service has been the extensive use of women. . . . That's even greater than nuclear weapons, I feel, as far as our own forces are concerned.

—General John A. Vessey, Chairman of the Joint Chiefs of Staff[7]

Since the (possibly mythic) Amazons and since Joan of Arc tormented the English, the image of the female warrior has had a hold upon our imaginations. Perhaps the reason is that the very thought of a great female military leader seems so *odd*. Whatever the case, historians have pointed out that women—including such heroines of the Revolutionary War as Molly Pitcher, Deborah Sampson, and Margaret Corbin[8]—have played a role in our military engagements.

More recently, the war in the Persian Gulf (and earlier, the invasion of Panama) displayed the courage of women soldiers for all Americans to see:

During the American invasion of Panama, an Army captain was sent with a platoon of soldiers to capture a Panamanian Defense Force guard-dog kennel. It turned out that the kennel contained more than dogs; inside there were also P.D.F. troops. The shooting began, and by the time it stopped the American soldiers had captured the kennel. The Army captain's first name was Linda. . . . On Dec. 20 [1989, Captain Linda Bray] made military and women's history.[9]

Yet, the question ultimately is not whether women soldiers are courageous—surely they are—but whether they are competent, whether they improve the effectiveness of the armed forces, and whether we as a society feel that women should have the same rights, responsibilities, and dangers as men. Should they be "unladylike" and kill our enemies?

The armed forces have changed dramatically since the mid-1960s. Before 1967, the services had a ceiling of 2 percent on the number of female soldiers. The need for "manpower" in Vietnam abolished this limit, but the real impetus for the changes in the gender mixture of the armed forces was the establishment of the All-Volunteer Forces in 1973. Since the elimination of the draft, the number of women in the U.S. military has steadily increased to 11 percent in 1989, the highest figure in NATO. Some commentators have suggested that women saved the all-volunteer military.[10]

An increasing number of positions in the military are open to women: 97 percent of the jobs in the Air Force and most jobs in the Navy and Army.[11] Thirty-five thousand women participated in Operation Desert Storm (6 percent of all U.S. troops), and eleven were killed.[12] But what about combat roles? What about being an infantry grunt, down in the mud and blood of foxholes? Congress, considering removing all restrictions on women in combat, is scheduled to examine the issue in 1993. In fact, there is evidence that the public supports the idea of women serving in combat. By a 52 to 44 margin, the public in 1991, after the Gulf War, approved of women in ground combat units.[13] As the nature of modern warfare has changed, the traditional distinction between the "front line" and "rear guard" no longer makes so much sense; surely women are as able to push buttons or fly planes as men, even if we must recognize they have differences in physical ability.

On the positive side, women are generally better behaved than men with fewer disciplinary infractions, and they are generally somewhat better educated than their male counterparts. However, they tend to leave the military sooner: It is not a career goal for many, but only a path to other goals. Also, women become pregnant while serving and may undermine the morale of their units. Finally, there remains the stubborn question as to what we as a society expect of our young women. Should they have the opportunities or responsibilities to perform all of the roles of young men, or should they be treated in a different way because of their gender. Here we return to questions of human nature and social organization.

The Social Democratic Point of View

Social democrats find discrimination on the basis of gender to be abhorrent. Yet, many also find a large military equally distressing. Should they favor equality so that women can be part of the war machine? It is not an easy choice. The heart of equality is being treated equally both in benefits and in costs. Supporting the rights of women to kill and be killed is a hard decision for many social democratic feminists. Still, if we need a military, as most social democrats would agree that we do, all groups should be treated equally.

Pacifism has traditionally been connected with feminist thought. Some feminists go so far as to suggest that if women were in charge, there would be no wars—would a mother tolerate war? In fact, it was widely believed in much nineteenth-century religion that women are more favorably disposed toward religion, love, and peace than are men. Contemporary feminism in part grew out of the antiwar movement.[14] Mary Jo Salter asks whether "we might not have invented war" had the world been populated only by women.[15]

Other social democrats point to tough political leaders such as Joan of Arc, Golda Meir, Margaret Thatcher, and Indira Gandhi and doubt that female leaders would be any softer than their male counterparts. These critics note that women are quite as capable of being tough as are males. Niceness, for these critics, is not a gender-linked characteristic.

Whether because of intellectual honesty or political survival, military sources suggest that women have been successful in the armed services, and, from this, the argument goes that they could perform all roles, including combat roles in a modern military. The military sociologist Charles Moskos found that women were as effective as men in an army exercise in Honduras.[16] Other data suggest that the gender ratio in an army unit has no effect on performance.[17]

Beyond these technical issues of efficiency, with which some conservatives argue, lie moral questions. Many social democrats support women in combat for ideological reasons—as a contribution to equity and as a fight against discrimination. They hate discrimination and constraints on an individual's right to choose an occupation. Social democrats note that some of the arguments raised against women in combat are similar to those once used against racial integration. The idea that the presence of women would affect male bonding sounds disturbingly similar to claims that black soldiers would make whites uncomfortable. Army Captain Carol Barkalow reports discovering in Saudi Arabia "a new type of relationship forming between men and women, one that has traditionally been described among men. It was a nurturing relationship based upon respect, based on sharing the same hardships."[18]

Ultimately, the problem as the social democrat sees it stems from sexism by males and some women. Air Force officer Cynthia Wright calls "the antiquated views of military men—and women . . . the most stubborn barrier to female acceptance in the military."[19] In fact, when the Israeli army decided to curtail the role of women in the army, it was not because of problems in the performance of the female soldiers, but rather because of "the frequency with which they were raped when captured and . . . [the] tendency of male soldiers to worry excessively about wounded women."[20] Lieutenant Sharon Disher puts the issue pungently: "So what if I get my guts blown all over the ship and it freaks the guys out? . . . They would freak out if another guy had his guts blown all over, too."[21] Why, asks the social democrat, should women find their choices limited by sexism.

The Libertarian Point of View

The establishment of the All-Volunteer Forces was a cause for rejoicing for libertarians. The coercion of the military draft was a major source of complaints, and, no doubt, some young men during the Vietnam War decided that they really were libertarians because of their personal opposition to being drafted. Now the draft has ended, and women volunteers decrease the likelihood of its return.

Libertarians, it must be noted, generally prefer a small military that does not become involved in overseas adventures, such as in Panama, Grenada, and Kuwait. None of these military actions were truly for national defense, but arguably for political ends. Libertarians are seen by some as being "isolationists," denying that the United States has any role as the police force of the world. Still, most libertarians would accept the legitimacy of some armed forces.

For libertarians, any government policy must be based on individual qualifications, and they would vigorously object to the military treating individuals as members of social groups. They would suggest that military positions, including combat, should be open to all those who volunteer and who meet whatever objective criteria are deemed appropriate. While libertarians do not feel that private discrimination should be made illegal, governmental discrimination is outrageous. The issue is one of individual rights.

The libertarians suggest that all recruits should be held to the same standards of physical and mental ability. Former New York City mayor Edward Koch remarked that "he didn't care what sex his firefighters were so long as they could carry a 206-pound mayor out of a burning room."[22] Yet, the military does not now judge on the basis of identical standards. Separate physical standards exist for men and women—a process called *gender norming*. Thus, women need to do significantly less well than men. Physical fitness standards require women to do 56 push-ups as compared to 80 for men. Isn't this a double standard in a situation in which the enemy plays by a single set of rules? One male Air Force captain is bitter:

> We are told to evaluate woman on a different scale than man. . . . A woman who is adequate is rated as outstanding, or who is unacceptable is rated acceptable. . . . We lie to the public, we lie to the Air Force, and most of all we lie to each other.[23]

Even supporters of women in the military, like Colorado congresswoman Pat Schroeder, feel that this double standard does women a disservice. It certainly flies in the face of the libertarian desire to treat everyone as individuals.

Within the military, the biggest losers from the exclusion of women from most arenas of combat are female officers, because advancement in the military typically relies upon combat command experience. Women officers are being denied opportunities for the "best" positions and promotions. As we speak of a "glass ceiling" in industry that prevents female executives from reaching the highest levels of corporate advancement, in the military there is a "lead ceiling." Unless you have seen bullets, you cannot be promoted to your top potential.

Not only is discrimination on the basis of gender alone unfair when mandated by the government, which is supposed to accord all citizens due process, it is also inefficient. Lieutenant Diane Mills, an air-weapons director in an AWACS unit at Tinker Air Force Base, was trained to direct fighters to intercept enemy aircraft. She explains, "Don't train me for a job and then tell me I can't do it because I'm female. That's a waste of the taxpayers' money—and a waste of my time."[24] There are few things that libertarians despise more than a waste of taxpayers' money. As recruitment to an all-volunteer army becomes increasingly difficult and as this high-tech military requires well-educated volunteers, women will simply be the most efficient and most productive choices.

War is a dangerous business. Bombs do not recognize gender. As Captain Barkalow emphasizes, ultimately we are talking about individuals and not groups. She notes:

> [The public] always say they wouldn't want to see their daughters in combat. What I ask them in return is, would you really want to see your *son* in combat? And isn't it the daughter's choice? One lesson our society learned in the Persian Gulf is that it is no more tragic to lose a mother, a sister, a daughter than it is to lose a father, a brother, or a son—and no less so. . . . No normal person wants to go into combat. Soldiers are the last people who want to. But we've volunteered. We understand our commitment. Everyone raises a hand, male and female, and swears to support and defend the same Constitution. Women are competent, capable and committed. We are an integral part of the best-trained military force in the world. The services should have the flexibility to assign the best-qualified person to the job, regardless of gender. That's the bottom line.[25]

For libertarians, the ability of the individual makes gender irrelevant to his or her treatment by the government. That is their bottom line.

The Conservative Point of View

Referring to the desolate mountain pass where many British soldiers lost their lives defending their Indian colony, conservative columnist Patrick Buchanan wondered, "Do we want coeds at the Khyber?"[26] Behind all of the questions and complaints about women in combat, the fundamental character of the "fairer" or "weaker" gender is the issue. Male society should not force women to do that sort of thing. Are we ready for large numbers of women to return home in body bags? Women are biologically necessary for reproduction (men are as well, but fewer men are necessary for population growth) and they are seen as selflessly devoted to their children. In addition, conservatives suggest that women are necessary for morality. General Robert H. Barrow put the argument dramatically in congressional testimony:

> Combat is . . . killing or capturing the enemy. It's KILLING. And it's done in an environment that is often as difficult as you can possibly imagine. Extremes of climate. Brutality. Death. Dying. It's . . . uncivilized! And women CAN'T DO IT! Nor should they even be thought of as doing it. . . . And I may be old-fashioned, but I think the very nature of women disqualifies them from doing it. Women give life. Sustain life. Nurture life. They don't TAKE it.[27]

Conservatives see military service for men as desirable in building patriotism and wonder whether it would be more appropriate to draft men, rather than to permit women to volunteer. Former Georgia representative Larry McDonald put it this way:

> We loudly proclaim that we don't have enough men and prove it by teaching our women how to use machine guns so that the men don't need to bother. We have 110 million male bodies, 108 million of which are not in service, and then claim that we need to send visibly pregnant women to Germany to beef up our forces there.[28]

Indeed, one of the most effective arguments used against the adoption of the Equal Rights Amendment to the Constitution was that it would force women to serve in combat.

Beyond the general issue of women's gender roles, conservatives make several points about their specific place in the military. One set of arguments is that women are not sufficiently competent or simply cannot fit in the military; another set suggests that the effect that they have on male soldiers is destructive.

With regard to the first set of arguments, we discussed the reality that on most tests of strength and physical endurance women as a group cannot measure up to men as a group. Many women who sign up for infantry training do not finish and transfer elsewhere. However, if this is the extent of the problem, we could simply assign to combat those women who passed the requirements, excluding the others, just as we do for men. In fact, women do serve on urban police forces, which must sometimes seem like combat.

Related to this argument is the claim that women, because of their instincts, cannot make good servicemen. Some suggest that women are too emotional or volatile. In short, for a variety of psychological and physical reasons, they just can't cut it. General Elizabeth Hoisington, a former director of the Women's Army Corps (the WACs) is blunt: "In my whole lifetime I have never known ten women who I thought could endure three months under actual combat conditions."[29]

Also, there is the "epidemic" of pregnancy among female soldiers, although conservatives admit that women alone are not to blame for this condition. Yet, if a pregnant woman is shot in the stomach are there two casualties or one? Brian Mitchell, a bitter critic of the "feminization of the military," notes that at any given time, 5 to 10 percent of all servicewomen are pregnant.[30] More than 1,200 pregnant women had to be evacuated from the Gulf, the equivalent of two infantry battalions. One ship became known as the "Love Boat" after 36 female crew members conceived. Of course, males had their share of problems: Sports injuries were the leading casualty producer in the Gulf War.[31]

Then there is the question of what the presence of women does to male soldiers. While it would be nice to treat women equal to men, few have ever described warfare as "fair." The goal of war is to win, and conservatives believe that if the presence of women hampers our fighting spirit, they should lose their "rights" for the higher goal of an effective national defense. As noted previously, the Israeli experience suggests that some male soldiers may be excessively concerned about women to the detriment of their jobs. One retired soldier claims that "the presence of women in military uniform has been instrumental in deterring many fine young men from the military. Men who like women resent their presence in an organization which has been a male domain."[32] Women allegedly destroy discipline by their "sexual presence"; they tempt men to break the honor code, and a few female soldiers may even have "turned tricks" as prostitutes. Further, they interfere with "male bonding," so important for establishing a tight-knit social unit. Some who emphasize this togetherness as the basis of an effective fighting spirit think that it is impossible that women could ever recreate this because sexuality and protectiveness would inevitably interfere.

Critics of this line of reasoning doubt some of the claims in terms of the evidence—a technical issue which I do not have the space to address—but, more than this, they claim that this is an example of "blaming the victim." Women, according to this view, have a right to be in the military if they are able, and what is the use of fighting if we find ourselves defeating our own values of equality and justice in the process. We can easily win the battle, but lose the "moral" war.

Military Women and Social Research

In his Inaugural Address President John F. Kennedy suggested that we ask what we can do for our country, not what our country can do for us. Yet, many of us expect that we will receive benefits from participating in civic life. Surely it cannot be denied that those who volunteer for military service do give of themselves to protect the rest of us and the values that we collectively hold. Yet, having said this, serving in the military benefits those who serve.

In their article, "Socioeconomic and Social Psychological Effects of Military Service on Women,"[33] Lois DeFleur and Rebecca Warner were interested in determining the effects of participation in the armed forces on women. To answer this question, they rely upon data collected as part of the National Longitudinal Survey's Youth Cohort in 1979. The sample was young women (and men) between the ages of seventeen and twenty-one; this research, therefore, has little to say about those who serve lengthy periods in the military or those who are in the officer corps.

Because of the amount of time it takes to make data available to researchers, the time it takes it conduct data analysis, write up the results, and then publish the finished article, we hope that sociological data have a long shelf life. What was true in 1979 might not have been true in 1985 because of changes in military recruitment, armed forces policies, economic changes in society, and the like. As you are reading about this study in the 1990s, the changes might be more dramatic. In learning about social research—in newspapers and textbooks—one should ask about the period in which the data were collected. Often, results remain generally stable, but this is not always so. Data that I report in this textbook were collected from the 1950s to the 1980s.

While few studies are repeated year after year, some studies are. While DeFleur and Warner's article reports data from one year, the survey that they are analyzing is a longitudinal survey, and it is possible to examine changes in these effects over time by examining data collected in other years.

Sociologists have frequently noticed that women's "nontraditional" employment (that is, employment in occupations in which women usually do not work) improve women's economic status, compared to "traditional" jobs that tend to be lower paying. There is less consensus about the effects of nontraditional work on women's self-concept. Perhaps few other jobs are as nontraditional as being in the military—a quintessentially masculine institution. DeFleur and Warner are not concerned about women's effects on the military, but on the military's effects on women.

DeFleur and Warner find that military service has benefits for young women. In terms of income, they discover that although young men earn more in civilian work, for young women this is reversed. Women are financially better off in the military than they are in the civilian labor market. Since men and women are paid the same in the military if they hold the same rank, these data suggest either that civilian wage scales are far from equal or that better qualified women enlist in the military, whereas better qualified men remain in civilian life. The differences may be a function of discriminatory civilian wage scales or different qualifications of civilian workers.

What happens when young women leave the military and look for employment? Are they paid more or less than nonveterans? Sociologists have proposed that the military can serve as a *bridging environment*, especially for women and minorities, in which they learn skills and achieve more education than would be possible in civilian life. The military provides a bridge between an individual's upbringing and the skills necessary to compete effectively in a job market that traditionally has been closed to him or her. In addition, the employment preferences given to veterans in civilian jobs helps these otherwise disadvantaged groups.

DeFleur and Warner discover that, in fact, female veterans do make significantly more than females of their age who did not serve in the military. This finding is particularly pronounced for nonwhite women, where the difference in pay is nearly 20 percent. Similar findings hold for men as well. While the data do not permit us to claim that the differences are *caused* by military service, as opposed to personal characteristics of the workers, the differences have been found in other research studies as well.

To address the effects of self-concept, the survey asked respondents to complete the Rosenberg self-esteem scale, a ten-question scale. DeFleur and Warner found that women in the military scored higher in self-esteem than civilian women (the effects for men were also significant, but smaller). Again, they cannot be certain that the military caused this difference, but the findings are suggestive.

While serving in the military is certainly not a panacea—harassment and tokenism exist—the data DeFleur and Warner present indicate that women can benefit from being in the military. We need more longitudinal research that would permit us to be certain that military employment was the cause of the effects, but for now we can feel reasonably confident in noting substantial variability between military and civilian women. In this, the authors implicitly adopt a social democratic perspective. They are examining group differences and find that this governmental institution seems to benefit an otherwise disadvantaged group. To the extent that military service stands for other nontraditional occupations, women should become fully integrated into all arenas of the U.S. economy with benefits for society and for the women involved.

Gender Roles and Military Service

The debate between conservatives and social democrats is a central one for understanding the relations between men and women in U.S. society. Over the past three decades, since the publication of Betty Friedan's *The Feminine Mystique* in 1962, the position of women in U.S. society has changed dramatically, and attitudes toward women have changed as well. All this has produced confusion, particularly in the less monumental but nonetheless significant aspects of life. Should men open doors for women? How should a liberated woman respond when a man offers to pick up the check? When should a gentleman give his seat to a lady? Who should invite whom on a date? Who is grading whom sexually? Many of the once taken-for-granted aspects of gender-role behavior are now openly questioned. These problems do not have the significance that equal job opportunities and pay have, but they may be more problematic since they rely on delicate face-to-face interactions. Because these are not conscious strains, they may not be easily fixable by a change in social policy.

Beneath this, there is an even more fundamental question. Should men and women behave identically? Some critics of feminism claim that the end result of that social movement will be two sexes of men. By this they mean that there is a danger of women acting like men. They will become aggressive, competitive, smoke more, drink more, have more heart attacks and ulcers, and eventually give up their edge in life expectancy. They will want to go into combat. Do we want a world of five billion "men"? Some feminists insist that it does not have to be this way; gaining equal opportunities does not necessarily mean that the traditional masculine styles of work remain dominant. Women can humanize corporations and perhaps even the military; with increased attention to personal needs and increased emphasis on interpersonal skills, the workplace can be changed. In this view, women need not stop being women (emotionally) in order to achieve occupational success. Others suggest that men and women can incorporate the "best" of both genders—an approach called *androgyny*. The difficulty with this is that it is not clear what constitutes the "best" aspects of each gender role. Finally, we might opt for an individualistic approach. Men and women might choose whichever "gender roles" (now no longer gender based) fit them best. According to this "humanistic" view, a person could be feminine, masculine, or androgenous. It is difficult to imagine how children will be socialized in such a situation or how we will learn to react to others with such a bewildering array of social types. But, at least, from this point of view, each person will to his or her own self be true.

The vast majority of Americans believe that men and women should have equal economic opportunities; however, few Americans would choose a world in which women and men acted identically. Biologically, men and women are permanently distinct, but even socially there is a belief in the desirability of difference. Although this may constrain some men and some women, and although the gap may need to be narrowed, the difference is likely to remain. In short, economically, most Americans are social democrats on this issue; socially they are, to some degree, conservatives.

Questions

1. Should married women with children stay home, as mothers, or should they work outside the home?
2. Are women still discriminated against in employment?
3. Do feminists necessarily believe that large governments are necessary?
4. Should women serve in the military?
5. Should women serve in combat roles in the military?
6. Should women be held to the same standards of physical ability as men, or should separate standards be set?
7. Does the presence of women affect "male bonding" and does this decrease military effectiveness?
8. Are women more pacifistic than men?
9. If women are more pacifistic than men, is this a function of culture or biology?
10. Would you be willing to serve in combat? Why?

For Further Study

Barkalow, Carol, with Andrea Raab. *In the Men's House: An Inside Account of Life in the Army by One of West Point's First Female Graduates*. New York: Poseidon Press, 1990.

Elshtain, Jean Bethke. *Women and War*. New York: Basic Books, 1987.

Levin, Michael. *Feminism and Freedom*. New Brunswick, NJ: Transaction, 1987.

Milkman, Ruth. *Gender at Work: The Dynamics of Job Segregation by Sex During World War II*. Urbana: University of Illinois Press, 1987.

Mitchell, Brian. *Weak Link: The Feminization of the American Military*. Washington, D.C.: Regnery Gateway, 1989.

Schneider, Dorothy, and Carl Schneider. *Sound Off!: American Military Women Speak Out.* New York: E.P. Dutton, 1988.
Schlafly, Phyllis. *The Power of the Positive Woman.* New Rochelle, NY: Arlington House, 1977.
Stiehm, Judith Hicks. *Arms and the Enlisted Woman.* Philadelphia: Temple University Press, 1989.
Yates, Gayle Graham. *What Women Want: The Ideas of the Movement.* Cambridge: Harvard University Press, 1975.

Notes and References

1. Ernest Jones, *The Life and Work of Sigmund Freud*, vol.2: *1909–1919: Years of Maturity* (New York: Basic Books, 1955), p. 421.
2. Gayle Graham Yates, *What Women Want: The Ideas of the Movement* (Cambridge: Harvard University Press, 1975).
3. George P. Murdock and Caterina Provost, "Factors in the Division of Labor by Sex: A Cross-Cultural Analysis," *Ethnology* 12(April 1973): 207.
4. *General Social Surveys, 1972–1990: Cumulative Codebook* (Chicago: National Opinion Research Center, University of Chicago, 1990), p. 247.
5. Andrew Cherlin and Pamela B. Walters, "Trends in United States Men's and Women's Sex-Role Attitudes: 1972 to 1978," *American Sociological Review* 46(August 1981): 453–460.
6. Talcott Parsons, Robert Freed Bales et al., *Family, Socialization and Interaction Process* (New York: Free Press, 1955), pp. 3–9.
7. Statement to the House Armed Services Committee, reported by *The Washington Post* (February 3, 1984): 12; cited in Brian Mitchell, *Weak Link: The Feminization of the American Military* (Washington, D.C.: Regnery Gateway, 1989), p. 3.
8. Helen Rogan, *Mixed Company: Women in the Modern Army* (New York: Putnam, 1981), pp. 119–147.
9. Anna Quindlen, "Forward March," *The New York Times* (January 7, 1990): 25.
10. "Soldier Boys, Soldier Girls," *The New Republic* (February 19, 1990): 9.
11. Donald G. McNeil, Jr., "Should Women Be Sent Into Combat?" *The New York Times* (July 21, 1991): E3.
12. David Hackworth, "War and the Second Sex," *Newsweek* (August 8, 1991): 25.
13. Barbara Kantrowitz with Eleanor Clift, "The Right to Fight," *Newsweek* (August 5, 1991): 23.
14. Sara Evans, *Personal Politics* (New York: Knopf, 1979).
15. Mary Jo Salter, "Annie, Don't Get Your Gun," *Atlantic Monthly* (June 1980): 83.
16. Charles C. Moskos, Jr., "Female GIs in the Field," *Society* 22 (September-October 1985): 28–33.
17. Karen O. Dunivin, "Gender and Perceptions of the Job Environment in the U.S. Air Force," *Armed Forces and Society* 15(1988): 73.
18. Carol Barkalow, "Women Have What It Takes," *Newsweek* (August 5, 1991): 30.
19. Cynthia Wright, "G.I. Jill," *The New Republic* (October 21, 1991): 16.
20. "Soldier Boys, Soldier Girls," p. 8.

21. Quoted in Jennet Conant, "Women in Combat?" *Newsweek* (November 11, 1985): 37.
22. Quoted in Hackworth, "War and the Second Sex," p. 26.
23. Ibid.
24. Quoted in Conant, "Women in Combat?" p. 37.
25. Barkalow, "Women Have What It Takes," p. 30.
26. Quoted in Helen Rogan, *Mixed Company* (New York: Putnam's, 1981), p. 18.
27. Quoted in McNeil, Jr., "Should Women Be Sent into Combat?"
28. Quoted in Rogan, *Mixed Company*, p. 19.
29. Ibid., pp. 24–25.
30. Brian Mitchell, *Weak Link: The Feminization of the American Military* (Washington, D.C.: Regnery Gateway, 1989), p. 6.
31. Hackworth, "War and the Second Sex," p. 29.
32. Quoted in Wright, "G.I. Jill," p. 17.
33. Lois B. DeFleur and Rebecca L. Warner, "Socioeconomic and Social-Psychological Effects of Military Service on Women," *Journal of Political and Military Sociology* 13(1985): 195–208.

CHAPTER SEVEN

Race and Ethnicity: Should Minorities Be Given Preferential Treatment in Hiring?

■ People say you can't judge a book by its cover. This folk belief, of course, extends beyond books to human relationships, and unfortunately, is as ignored in this case as it is in the case of books. The melancholy fact is that people act toward others on the basis of their racial, religious, national, or ethnic category.

While many people diligently try to rid themselves of all discriminatory tendencies and sincerely believe that prejudice on the basis of another's race, color, or creed is morally objectionable, this attitude is rare in the history of humankind. Few societies have been without ethnic or racial prejudice. To be without any prejudice is to be convinced that your genetic or social group is without special merit ("the chosen people," "the best and brightest," "the center of the universe"). This totally nonegocentric attitude is rare. Indeed, the names of many tribal groups throughout the world label that group as special. For example, Hottentot means "the people." Killing in the name of race and ethnicity still occurs frequently today. The moral belief held by many Americans that no group is better than any other must seem unusual and incomprehensible to some.

Despite our belief in racial and ethnic equality, prejudice is still very much with us. Equality is easy to mouth but difficult to maintain. Most Americans recognize that prejudice and discrimination still exist against many racial and ethnic groups. The term *race* in this context refers to significant genetic differences between individuals and groups and is typically related to skin color and also to other anatomical features, such as the shape of facial features and average height. We still know too little about other genetic features that are related to race, particularly cognition and intelligence, to make any definitive statements. For example, although

African Americans on average regularly score lower on some standard intelligence (IQ) tests than white Americans, the reasons for this difference are hotly debated—with test biases and environmental factors being put forth as alternatives to a genetic explanation. Until there is definitive proof of genetic racial differences in cognition and behavior, it is best to assume that "racial" differences in test scores are due to environmental differences and, therefore, are subject to change.

Ethnicity refers more directly to culture. Ethnic groups are groups of people that share a culture and perceive themselves as cultural groups. When members of such groups regularly marry within their own group, they may have common genetic traits (such as some hereditary diseases), but typically the genetic component of ethnic groups is less salient than their cultural unity.

Unless you happen to be a white, male Episcopalian from Vermont and of English descent (on both sides of the family), you have probably experienced some form of prejudice or discrimination. Even if you are one of the very few who do fit this facetious description, your mother or sister may have been discriminated against. (See the discussion on gender roles in Chapter Six.) Very few people have not experienced some kind of discrimination, but some groups have suffered more than others. African Americans and Native Americans, for instance, have been the victims of slavery and genocidal wars. American Jews have found their synagogues defaced with swastikas; Japanese Americans were unfairly placed in internment camps during World War II, and Polish Americans, until recently, have been regularly portrayed as ignorant boobs on television. The large *majority* of Americans are members of racial or ethnic groups that have been the targets of prejudice and discrimination.

Sociologists distinguish between the concepts of prejudice and discrimination. *Prejudice* refers to a negative attitude toward members of some group because of their perceived characteristics. Obviously, those characteristics that typify a group do not apply to all or even most group members (e.g., African-Americans being musical, the French being culinary geniuses, or the English keeping a stiff upper lip). Whereas prejudice refers to attitudes, *discrimination* refers to behavior that is directed against a group or its members—in particular the refusal to provide opportunities or rewards to members of a group even though they are qualified. Although the extent of prejudice and discrimination has declined in the United States over the past few decades, both remain ingrained in segments of our society.

Difficulty in ethnic and race relations can occur on several levels. Prejudice and discrimination are individual-level concepts; that is, they are things individuals feel and do because of personal traits (for example, an authoritarian personality) or experience (such as never having had contact with a member of a minority group). On another level, racial or ethnic groups may be harmed without anyone deliberately or maliciously planning to do so. Sociologists term this *institutional racism* or *institutional discrimination*. This refers to established, customary ways of doing things that keep a minority in a subordinate position. For example, many minorities are channeled into low-paying, dead-end jobs because of poor education, which means they are unable to move to better neighborhoods. No one person has forced them to take these jobs, ostensibly it was their own choice, but their social circumstances or environment makes it difficult to improve their lot.

It is relatively easy to see the effects of this treatment on minorities, but it is not necessarily clear what the consequences are for society. Sociologists differ on their interpretations of the effects that intergroup relations have on a society. Some functional theorists argue that racial and ethnic segmentation, unpleasant as we might find it, has a hidden or latent benefit for society as a whole, in that it provides for a division of labor. Someone must do the physically demanding, low-paying, dirty jobs; by categorizing some people as second-class citizens, society has a supply of cheap labor. Sociologists refer to this difference in labor costs between racial or ethnic groups as a *dual-labor market*. Conflict theorists, while not disagreeing that there must be a division of labor, would emphasize that all of society is not benefiting from this situation, but only certain segments: the powerful and wealthy members. Open conflict between groups may be necessary in order to increase the standing of the subjugated groups. While functional theorists imply that large-scale social movements indicate a functional imbalance in society, conflict theorists are more likely to welcome such movements as a sign that a society is still changing and growing. Such movements may represent a healthy redistribution of power and resources. Although neither approach welcomes racism and prejudice, they approach the problem from different angles.

■ Question:

Should Minorities Be Given Preferential Treatment in Hiring?

"Affirmative action" has become a prominent part of the political lexicon within the past two decades, and no time more so than in the bitter debate in 1991 over the nomination of Clarence Thomas to the U.S. Supreme Court, in the campaigns of David Duke for senator and governor of Louisiana, and in the memorable political advertisement for Senator Jesse Helms in which a white hand crumples a letter of rejection for a job that was given to an African American. Americans recognize that certain groups are underrepresented in some jobs and overrepresented in others. African Americans and Hispanics represent about one-fifth of the U.S. population, but are 20 percent of sociology professors black or Hispanic? Are 20 percent of the bankers or astronauts black or Hispanic? Are 20 percent of all cleaning women, farm laborers, and dishwashers black or Hispanic?

The list of statistics demonstrating that African Americans and Hispanics are disadvantaged is almost endless. For example, the median African-American family income was 60 percent of that of whites in 1987, a figure that had changed little during the previous two decades. Black levels of unemployment are approximately twice those of whites. A smaller percentage of blacks than whites attend college. Despite these inequalities, most overt discrimination has vanished. Employers no longer tell African American applicants that they have been rejected *because* they are black. Nevertheless, it is understandable why many African Americans, after listening to this list of statistics, feel discrimination is in the minds of many white Americans, if not on their tongues. Experimental studies in which similarly qualified African Americans and whites visit employment agencies find that the whites are more likely to be offered positions.

Since we can assume that the reason there are fewer white Americans, proportionately, among farm laborers or menial workers is not because they are discriminated against, the real question is what can be done to increase the number of minority professionals, white-collar workers, and skilled craftspeople. To see this as a *problem*, we must make two important assumptions: The first assumption is that minority members wish to hold these positions, that is, that they are in the labor pool but are not being hired. The second assumption is that enough minority applicants have the *minimum* qualifications necessary for employment. Although specific job classes may not meet these assumptions, we shall assume for our discussion that these two assumptions have been met.

In order to correct the absence of minorities in employment, affirmative-action programs have been instituted. The term *affirmative action* is tricky to define precisely. Its meaning has changed with time and with circumstances. The first formal government action on the subject of racial discrimination was Executive Order 8801, issued by President Franklin Roosevelt on June 25, 1941. The order barred discrimination in defense industries and government because of race, creed, color, or national origin, and stated that "it is the duty of employees and of labor organizations . . . to provide for the full and equitable participation of all workers in defense industries."[1] It was not until 1961 that the phrase "affirmative action" was used in a government order. President John Kennedy, in requiring government contractors to recruit workers on a nondiscriminatory basis, wrote: "The Contractor will take affirmative action to ensure that applicants are employed, without regard to their race, creed, color, or national origin."[2] No longer was it enough for employers to refrain from discrimination, now they had to actively *recruit* applicants who belonged to minority groups.

This position, calling for affirmative action in recruitment (but not in hiring), was the policy of the Reagan administration.

During the mid-1960s, people went further and assumed that *hiring* should be "without regard to race and ethnicity." By the late 1960s and through the 1970s, this "race-blind" view took another turn. It was not enough for employers merely to recruit minority workers openly. Increasingly, they were expected, or even required, to balance the number of minorities in their work force. By 1971, under the Nixon administration, federal orders demanded the establishment of goals and timetables for increasing minority employment. For some, these phrases and the way they are implemented smack of quotas and "reverse discrimination" against groups like Jews, Italian Americans, and Polish Americans who are defined as part of the "majority." If the work force is not integrated according to the estimated racial composition of the pool of workers, the employer has the burden of proof to demonstrate that there is no discrimination. The angry debate over the 1991 Civil Rights bill, finally passed by Congress and signed by President Bush, consisted of how large a burden of proof businesses have in such situations and whether this would lead to informal "quotas" to avoid possible lawsuits.

The 1978 Supreme Court ruling on Allan Bakke's case (*Regents of the University of California* v. *Allan Bakke*) was a blow to affirmative action. The Court found that the University of California at Davis Medical School could not exclude nonminorities by reserving a precise number of places for minority applicants—a fixed quota. Most Supreme Court decisions since then have supported programs that have targets and goals, although with the more conservative court of the late 1980s and 1990s, this may be changing. This difference between quotas and goals is, according to critics, one of semantics rather than substance. In a world with limited resources, the fact that one person or group gets something means that other people or groups do not. The question then is should people who belong to a minority be given preference in hiring if they are equally or slightly less qualified— provided that they meet the minimum requirements necessary for doing the job? Should "preferential treatment" be a matter of government policy?

Throughout the last few pages I have been using the terms "majority" and "minority" quite deliberately, but it is not always clear who comprises these groups and who should be the beneficiary of preferential hiring programs. To the extent that women as a group are victims of discrimination, they can be considered a "minority" even thought they are a numerical *majority* of the population. They are, in other words, a majority with the power of a minority. Also, other groups that are covered by affirmative-action plans have changed somewhat over the years and for particular purposes. The 1977 Public Works Employment Act requires that 10 percent of all federal public works contracts be reserved for "minority-owned" construction firms. Minority, in 1977, was defined as black, Spanish-speak-

ing, American Indian, Eskimo, Aleut,[3] and Asian. One might ask why a
language group was included, since speaking Spanish implies neither race
nor ethnicity. Furthermore, the inclusion of Asians might strike one as
unusual if the concern is to help the disadvantaged. Although Chinese
Americans and Japanese Americans have both suffered discrimination, as
have Jews and Finns, they have higher incomes than many of the ethnic
groups not included, such as German, Irish, Italian, or Polish-Americans.[4]
Clearly such a criterion is based primarily on skin color and not entirely on
being disadvantaged. Thus, it is not surprising that Jews, Italian Americans,
Polish Americans, and other "nonminority" groups with histories of discrimination and current economic problems should feel resentment toward
a system that rewards others and ignores their troubles. The decision of
which groups deserve special treatment is a complicated one grounded in
politics as well as in economic circumstance.

The Social Democratic Point of View

Preferential hiring, even that which is government mandated, poses little
problem for the social democrat. Individuals have always been treated as
members of groups, often to their detriment; now it is time to right that
wrong. Government at its most moral should intervene to insure that no
group is being systematically denied justice and equal treatment. Even if it
means a few people who belong to the majority group are denied jobs,
society must help disadvantaged people to compete *fairly*, and in the process
break down class boundaries that are tied to group membership. Equal
opportunity, alone, ignores the heavy weight of history and oppression.
Lyndon Johnson expressed this sentiment in his famous address at Howard
University:

> Freedom is not enough. You do not wipe out scars of centuries by saying "now
> you're free to go where you want and do as you desire." You do not take a
> person who for years has been hobbled by chains and liberate him, bringing
> him up to the starting line of a race and then say "you're free to compete" and
> justly believe that you have been completely fair. All of our citizens must have
> the ability to walk through those gates; and this is the next and most profound
> stage of the battle for civil rights.[5]

The social democrat recognizes the effects that historical injustice has
on groups. Regardless of whether this injustice is equally applicable to
everyone within a group (for example, injustice may be less for the son of
an African American doctor than for the son of an unemployed single
mother living in a slum), it is group justice that is central. This justice will
have benefits for the society as a whole in that it produces a "truly open"

society in which all groups can participate equally. The *Philadelphia Evening Bulletin* editorialized on the value of preferential admission to medical schools in light of the *Bakke* case:

> Some people argue that to provide special consideration for black students is to discriminate against whites. The sad fact is that if the effects of years of discrimination against minorities are to be undone, for awhile some individuals in the majority are going to suffer deprivation. That isn't pretty, but it is a fact.... Until effective equal opportunity programs have made it possible for minorities to catch up with the rest of society—and that will take decades— minority people must receive some special consideration. That way the ideal of a truly open society will be brought closer to reality.[6]

Likewise, white students are told by supporters of affirmative action: "You have benefitted in countless ways from racism, from its notions of beauty [and] its exclusion of minorities in jobs and schools." "For most of this country's history, the nation's top universities practiced the most effective form of affirmative action ever; the quota was for 100 percent white males."[7]

Some people argue that without meaningful affirmative-action programs, we are courting disaster. It is in the interest of society to protect itself by ensuring justice for everyone. George McAlmon, a director of the Fund for the Republic, observed that millions of Americans, the chronically unemployed and the propertyless, could actually do better under communism. Why, then, should they be committed to free enterprise and private ownership? What morality prevents these citizens from engaging in violent and destructive behavior?[8]

Supporters of preferential hiring point out that hiring criteria may systematically discriminate against minorities because they use measuring sticks that are particularly favorable to the majority. Scores on standardized tests, past work histories, and attendance at prestigious schools are only some of the criteria that are used to predict success. Moreover, supporters of preferential hiring note that not all hiring and admission are based on criteria that predict success.[9] For example, some schools give preference to in-state residents and athletes. Some unions make it impossible for anyone but relatives of members to join. Some organizations give special weight to veterans. Some employers prefer individuals who are married or who dress in a particular style. Thus, consideration on the basis of race is not unique, but is only one more means by which people are hired. The existence of seniority is another indication that "ability" is not the only criterion for employment. In many companies, when employees have to be laid off, it is those who were last hired who will be first fired. This flies in the face of the belief in merit as the sole means of judging people. Why not lay off those workers who are least qualified? Such a process, however, would prove offensive to many unions; the seniority system assumes that there is a level of competency above which ability does not really matter. Once people have met the level of acceptability, termination should be on the basis of years with the company. Without seniority, companies might choose to hire only young, and cheap, workers and replace them when they become older and more expensive.

Social democrats see the controversy over preferential hiring as an issue that involves the rights of groups, rather than those of individuals. The question for them is how we can ensure equitable representation for disadvantaged groups, rather than how individuals can be treated fairly. Frequently, the major concern is ensuring "equal representation." Although some writers[10] have claimed that this need not derogate individual rights since there are other factors involved in hiring, others have vigorously criticized this position,[11] suggesting that invidious discrimination is inevitably involved. Surely in some cases whites are being denied rewards that would otherwise be theirs if there was no program of preferential hiring. The social democrat's concern then is with equalizing the positions of groups and lessening class differences, rather than ensuring that people are treated equitably as individuals. Supreme Court Justice Harry Blackmun stated this effectively in his dissent in the *Bakke* case: "In order to get beyond racism, we must first take account of race. There is no other way."[12]

The Libertarian Point of View

The 1992 platform of the Libertarian Party clearly and emphatically states the party's position on preferential hiring:

> Discrimination imposed by the government has brought disruption in normal relations of people, set neighbor against neighbor, created gross injustices, and diminished human potential. Anti-discrimination enforced by the government is the reverse side of the coin and will for the same reasons create the same problems. Consequently, we oppose any government attempts to regulate private discrimination, including discrimination in employment, housing, and privately owned so-called public accommodations. The right to trade includes the right not to trade—for any reasons whatsoever.[13]

For the libertarian, the rights of the individual must remain paramount. This includes property rights and the right to trade or not trade. Thus, libertarians assent to what may seem to be a paradoxical position: Individuals have the right to ignore the "equal rights" of others. This position, however, is only paradoxical until one considers the libertarian concept of freedom. People have freedom to do what they wish, providing it does not coerce others; they do not have the freedom to make others act toward them in any particular way.[14] This is based on the view that each individual has the freedom to acquire as much power and wealth as he or she wishes—a philosophy perhaps more applicable in the ideal world in which all are created equal than in the real world in which some are born with social handicaps.

The libertarian is particularly incensed by the government's attempt to intervene in human relations. Most libertarians do not personally support discrimination; yet, they don't see discrimination by its nature as being coercive. In this sense, the libertarian believes voluntary preferential treatment plans are acceptable, although not desirable. If white employers choose to hire all whites (or, for that matter, all African Americans), this would not require any kind of government intervention because the employers are engaging in their own rights to use their resources as they see fit. To the extent that affirmative action is a voluntary decision by the employer, and not coerced by the government, then the libertarian would not stop it.

A controversial court case, *Kaiser Aluminum & Chemical Corporation* v. *Brian F. Weber et al.*, illustrates the conflict for libertarians posed by private decisions versus government interference. In 1974, Kaiser Aluminum & Chemical Corporation and the United Steelworkers of America agreed to set up skilled-craft training programs at fifteen Kaiser plants around the country. Half of the positions in the programs were set aside for minorities and women. Whites who could enter the program were determined by seniority (who had worked at the plant longest), and the minorities and women were selected by a separate seniority list. Such a program was easily justified because of the very low representation of women and minorities in these mostly all-white male jobs. When Brian Weber, a white male laboratory analyst, applied for this training program, he was rejected because he did not have enough seniority. He then learned that several of the minority applicants accepted from the other seniority list had less seniority than he had. He subsequently charged racial discrimination under the 1964 Civil Rights Act.

When the case finally wound its way to the Supreme Court, the Court decided by a vote of 5 to 2 that the Kaiser plan was legal under the 1964 Civil Rights Act, even though the act appeared to outlaw discrimination on the basis of race or ethnicity. Weber contended that if he were African American he would have been trained, a point that was not contested. The Supreme Court majority brushed aside the surface reading of the law and pointed to its intent: to reduce discrimination in employment. Pertinent to libertarian theory was that, ostensibly, this was a private decision that was not directly dictated by the government. Kaiser could, if it wished, train and hire whatever percentage of minorities it chose provided it did not discriminate against minorities, which all agreed was illegal under the Civil Rights Act. Although some noted that government intervention was not totally absent, in that Executive Order 8801 did call for federal contractors to take "affirmative action" to ensure that minorities were represented in the work force by telling companies they could lose their federal contracts, the coercion was indirect. Still, it is ironic that the supporters of civil rights were now taking a similar position to those such as Senator Barry Goldwater who, speaking against the Civil Rights Act, said employers should have the *freedom* to take race or ethnicity into account in hiring.[15] A business should choose the best person for the job *regardless of race* or it will suffer by having a less qualified work force than its competitors.

There is a second part of the libertarian attitude toward preferential hiring that finds such practices abhorrent. The libertarian philosophy is based on the moral stature of the individual. Libertarians believe every person should succeed or fail by virtue of his or her own abilities. Preferential hiring violates this belief by promoting some citizens simply because they are of a different race or ethnic group over others who are "objectively" more qualified. While libertarians would acknowledge that other non-ability-based criteria are used in judging hiring, these are equally as questionable as race or ethnicity as a means for making a hiring decision. Libertarians agree with Supreme Court Justice John M. Harlan who says "the Constitution is color-blind and neither knows nor tolerates classes among citizens."[16] Furthermore, preferential treatment is akin to punishing the children for the sins of the fathers. Brian Weber did not discriminate against minorities; American society did. Yet, it is Brian Weber who is forced to carry the burden. People are made to suffer for acts that have been perpetrated by other people. Many libertarians see this as unfair, even if they might be satisfied with the end result. In this case, the ends truly do not justify the means.

The Conservative Point of View

It is ironic that some who at one time felt African Americans were inferior and not deserving of any but the most menial jobs are now in the forefront of those who call for scrupulously equal treatment. In our current political debate, white males, in an ironic, if cruel, twist, appropriated the language of victimization to prevent the gains of those who had been oppressed.[17] Perhaps they should be given the benefit of the doubt; just as we give the benefit of the doubt to the social democrats who once spoke out in support of the Civil Rights Act saying it would not mean special treatment for minorities.

Consider, as an example of conservative thought, the blunt comments of the late William Loeb, the ultraconservative editor of the *Manchester (N.H.) Union Leader*, writing about preferential admission to graduate school:

It makes no sense to try to make up for the wrong of discrimination against blacks in the past by now discriminating against whites. What we are trying to do in this country—at least what this newspaper thought we were trying to do in this country—is to find the ablest people in our society and give them the best possible education so that they can then best serve the nation. . . . If we are going to lower the standards and say to incompetent black students, "You may not have any brains, but we will let you in college anyway because years ago we discriminated against blacks," at the same time we would be saying to many white students, "You are more qualified, by the proven level of your intelligence and your entrance examinations, to become a lawyer or doctor or architect, etc., but we're sorry, old boy or old girl, you will have to step aside and let this less qualified black take your place because we are discriminating now in favor of blacks."[18]

Increasingly, it is not old-line white conservatives who question the principles of affirmative action, but articulate, conservative African-American intellectuals, who wonder whether the effects of these proposals do not create self-doubt and public misgivings about equal treatment. They wonder if affirmative action mainly aids the children of African-American lawyers and doctors, doing little for inner-city youth. The number of Clarence Thomases is multiplying, as the number of African-American professionals, many of whom were helped through affirmative-action programs, similarly increases.

Although libertarians and conservatives share a distaste for programs of preferential hiring for minorities, they dislike them for somewhat different reasons. The libertarian focuses on the unfairness to the individual, while the conservative suggests that the new system is unfair to the majority group and perhaps, in the long run, to the minority group, whose members question their own abilities. Of course, many who argue against preferential hiring use both sets of arguments and may not even distinguish between the two, but the bases of the arguments are different. The conservative dislikes the radical change the concept of preferential hiring will bring in the relationship between employers and workers and the government-sponsored changes that will affect race and ethnic relations. The conservative maintains that all citizens increasingly believe that race should not be a factor in hiring, and, so, they do not like the government attempting to alter public values, instituting in their place sanctioned discrimination against unprotected groups (whites). African-American economist Thomas Sowell, a vocal conservative critic of preferential hiring, notes that by including women under the banner of affirmative action, "discrimination is legally authorized against one third of the U.S. population (Jewish, Italian, Irish [males])—and for government contractors and subcontractors, it is not merely authorized but required."[19] Leonard Walentynowicz, executive director of the Polish-American Congress, emphasizes this point: "If America's job opportunities and money are to be parceled out to groups, we are a definable group, and we want our share."[20] If preferential treatment is extended to every group that is underrepresented in the upper levels of the work force, what will this do to those groups that are overrepresented? Jewish leaders, for example, worry that a strong and large-scale program of preferential hiring would actually be anti-Semitism in disguise.

Conservatives also point out that despite the continuing steps that have been made toward affirmative action and preferential hiring, many political leaders and most Americans—white and African American—oppose it. The policy changes during the growth of affirmative action demonstrate the clout of an unelected bureaucracy, which runs the day-to-day operation of government, not the clout of a majority of citizens. Thomas Sowell offered some concrete support for this argument:

> The insulation of administrative processes from political control is illustrated by the fact that (1) administrative agencies went beyond what was authorized by the two Democrats (Kennedy and Johnson) in the White House who first authorized "affirmative action" in a sense limited to decisions *without regard* to group identity, and (2) continue to do so despite the two Republican Presidents (Nixon and Ford) who followed, who were positively opposed to the trends in agencies formally under their control as parts of the Executive branch of government.[21]

Surveys, too, indicate that the American public is overwhelmingly (83 percent) opposed to preferential treatment in hiring,[22] and 64 percent of African Americans reject preferential treatment.[23] Thus, the conservative claims, government policy flies in the face of public opinion and social tradition. Regardless of whether white Americans discriminated against African Americans, people should hire the best person for the job. It is this belief that is being undercut by a government that conservatives are afraid will only succeed in promoting racial tension. The leading conservative journal, *National Review*, suggests, perhaps sarcastically, that it would be simpler if Congress passed a "Black Reparations Act"—a point of view with which some social democrats might sincerely agree, in spirit, if not in name, and, indeed, had been suggested in the turbulent 1960s by social democrats.

African-American Unemployment and Social Research

By the 1990s, on most indicators of race relations, African Americans have improved their standing relative to whites. Youth employment for African Americans, however, seems to show an opposite trend. In 1954, the difference between black and white unemployment rates for young people between the ages of sixteen and twenty-four was 5.9 percent (with young blacks being less employed). As of today, this rate has nearly tripled. On the surface, this suggests that racial prejudice in employment has not only not lessened, it has substantially increased.

This view, however, is perceptively challenged by two statistically sophisticated sociologists, Robert Mare and Christopher Winship.[24] They argue that these statistics are not as depressing as they appear at first because the magnitude of the black-white unemployment differences in the 1950s is actually masked by other aspects of race relations.

To study unemployment rates, one must depend on statistics that have been collected by the U.S. Bureau of the Census in its *Current Population Surveys*. This type of research is known as *secondary data analysis*; that is, researchers analyze data that were collected for another purpose. Such a methodology, of course, is much less costly than doing original research. Large amounts of data that were originally collected for one purpose may be used in numerous other studies. (Only the federal government has the resources to engage in this kind of data collection—a point with which the libertarian would groan in agreement.) The weakness of this approach is that the data have been collected by someone else; thus, the original research may have omitted certain crucial questions. Particularly when using government data, there may be a conservative bent to the research in that the questions asked are those to which the government in power wants answers and that the powerful consider to be important. Also, the nature of the massive data collection typically provides little of the detailed information about people that interactionists would insist on to understand how people make their decisions.

Mare and Winship suspect that certain changes in the choices made by African-American youths would explain their lower rates of employment. Specifically, Mare and Winship note that African-American youths are attending school longer than they had previously and that they are entering the military at rates that are higher than that of whites. Furthermore, once they leave these institutions, they have some difficulty finding a job—not because they are black (or not completely so) but because they have had limited work experience. Finally, more of the most qualified African-Americans attend college and enter the military, although currently the proportion of African Americans attending college has begun to decline and the size of the military is shrinking. The most highly employable African Americans remain out of the job market for many years—a process that Mare and Winship call *creaming*. In the 1950s, blacks would enter the job market immediately after leaving school, and so had a "jump" on whites who completed their schooling. If schooling and military service had been held constant in evaluating the 1950s statistics, the employment difference between African Americans and whites would have been much larger.

Such results prove comforting to the conservative, although the authors would disagree that they are sympathetic with conservative views.

These data, however, echo the conservative belief that if African Americans become educated, their employment opportunities will open up. Says the conservative, once African Americans leave school and the military (and, thus, are no longer youths), their employment patterns will be much like whites. This is perhaps too rosy a scenario for the immediate future, but Mare and Winship's article does remind us that we must be very careful in analyzing social statistics—what they suggest on the surface may be different from what a careful sociological analysis will demonstrate. This study does not address the type of jobs blacks and whites are able to obtain, nor does it demonstrate that there is no discrimination against middle-aged African Americans. Still, we can take some measure of comfort in Mare and Winship's conclusion:

> The growing race difference in employment is, in part, a consequence of otherwise salutary changes in the lives of young blacks, especially increased school enrollment and educational attainment. . . . Our results suggest . . . that worsening labor force statistics for black youths do not denote increasing racial inequality, but rather persistent racial inequalities previously hidden by race differences in other aspects of young adulthood.[25]

Because the authors believe there are still underlying racial differences, they would probably oppose eliminating affirmative-action programs. Their analysis, however, might be used by conservatives to suggest that African Americans can make it on their own.

Race Relations and Preferential Hiring

The question of preferential hiring, affirmative action (as supporters call it), or reverse discrimination (as opponents call it) will not disappear until all groups in our society are integrated into the work force in proportions equivalent to their number in the population. As much as any issue discussed in this book, this is a highly personal one because it will affect your success in this world. It is easy for those who already have it made to support affirmative action: It won't hurt them. It is equally easy for those who are racially prejudiced to use opposition to reverse discrimination as a guise for their own bigotry. But it is you who will be applying for jobs and for graduate school, and you will be helped or hindered by these rules.

Despite the fact that some individuals will be affected, we should remember that we are dealing with relatively small numbers; most affirmative-action goals will not dramatically limit the opportunity for young white males to advance, nor will they permit minorities to enter into the economic mainstream overnight. They represent a commitment by our society to do better than we have in the past in ensuring equitable participation by all. Whether this is the proper means by which we should reach this goal depends on which social policy perspective you find most appealing.

The three views provide different answers to the legitimacy of preferential hiring based on race. The libertarian, who believes in freedom and individual action, suggests that individuals have the right to hire whomever they choose, including hiring only African Americans. Yet, the idea of hiring on the basis of race suggests that the supporter of affirmative action wishes that all groups are equally successful, or have equality of outcome. Most libertarians reject this notion as inequitable and claim that it will ultimately weaken motivation to succeed. Why work hard as an individual if your group membership will gain those rewards for you?

The social democrat supports preferential hiring, and state-managed equality, from a desire to narrow the group differences between African Americans and whites. The social democrat argues that the differences between African Americans and whites are not due to innate differences in ability but because the group of which they are members faces discrimination that is difficult to overcome without extra assistance. Fairness demands that people should not be denied the fruits of society simply because they were born into a certain group.

Although conservatives find discrimination against minorities to be pernicious and immoral, they do not object to the existence of classes in society. Conservatives believe in class mobility, but they do not equate wealth with happiness and goodness, as the other philosophies seem to. Conservatives suggest there is no reason why a working-class family cannot be as happy as a rich one—a comforting belief if you happen to be rich and oppose change, or if you are poor and doubt the possibility of change. If we can evolve into a society that judges only ability, everyone will have an opportunity to succeed. A well-adjusted society for the conservative is a stable and orderly one. Seen in this light, conservative social theory has a close resemblance to functional theory in its emphasis on social equilibrium.

Consider one final, difficult question. Why should we not discriminate? What is wrong with wanting to be with people like ourselves and giving them those rewards that we can offer? Today, most people reject discrimination without considering why they should. Why is racial discrimination wrong? Have we created a society in which we have no loyalty to our own group?

The answer ultimately comes down to a question of how we choose to define "our group." As interactionist theory tells us, the meaning of things is not inevitable. Skin color is one very salient way in which people differ, but then so is height, hair color, and regional accent. A person is not "black" or "white," "redheaded" or "blond," but a particular shade. Also we must select which categories are most important to us. Are we "brunettes" or "whites?" If a person is a Russian emigrant, is he or she a Soviet emigré or a person who escaped Czarist pogroms at the turn of this century? Are

Chinese Americans and Japanese Americans both Asian Americans or are they two different cultural groups? What about Vietnamese and Cambodian immigrants? Are Floridians and Georgians both southerners, or should they be distinguished?

It is not my intention to end this chapter with a syrupy plea for tolerance; I only suggest that the group you identify with is not carved in stone but is a social decision. Whatever group you see yourself as belonging to, there are some who resent and dislike that group, while others may choose to place you into other groups that may categorize you to your disadvantage. While group loyalty and solidarity have positive aspects, they carry with them the sense that outsiders do not deserve equal treatment.

Questions

1. What does affirmative action mean?
2. Is reverse discrimination ever justified?
3. If there were no discrimination today, should preferential hiring be used to eliminate the remnants of discrimination in the past?
4. Under what circumstances should individuals be treated as members of racial groups?
5. What groups in our society should receive preferential treatment in hiring?
6. Why are most Americans (African American as well as white) opposed to preferential hiring?
7. Are numerical racial quotas for hiring ever justified?
8. Should government be involved in ensuring affirmative action, or should it be handled voluntarily?
9. Should government contracts be given to companies that do not have many minority workers, even if it cannot be demonstrated that they have intended to discriminate?
10. Is racial or ethnic prejudice and discrimination ever justified?

For Further Study

Carter, Stephen L. *Reflections of an Affirmative Action Baby.* New York: Basic Books, 1991.

Dworkin, Ronald. *Taking Rights Seriously*. Cambridge: Harvard University Press, 1977.

Fullinwider, Robert K. *The Reverse Discrimination Controversy: A Moral and Legal Analysis*. Totowa, NJ: Rowman and Littlefield, 1980.

Glazer, Nathan. *Affirmative Discrimination: Ethnic Inequality and Public Policy*. New York: Basic Books, 1975.

Lynch, Frederick R. *Invisible Victims: White Males and the Crisis of Affirmative Action*. New York: Praeger, 1991.

National Research Council. *A Common Destiny: Blacks and American Society*. Washington, D.C.: National Academy Press, 1989.

Sowell, Thomas. *Preferential Policies*. New York: William Morrow, 1990.

Steele, Shelby. *The Content of Our Character: A New Vision of Race in America*. New York: HarperCollins, 1990.

Wilson, William J. *The Declining Significance of Race*. Chicago: University of Chicago Press, 1978.

Notes and References

1. Quoted in Nijole V. Benokraitis and Joe R. Feagin, *Affirmative Action and Equal Opportunity: Action, Inaction, Reaction* (Boulder: Westview Press, 1978), p. 7, quoting *Federal Register* 6, no. 3109, 1941.

2. Ibid., p. 10, quoting *Federal Register* 26, no. 1977, 3 C.F.R., 1959–63, comp. 448, pt. 3, 301(1).

3. The Aleuts are a small group (population of 2,000) who inhabit the Aleutian Islands, which stretch out to the southwest of Alaska. They have a distinctive language, culture, and racial composition.

4. Thomas Sowell, "A Dissenting Opinion About Affirmative Action," *Across the Board* 18 (January 1981): 66.

5. Quoted in D. Stanley Eitzen, *In Conflict and Order: Understanding Society*, 2nd ed. (Boston: Allyn and Bacon, 1982), p. 332.

6. Editorial, *Philadelphia Evening Bulletin*, September 25, 1977.

7. Randall Kennedy and R. Richard Banks, quoted in Stephen L. Carter, *Reflections of an Affirmative Action Baby* (New York: Basic, 1991), p. 19.

8. George A. McAlmon, "A Critical Look at Affirmative Action," *The Center Magazine*, 11(March 1978): 45–56.

9. Derek Bok, "The Case for Racial Preferences: Admitting Success," *The New Republic* (February 4, 1985): 15.

10. Ronald Dworkin, *Taking Rights Seriously* (Cambridge: Harvard University Press, 1977).

11. Ronald Simon, "Individual Rights and 'Benign' Discrimination," *Ethics* 90 (October 1979): 88–97.

12. Quoted in J. S. Fuerst and Roy Petty, "In Defense of Managed Integration," *Commonweal* 113 (February 14, 1986): 77.

13. 1992 Platform of the Libertarian Party.

14. Scott Bixler, "The Right to Discriminate," *Freeman* 30 (1980): 358–376.

15. William F. Buckley, Jr. "Double Thought," *National Review* 31 (August 3, 1979): 990.
16. In Harlan's famous dissenting opinion to the case of *Plessy* v. *Ferguson* in which the court majority legalized "separate but equal" treatment for blacks.
17. Michael Eric Dyson, "Deaffirmation," *The Nation* 249 (July 3, 1989): 4.
18. William Loeb, editorial, *Manchester (N.H.) Union Leader*, November 22, 1977.
19. Sowell, "A Dissenting Opinion About Affirmative Action," p. 66.
20. Quoted in "What the Weber Ruling Does," *Time* 114 (July 9, 1979): 49.
21. Sowell, "A Dissenting Opinion About Affirmative Action," p. 67.
22. Charles Lawrence, "The Bakke Case: Are Racial Quotas Defensible," *Saturday Review* 5 (October 15, 1977): 15.
23. Sowell, "A Dissenting Opinion About Affirmative Action," p. 67.
24. Robert D. Mare and Christopher Winship, "The Paradox of Lessening Racial Inequality and Joblessness Among Black Youth: Enrollment, Enlistment, and Employment, 1964–1981," *American Sociological Review* 49 (February 1984): 39–55.
25. Ibid., p. 54.

CHAPTER EIGHT

Family: Who Should Be Allowed to Adopt?

■ When politicians scramble for votes, they often stress their love for family—their own and others—and may speak of the United States as being one family. The family is one of the grand rhetorical images in the arsenal of any public speaker. And, of course, the family influences us more than we know in our socialization, culture, education, income, and class position. Most of us have had the experience of growing up in a family, and whatever we might think of that experience, there is no denying that we have been much influenced by it. Most of us (96 percent) choose to repeat the pattern at least once in our lifetime.

The family is a central building block of society. But what is a family? Many family structures are possible with widely different roles for the participants. Basically, a *family* is a long-term social arrangement in which people who are related through marriage, birth, or adoption reside together as an economic unit and raise children. Sociologists distinguish between a person's family of origin (the unit he or she was born into) and a person's family of procreation (the unit in which he or she rears offspring).

Because of its role in propagating and socializing the species, the family is the most basic of all social institutions. Social order would not be possible without *some* institution that performs the tasks we expect of the family. In Israeli agricultural communes (kibbutzes) most child care is organized collectively, but the intense social integration and similarity of goals of the participants makes this unusual form of child rearing possible.

Functionalists see the family as a convincing example of the necessity of social institutions. Families provide the following important social functions in most societies:

1. They regulate and control sexual behavior—determining who will mate with whom. Since intercourse typically involves an intense social and emotional relationship, changing the relations of the two people and their relations with others in society, no society can permit totally free and open sexual behavior. Such free sexuality would produce

severe and changing lines of stress because relationships would never be stable.

2. The family provides for the stable replacement of the population. No society can exist for long if the death rate remains higher than the birth rate.

3. Along with the creation of new members, the family provides an efficient means by which these individuals learn the rules and values of a culture. The family is the first, and perhaps most important, means of socialization.

4. The family provides a means by which children are fitted into a social structure. Some families are wealthy and powerful ("the elite," "the blue bloods," "the Four Hundred"), while other families are stigmatized as poor, homeless, or uneducated. The children of these families are branded with the position of their parents.

5. The family distributes goods. It is a micro-social welfare agency in providing food, shelter, interaction, and other needs.

The functional services provided by families, however, are only part of the picture. The conflict theorist, while not denying that the family may efficiently provide for certain important societal needs, also sees its darker side. Most societies are patriarchal. That is, men control the major forms of decision making. Despite the joke made by some chauvinists that "the only way for women to gain equality is for them to come down off their pedestal," most important decisions in a traditional family are made by the husband. He decides where the family will live (the right of domicile), how the family budget will be spent, and, in large measure, what the wife shall do (whether she can or must work outside the home). Although this has changed substantially in the last three decades, husbands still have more power than wives in many marriages. This lack of power suggests that the family system may oppress women. Friedrich Engels,[1] Karl Marx's co-author of the *Communist Manifesto*, argued perceptively that the family system represents the first instance of repression in history and that the relationship between husband and wife is the model on which other types of economic oppression are based. Marx and Engels make the analogy of a wife as a prostitute: both provide sexual favors in return for money and goods.[2] The domination of the male over the family is also seen in the recognition of family violence. While the image of the family in our society is of a loving "team," this team is often racked by disputes and, sometimes, even bloodshed.

Sociologists distinguish between *nuclear families* and *extended families*. The former refers to the kinship unit that is composed of parents and children, whereas the latter includes other relatives, especially "grown children" and grandparents. Nuclear families are particularly characteristic of our highly mobile society in which each adult generation has sufficient resources to live independently. Some have argued that the Social Security system, with its payments to senior citizens, is in part responsible for the decline in extended families. But an increasing number of families fall into neither category. These are "families" that have a single head of household, typically a single mother. These families pose many challenges to the traditional sociological explanations of family life.

Another feature of our mobile society is the extent to which the choice of marriage partners is relatively unconstrained by geographical proximity. Although location is still a good predictor of whom one will marry, it is not as adequate a predictor as it was a few decades ago. A person is more likely today than before to meet his or her mate at school, work, or at a nonneighborhood social event. Despite this, the choice of a marriage partner is still based largely on *homogamy*—that is, the attraction and marriage of partners with similar social backgrounds. Those people who are least likely to marry each other are also the ones who are most likely to get divorced. The greater the similarity of social experiences, values, beliefs, and expectations, the more likely will we celebrate a marriage and then raise a family.

■ Question:

Who Should Be Allowed to Adopt?

"Compared with childbirth, adoption is a civilized business. The preliminaries involve more red tape than passion. The delivery of the child occurs in an office rather than in a hospital. It is free of panic, agony, and danger."[3] Yet, adoption is not free of emotion; there is joy, and, if the birth mother is present, sadness. Few images are as sad as a child who is unwanted, who has no home. Every child deserves a family—a happy, loving family. Once the primary purpose of adoption was to fill a family need; today adoption is supposed to be for the child, and adoption procedures are to be in the child's "best interests." But we do not always know what these are; nor do we know for sure what kind of home provides the best upbringing.

Adoption has had a long history, going back beyond the time when Pharaoh's daughter discovered young Moses in the bulrushes. Romulus and Remus, the founders of Rome, were supposedly adopted by a she-wolf and suckled by her. Oedipus was adopted so as to make the murder of his "true" father and marriage to his "true" mother inevitable. The great legal code of Hammurabi contained a detailed treatment of adoption in ancient Babylonia.

The longevity of adoption is but one testimony to its success. Many studies of adoption[4] indicate that children so placed are quite happy and healthy, even compared to children who are raised by their birth family.

Since the adopting families often have more social status and wealth than the families of birth, this suggests both the power of environment and the flexibility of children in overcoming difficult circumstances.

The present adoption situation demonstrates convincingly the power of rapid social change. Twenty years ago, the adoption problem was the reverse of what it is today. At that time there were too many babies and not enough adoptive parents. Today we have a "baby shortage." There is far more demand for certain types of infants than there are infants to meet the need. According to the Bureau of the Census, in 1986 only 51,000 babies were adopted by nonrelatives, compared to 89,000 in 1970.[5]

Why has there been such dramatic change? Several factors are involved. With the change in sexual morality and tolerance for different life-styles, it is more acceptable for a single mother to keep her child. In the late 1960s, it was estimated that 80 percent of single mothers gave up their children for adoption; a decade later 80 percent were keeping their children.[6] Schools have made special provisions so that pregnant teenagers will not have to drop out. Second, new methods of birth control and more education about them have decreased the proportion of "accidents." Third, there are more government programs to aid poor, unmarried mothers. Having a child out of wedlock is less of an economic hardship with such programs. Finally, the Supreme Court decided in January 1973, in *Roe* v. *Wade*, to legalize most abortions. Among the unintended consequences of this controversial decision was a decrease in the number of babies available for adoption. Why would a woman wish to deliver a baby she knew she would not keep? Only ethical considerations would lead to that decision, but that has not been enough in many cases. As the supply of babies has dwindled, people have struggled to adopt; now it is virtually impossible to adopt a healthy white infant unless you pass rigorous screening and can prove you are infertile—and even then your chances are uncertain. This has given social workers enormous power in determining who is fit to raise the small number of children available. It has also given rise to the development of alternatives: surrogate motherhood and (more commonly) adopting infants from the Third World (notably Korea, Central and South America, the Philippines, and the Indian subcontinent). From 1981 to 1987, the number of foreign adoptions nearly doubled, to over 10,000 each year,[7] even though some of these nations are now rethinking their policies. We maintain a substantial "trade deficit" in babies.

Putting aside surrogate mother contracts, there are three types of nonkin adoptions: agency adoptions (the white market), independent adoptions (the gray market), and baby selling (the black market). The first is the most common form of adoption when relatives are not adopting. The mother signs away her rights to the child to a social welfare agency (either public or private), and the agency's social workers find suitable parents, with the approval of the courts. In independent adoptions, which are legal in all but four states, adoptive parents and mothers who choose not to keep their children find each other (often through middlemen, such as friends or lawyers) and arrange to have the child transferred. Under this system, money is not supposed to change hands other than for the mother's medical expenses and a reasonable lawyer's fee—an approach that some states are using for surrogate motherhood. Black-market adoption is identical to independent adoption except that the money paid is considerably higher, and the transaction amounts to "purchasing" the child. I shall discuss this further in considering the libertarian point of view.

Considering the reality of the baby shortage, it is significant that there are 120,000 to 140,000 children in foster care ("temporary" homes paid for by the state),[8] a figure that is now made more tragic by the increasing number of abandoned newborns of AIDS-infected mothers. Obviously, these children are not included in discussions of the baby shortage, despite their lack of homes. These children are racial minorities, older children, the handicapped, the chronically or fatally ill, and the troubled. Our society treats these children as "damaged goods." If those of us who are white consider the matter honestly, we probably long for the healthy blue-eyed, blond cherub and consider the others poor second choices.

The baby shortage has forced potential parents to consider these "hard-to-place" children. Even though they may not be their first choices, these children can still love and be loved. Simultaneously, there has been pressure to broaden the definition of who can adopt a child. In particular, single women (and some men) have argued for their rights to adopt, noting that in 1980 some 12.6 million children under the age of eighteen lived with only one of their natural parents. Adoption by single parents through adoption agencies is a fairly recent phenomenon. Even though there is little evidence that having a single parent harms a child, it was not until the mid-1960s that adoption agencies finally agreed to consider single parents.

A second controversial issue is transracial adoptions. The first recorded case in the United States occurred in Minneapolis in 1948 when a white family adopted an unplaceable black child. By 1971, 35 percent of all black adopted children were placed in white homes. While this percentage has decreased dramatically because of the objections from the African-American community, there are still transracial adoptions (particularly of foreign children), and a recent court ruling has said that race cannot be the *sole* criterion for African-American foster care placement. By the mid-1970s, it was estimated that 15,000 African-American children lived in white homes.[9] This could be interpreted as either a hopeful sign for a truly multiracial society or an example of "cultural genocide." Current figures are not available, but, if foreign adoptions are excluded, they would be much lower.

The Libertarian Point of View

What would a system of adoption with minimal state involvement look like? According to some libertarians, it would be a "stork market." In a provocative article, two libertarians, Lawrence Alexander and Lyla O'Driscoll, argue that people should be allowed to sell their rights (and duties) as parents. A mother who did not wish to keep her child could just go to an adoption market and sell her interest in the child for whatever she could receive.[10] Note that parents would not sell their children (children are not property, even for the libertarian) but rather would sell their parental rights and duties.

Alexander and O'Driscoll contend that our current system also constitutes a market, but is simply not recognized as such. In independent adoption, for example, prospective parents are permitted to pay for the mother's medical expenses, and we are not upset by this payment. Surely this is not all that a woman loses by being pregnant. Pregnancy is not a wholly pleasant experience, and a pregnant woman may lose many opportunities. The libertarian believes that it is only reasonable for a mother to be compensated for those lost opportunities. Rather than having cash paid under the table, the system should be open, avoiding the fraud and blackmail that now occur in the black market. For the libertarian, the major problem with the black market is that it is illegal and so attracts criminals, leads to illegal behavior, and stigmatizes "honest" citizens.

Critics might ask whether a couple can truly love a child they have purchased. What would their motives be for such a transaction? Although there is no direct evidence on this point, Alexander and O'Driscoll use the analogy of buying a pet:

> In transactions regarding pet animals, people do not . . . seem to believe . . . that those who *buy* pets are likely to have motives or expectations different from—or less suitable than—the motives or expectations of those who pay no cash price. Nor do they seem to think them less likely to love and care for the pet once they have it, or that their having paid cash (as opposed to some other or no medium of exchange) is itself likely to corrupt their attitude toward the pet. Indeed, some who have young animals to distribute prefer to charge at least a nominal cash price rather than to give the animal away; they apparently believe that, other things being equal, the purchaser's willingness to make an explicit sacrifice is a sign that the pet is "really wanted" and will be given good care.[11]

Libertarians assert that under our current system money is involved in all the adoption markets. Adoption agencies regularly consider the financial status and the "cultural atmosphere" of the applicants; the amount of income one has contributes to the likelihood of being able to adopt. Even though being rich does not guarantee that someone will be a good parent, and being poor does not mean that he or she will be a poor parent, most people would probably entrust a child to the family with more wealth, status, and education because care and love are difficult, if not impossible, to measure. If you had to choose an adoptive parent, not knowing their capacity for love, what factors would you look for? Baby selling, while not without flaws, insures that the purchased child will be wanted and that the family will have the resources to care for him or her.[12]

Recently, the discussion of baby selling has taken a particularly controversial turn with the publicity attached to surrogate motherhood. In the past, there had been instances (in the "black market") of couples paying pregnant women to carry a baby to term ("birth"). Recently, infertile couples are contracting with women to be impregnated with the husband's sperm or the couple's impregnated egg. As a result of medical technology, such has become possible, even routine. But morally this raises numerous questions. While some surrogacy contracts work well, in others the surrogate objects to giving up the child.[13] The "Baby M" case was such an instance. Despite a seemingly legal "contract" with Elizabeth and William Stern, Mary Beth Whitehead, the surrogate mother, decided that she wished to keep "her" child. After a bitter trial and appeal, the New Jersey Supreme Court ruled that the contract violated New Jersey's adoption laws, revoking the adoption of the child by Elizabeth Stern, restored visitation rights to Mary Beth Whitehead, but left the father, William Stern, with custody of "Baby M."

Despite an intricate and legalistic contract, which specified reduced payment for "damaged goods," the courts have found surrogacy covered by laws against "black-market babies." Different states have handled the problem differently; where one resides determines the possibility of surrogacy. Michigan forbids commercial surrogacy, whereas Nevada exempts surrogate contracts from the ban on payments connected with adoption.[14] While recognizing certain special problems inherent in these contracts, the libertarian believes that such contracts should be legal, although the all too frequent regrets of the surrogate mother surely cast a pall over the enterprise. No matter how "rational" we wish to be, the lure of a child one has been carrying for nine months is difficult to resist. But so is the hope of infertile couples being able to obtain a child who is "genetically" their own.

Critics raise numerous questions about whether there should be any control on costs, what happens in the event of a miscarriage, who can enter into such contracts (only infertile, heterosexual couples?), what counseling and informed consent are necessary, or does the contract become null and void if the fetus is discovered to have a birth defect. The questions and the moral problems that ensue seem endless, but so is the potential joy.

The libertarian is always concerned about the state intruding into people's lives. Some resent the "home visits" that adoption agencies make to prospective clients, suggesting that it would be logically consistent for state welfare officers to pay the same "home visits" to prospective parents before licensing them to have children—an image consistent with George Orwell's *1984*. Libertarians believe, within broad guidelines (for example, preventing extreme child abuse), parents should be allowed to raise children as they wish. Just as the state should not tell biological parents how many children they should have and how to raise them, they should apply this restraint to adoption.

The Conservative Point of View

For the conservative, the family is the cornerstone of society. Organized society cannot exist without the family—it is a sacred institution. Conservatives have none of the cold, rational calculation of the libertarians when it comes to buying and selling babies. There is something grossly offensive about such a practice. Perhaps it is the mixing of "filthy" money with "pure" love that is so disturbing. Conservatives look upon adoption as a beautiful and important relationship. By adopting a homeless child, a family can socialize the child properly.

But what is a family to a conservative? For many it is the "Walt Disney model of daddy coming home to mommy in the house with a white picket fence and the boy, the girl and the dog running out to greet [him]."[15] Single parents, handicapped parents, homosexual parents, older parents, and ill parents run families, and they often do so well. But such families are not likely to receive a healthy adopted child. In her study of transracial adoption, Joyce Ladner learned that most adoption agencies had a fairly restrictive list of criteria, given the shortage of babies. These requirements include (1) Both parents have a publicly declared religious faith. (2) Both parents have the same religious faith. (3) They have good physical and mental health. (4) The husband is employed. (5) The wife is a housewife and not otherwise employed. (6) They have a middle-class income and life-style, including a separate room for a child. (7) They cannot be too old or too young—they must be the age they would have been had the wife given birth. (8) They should not be too intense about their desire for a child, nor too uncaring. If your parents wished to adopt you, given all these requirements, would they have been allowed to? Mine wouldn't. Ladner suggests that these criteria have the effect of "screening out" parents, rather than "screening them in."[16] When one adds to this that the cost of adoption is nearly $10,000, few potential parents qualify.[17] Inevitably, the social worker plays God choosing among well-heeled applicants. One can argue for each of these criteria (which have been liberalized to some extent in the fifteen years since Ladner's study), but taken together they exclude many good parents and may cause some couples to shade the truth and present themselves in the best light possible. Given the shortage of babies, do these requirements make for the best possible adoptive parents and serve the best interests of the child?

Ultimately, for the conservative, the goal is to place each child in a warm, welcoming, stable family. Joseph Goldstein, Anna Freud, and Albert Solnit, writing from a psychoanalytic perspective, feel that the goal of child placement (with the exception of violent juveniles)

> is to assure for each child, membership in a family with at least one partner who wants him. It is to assure for each child and his parents an opportunity to maintain, establish, or reestablish psychological ties to each other free of further interruption by the state. . . . The intact family offers the child a rare and continuing combination of elements to further his growth: reciprocal affection between the child and two, or at least one, caretaking adult; the feeling of being wanted and therefore valued; and the stimulation of inborn capacities.[18]

The conservative, like the libertarian, objects to state intervention except under the greatest provocation. Where the libertarian values the freedom of the individual actor, the conservative points to the necessary stability of a family; even a bad family might be better than a good, temporary foster home.

One of the areas in which the debate over adoption is particularly intense concerns whether a single person can adopt a child. Is a two-parent home always preferable to a single-parent home? Conservatives would say yes, and this appears to be the sentiment of most Americans, despite considerable evidence that a single-parent home is not necessarily a disadvantage to a child.[19] In 1969, *Good Housekeeping* magazine conducted a survey of its readers, asking; Should a single person adopt a child? Of those responding, 73 percent favored the idea while 23 percent opposed it. But even those who supported the idea did not believe that a single-parent home was as good a setting for bringing up a child as one with two parents present.[20] The sentiment generally suggests that "one parent is better than none," just as it is better to have one eye than to be blind. Howard Stein, the executive director of Family Service of Westchester (N.Y.), however, does not completely agree. He feels "a child really needs both parents—the parent of the same sex to identify with and of the opposite sex as a love object to fix on. A boy brought up only by a woman faces serious psychological hazards; a girl without a father may be limited in her responses. Any child growing up in a one-sided household is deprived of an important life experience and may be poorly prepared for his or her own marriage and parenthood."[21] While this may be somewhat exaggerated, few people would claim the single-parent home is the best of all possible worlds. Thus, single parents who wish to adopt must settle for the less desirable children. Such a situation is ironic. These children with special needs are precisely those for whom two parents are particularly desirable, but they are rarely the first choice of first-choice parents. Conservatives believe in the importance of families, but the question of what constitutes a family is something of a puzzle.

The Social Democratic Point of View

The social democrat does not see anything inherently wrong with agencies of the state intervening in family life if the welfare of a child is at stake. The question is, What should the government do? What image of the family should it encourage? What is the best upbringing for a child? In this section I examine one particularly thorny question: Are transracial adoptions morally justified or do they reflect a form of prejudice? This question is particularly difficult for social democrats because their emphasis on equality may lead to opposite answers.

The first transracial adoption occurred in the late 1940s, but it was not until the late 1960s that many white families began to adopt African-American children. By this time, the shortage of healthy white infants was increasing and the overt racial discrimination that had characterized U.S. society was decreasing. By the early 1970s, over one-third of all adopted African-American children were adopted by white parents. In 1972, a federal court struck down a Louisiana law that prohibited such adoptions. Ironically, this same year the National Association of Black Social Workers went on record as being "in vehement opposition to placing black children in white homes."[22] At the same time the battle had been won against white racists in the South, arguments similar to those being used by segregationists were advanced by African-American professionals. These arguments pitted the image of a society in which there would be no race consciousness against one in which all racial groups would retain their own identity. Social democrats were caught in the middle.

Those who argue in favor of transracial adoption contend that society's goal should be a multiracial society, a melting pot—with race not particularly salient. Race mixing is healthy and is to be encouraged. The mother of an African-American child and a Hispanic child expresses this view:

> In our experience the multicultural family has become something positive, something to celebrate. We tell our children that because we are a family, each of us can share in the cultural heritage of all the rest: "Thanks to Mark, we can all celebrate Martin Luther King Day, thanks to Adam we can all have birthday pinatas, thanks to Daddy we can all wear green for St. Patrick's Day, and thanks to Mommy we can all eat garlic bread." Although parenting a multi-

cultural family is a challenge, it suggests practical ways to embody spiritual values in the daily life of the most intimate unit of society.[23]

Some supporters of transracial adoption justifiably point out that the policy now generally adhered to in the aftermath of the objections of African-American social workers is an instance of reverse discrimination. Although black parents adopt at the same rate as white parents (controlling for their income), there are not enough black parents to meet the demand. There are two major reasons for this: (1) there is a smaller *percentage* of African-American middle-class parents than whites, and (2) fully 40 percent of the children put up for adoption are African American. White people who want to adopt black children have been turned away by welfare agencies, causing black children to wait twice as long as whites to be placed.[24] After a Connecticut court decision that ruled that a white family could not adopt an African-American child it had raised from birth, civil rights leader Roy Wilkins commented that this policy:

> has the effect of depriving otherwise-adoptable black children of a stable, loving family life. The state which permits such archaic considerations as the race of the prospective parents to bar an adoption bears a heavy responsibility for cruelty to children by sending them instead to institutions or passing them from one foster home to the next. . . . To render a black child "unadoptable" or label his white foster parents "unable" or unfit to adopt him on the grounds of racial incompatibility would be the advice of the segregationist.[25]

And so it is. A Pennsylvania court has ruled that John and Marilyn McLaughlin, a white foster couple, could keep Raymond, a young African-American child, who was abruptly taken from them for no reason other than race. The court ruled that race could not be the sole criterion for determining foster placements. What difference, after all, does race make?

For some, race does make quite a difference. Opponents of transracial adoptions say that the white demand for African-American babies did not begin until after whites learned they could no longer adopt healthy white babies. African Americans saw that in many (although not all) cases whites who were given black babies did not qualify for white babies.[26] Just as the white parent may see an African-American baby as a second choice, the African-American adult may see the white parent as inferior. African Americans are now recommending that adoption agencies make an intense effort to find black parents to adopt black children, even if it means altering their criteria of income and home ownership and subsidizing some of these adoptions. Agencies responded by liberalizing standards for minorities. In 1986 half of minority adoptive parents had incomes below $20,000 a year, compared with only 14 percent of white adoptive parents.[27]

Opponents of transracial adoption see adoption as a political issue with racial and class implications. Mary Benet notes that more recent doubts about adoption stem from today's controversies over inequality, imperialism, and the nature of the family itself. . . . Adoption has usually meant the transfer of a child from one social class to another slightly higher one. Today, as always, adopters tend to be richer than the natural parents of the children they adopt. They may also be members of a racial majority, adopting children of a minority; or citizens of a rich country, adopting children from a poor one.[28]

The contention is that the members of the upper class use minority or Third World children for their own pleasure, sometimes wiping out the culture of those they adopt. One African-American man sees the issue in genocidal terms: "Transracial adoption is one of the many conspiracies being waged against Black people. It is one of the white man's latest moves to wipe out the last vestiges of our culture, if not us. He made progress in brainwashing us and our young with his churches, his schools, and birth control. And now he wishes to use his latest trick of mental genocide."[29] This may be an extreme statement, but it captures the sensitivity of African Americans toward the preservation of their heritage. While caring white parents can certainly teach African-American history and literature, they cannot teach a child what it means to be black in white-majority America. Since the United States is likely to remain color-conscious, some argue that a strong African-American identity is necessary. This may pose a particular problem once the African-American child has reached adolescence and must deal with white political institutions and also with his or her own sexuality in a largely white community. While the testimonies of many parents and children suggest that transracial adoptions are successful, the difficulties of such adoptions cannot be easily dismissed.[30]

Social democrats want to recognize both of these impulses: the desire for a color-blind society and the desire for a society in which all people are proud of their "roots." For now, most people involved in adoption accept that racial matching is desirable and many African-American children remain in foster care.

Transracial Adoption and Social Research

Sometimes the best way to find out about someone's behavior is simply to ask him or her directly. If we wish to understand white parents who have chosen to raise African-American children—their attitudes toward their responsibilities, their philosophy of upbringing, their views on how their neighbors feel, and their fears of the future—we could sit down with them and discuss their concerns. This is precisely what Joyce Ladner, a prominent African-American sociologist, decided to do in her study, *Mixed Families*. Recounting her experience, she remembers she started her research project

with considerable skepticism of whether white parents had the abilities
necessary to raise African-American children. But she was also convinced
that every child had the right to a happy and stable home life. These two
attitudes influenced her research.

An important methodological issue raised in this study is the question
of whether a sociological researcher can conduct racially sensitive research
with members of another race. Ironically, Ladner had been a militant who
questioned the value of white sociologists examining African Americans.
Here, some years later, she found herself conducting personal interviews
with whites on their racial attitudes.

In conducting in-depth interviews, a sociologist must be able to make
his or her informants open up and reveal their honest and private
thoughts—those they might only reveal to their closest friends. Good
interviews have the ring of truth and, sometimes, the sting of pain. Poor
interviews consist of subjects rattling off what they think the researcher
wishes to hear. Interviews, like participant observation, involve understanding the subject; thus, they usually produce sympathetic accounts. It is
hard to paint someone you know well, and who has been friendly, as a bad
person. This is true in Ladner's study of 136 parents in six states and the
District of Columbia. Since the focus is on white parents, the study "dis-
covers" that white parents can raise African-American children.

It would be unfair to characterize this study as suggesting parental
race does not affect child rearing. Ladner believes deeply that African-
American children should have their own racial identity and that their
white parents face difficult challenges in ensuring that this sense of black-
ness is not lost. While she respects most of the parents in the study and
indicates that most appear to be doing a good job in raising their children
(recall that she has no objective measures), Ladner would clearly prefer for
there to be enough African-American adoptive parents to go around. She
summarizes the challenges to white parents of African-American children
as follows:

> Adoptive parents need to be exceptionally strong, well-adjusted, inde-
> pendent-minded, confident individuals who are more prepared for failure in
> the childrearing than are birth parents. The added dimension of transracial
> adoption is obvious. It requires courage, commitment, independence, and
> sensitivity to undertake this awesome responsibility in bringing up a healthy
> child. . . . The racial attitudes and behavior [of the parents] as well as their
> attitudes toward adoption itself will, more than anything else, determine these
> children's outcomes.[31]

Perhaps the most compelling portion of her study, as is often the case
in in-depth interviews, is the testimonies of the participants. Although
Ladner worried about whether she would receive honest comments, and
although not all subjects may have been candid, there are enough "honest-

sounding" accounts for us to be able to better understand these people's lives. Consider for example, the ambivalent remarks of one white father: "It is very painful for me to listen to blacks criticize me for what I have done, even if I know that they don't personally know *me*. I used to dismiss their criticisms as trite, irrelevant, and irresponsible. One day I asked myself, 'How would I feel if I were them?' I then realized that I could understand their anger and frustration, even when I also know that many of these children wouldn't have homes if whites had not adopted them."[32] Ladner's interviews may remind us that ultimately we are talking about people who feel pain, anger, and joy. But aside from this, if we look at each individual as an individual, we do not have certain guidelines for determining the amount of good or harm these parents do. Ultimately, despite its virtues, the in-depth interview does not give us a *numerical estimate* of the extent of the crucial variables of good or harm.

Ladner's position falls between the two poles of the social democratic argument described in this chapter. On the one hand, she points out that in the real world, race does make a difference and that it should make a difference. Thus, she has a preference for black homes for black children, which is in line with the wishes of African-American social workers. On the other hand, Ladner does not forget that these children are children, and, while transracial adoption poses special problems, she does not advocate stopping it. Most of these children, she suggests, are being raised lovingly and well.

Adoption and the Family

It is ironic that a healthy, white infant put up for adoption is likely to be placed in the "ideal American family," while babies reared in their families of procreation are often not so fortunate. Such are the whims of biology that many couples who are unable to have the perfect children they have been told they are supposed to have must compete with each other for a few children, sometimes paying tens of thousands of dollars to give "someone else's child" the upbringing their biological child would have had. Because of the competition, adoption agencies are able to place children in families that meet the agencies' image of what a family should be. Even many children who are ill or "damaged"—but "perfect" in their love and humanity—are placed in permanent homes rather than going to foster homes and institutions.

How we treat children reveals a great deal about what we think about ourselves. First, the existence of the highly bureaucratic and careful adoption procedure suggests that we do not trust individuals to make personal arrangements for their children—perhaps a consequence of a large and complex social system. "Experts" have the power to make decisions about who should get which children. Second, by placing the "most desirable" children with the "most desirable" parents, society underlines its support for the social elite. Yet, unlike some cultures, we do not let unwanted children die. We do not leave them out on the hillside in the middle of winter to fend for themselves. We place unwanted children with parents who will make a special effort to raise these children. But we are torn between "the best interests of all children" and the desire to maximize our human capital by giving special treatment to the healthy white child.

One question involving how we maximize our human capital is whether we should match parents and children racially and culturally. There is a belief that demographic considerations (race, religious background, ethnicity) should not make any difference. Why should an African-American child not be reared at birth by orthodox Jews and become a member of a Hasidic synagogue? Some people would reply that a person's roots are genetic and that religion, ethnicity, and race should not be lightly discarded. Furthermore, changes in a child's ethnicity or religion have political implications if duplicated often enough; such a pattern of adoption might be enough to do away with a culture, a set of beliefs or traditions of a group—a charge made by Catholics when it was their children who were put up for adoption to Protestant families. Of course, with race, parents and children can never escape public recognition and perhaps stigma. Americans are of two minds about what to do with matching children to parents. What we consider legitimate for race and, to some extent, for religion would seem ludicrous if we extended it to political beliefs or leisure preferences.

Adoption reminds us that biology is not the only basis on which a family can be built. Just as husbands and wives can love each other, even though they are not biologically related, so, too, can they love someone else's biological child. The social bonds in the family are as strong as any biological bond. Furthermore, the success rate of adoption gives testimony to the fact that, whatever our feelings about our own families of origin and procreation, the family remains a viable and much needed institution.

Questions

1. Should the rights to raise unwanted infants be bought and sold openly?

2. Should the government subsidize parents to adopt certain types of "hard-to-place" children?

3. If you were to be adopted, what kind of parents would you wish to have?

4. Should single parents be allowed to adopt children? Should they be allowed to adopt children only after no other suitable parents can be found?

5. Should white parents be allowed to adopt African-American children? Should they be allowed to adopt African-American children only after no suitable African-American parents can be found?

6. Should adoption agencies attempt to match the background of the mother with the background of the adoptive parents?

7. Should adoption agencies attempt to place children with parents of the same religion as the mother?

8. Should homosexual couples be allowed to adopt children?

9. If you learned that you or your spouse were infertile, would you attempt to adopt a child?

10. Should commercial surrogate motherhood be permitted?

For Further Study

Alexander, Lawrence A., and Lyla H. O'Driscoll. "Stork Markets: An Analysis of 'Baby-Selling,'" *Journal of Libertarian Studies* 4(1980): 173–196.

Anderson, David C. *Children of Special Value: Interracial Adoption in America.* New York: St. Martin's Press, 1971.

Benet, Mary K. *The Politics of Adoption.* New York: Free Press, 1976.

Field, Martha A. *Surrogate Motherhood: The Legal and Human Issues.* Cambridge: Harvard University Press, 1990.

Goldstein, Joseph; Anna Freud, and Albert J. Solnit. *Before the Best Interests of the Child.* New York: Free Press, 1979.

Hartman, Ann. *Finding Families: An Ecological Approach to Family Assessment in Adoption.* Beverly Hills: Sage, 1979.

Kane, Elizabeth. *Birth Mother: The Story of America's First Legal Surrogate Mother.* New York: Harcourt Brace Jovanovich, 1988.

Ladner, Joyce A. *Mixed Families: Adopting Across Racial Boundaries.* Garden City, NY: Anchor, 1977.

Morris, Steven. "The Fight for Black Babies," *Ebony* (September 1973): 32–42.

Simon, Rita, and Howard Altstein. *Transracial Adopters and Their Families.* New York: Praeger, 1987.

Notes and References

1. Friedrich Engels, *The Origin of the Family, Private Property, and the State* (New York: International Publishing, 1942, orig. 1884), pp. 59–60.

2. Karl Marx and Friedrich Engels, *The Communist Manifesto* (Arlington Heights, IL: AHM Publishing, 1955, orig. 1848), pp. 27–29.

3. David C. Anderson, *Children of Special Value* (New York: St. Martin's Press, 1971), p. 1.
4. Joyce A. Ladner, *Mixed Families* (Garden City, NY: Anchor, 1977), pp. 148–149.
5. U.S. Department of Commerce, Bureau of the Census, *Statistical Abstract of the United States, 1991* (Washington, D.C.: Government Printing Office, 1991), p. 376.
6. Harold Kennedy, "As Adoptions Get More Difficult," *U.S. News and World Report* (June 25, 1984): 61.
7. U.S. Department of Commerce, Bureau of the Census, *Statistical Abstract of the United States, 1991*, p. 376
8. Ann Hartman, *Finding Families* (Beverly Hills: Sage, 1979), p. 14.
9. Ladner, *Mixed Families.*, p. 248.
10. Lawrence A. Alexander and Lyla H. O'Driscoll, "Stork Markets: An Analysis of 'Baby-Selling,'" *Journal of Libertarian Studies* 4(1980): 174; see also Elizabeth M. Landes and Richard A. Posner, "The Economics of the Baby Shortage," *Journal of Legal Studies* 7(1978): 323–348.
11. Alexander and O'Driscoll, "Stork Markets: An Analysis of 'Baby-Selling,'" p. 187.
12. Alexander and O'Driscoll (ibid., p. 196) suggest that there should be a minimum age above which a child cannot be "sold." This age should be lower than the age at which the child becomes aware of the market. Otherwise, the child might worry that he or she could be sold to buy a new car—and rightly so.
13. Elizabeth Kane, *Birth Mother: The Story of America's First Legal Surrogate Mother* (New York: Harcourt Brace Jovanovich, 1988).
14. "Birth Marketing," *Commonweal* 114(December 4, 1987): 692; "Unnatural Acts," *Commonweal* 115(October 21, 1988): 550.
15. Cynthia D. Martin, *Beating the Adoption Game* (La Jolla, CA: Oak Tree, 1980), p. 193.
16. Ladner, *Mixed Families.*, pp. 218–219.
17. Philip J. Hilts, "New Study Challenges Estimates on Odds of Adopting a Child," *The New York Times* (December 10, 1990): B10.
18. Joseph Goldstein, Anna Freud, and Albert J. Solnit, *Before the Best Interests of the Child* (New York: Free Press, 1979), pp. 5, 13.
19. Alfred Kadushin, "Single-Parent Adoptions: An Overview and Some Relevant Research," *Social Service Review* 44(1970): 263–274.
20. "Should a Single Person Adopt a Child?" *Good Housekeeping* (August 1969): 12.
21. Ibid., p. 14.
22. Carole Klein, *The Single Parent Experience* (New York: Walker and Company, 1973), p. 96.
23. Quoted in Jane Zeni Flinn, "Many Cultures, One Family," *America* (October 21, 1981): p. 261.
24. Melinda Beck with Elisa Williams, "Willing Families, Waiting Kids," *Newsweek* (September 12, 1988): 64.
25. Roy Wilkins, "What Color Is Love?" *OURS* (March/April 1980): 33.
26. Ladner, *Mixed Families.*, p. 231.
27. Beck with Williams, "Willing Families, Waiting Kids," p. 64.
28. Mary K. Benet, *The Politics of Adoption* (New York: Free Press, 1976), p. 12.
29. Ladner, *Mixed Families*, p. 88.

30. Rita Simon and Howard Altstein, *Transracial Adoptees and Their Families* (New York: Praeger, 1987).
31. Ladner, *Mixed Families*, p. 257.
32. Ibid., p. 212.

CHAPTER NINE

Education: Should Books in Public Libraries Be Censored?

Mine eyes have seen the glory of the burning of the school.
We have tortured all the teachers,
We have broken every rule,
We are marching down the hall
To hang the principal,
Our gang's marching on.
Glory, glory hallelujah,
Teacher hit me with a ruler;
I hit her on the bean
With a rotten tangerine
And she ain't no teacher any more.[1]
(Sung to the tune of "The Battle Hymn of the Republic")

■ As the preceding ditty suggests, school and learning need not be synonymous. In its 1983 report, *A Nation at Risk: The Imperative for Educational Reform*, The National Commission on Excellence in Education notes that 13 percent of all seventeen-year-olds are functionally illiterate (as high as 40 percent among minority youth), College Board Scholastic Aptitude Test scores declined consistently from 1963 to 1980, and only one-fifth of all seventeen-year-olds can write a persuasive essay.[2] Schools are neither necessary nor sufficient for education and, in fact, many people become educated outside of a formal school setting. Nevertheless, by educating children in large groups and processing them through a formal organization, schools are efficient. Despite the problems that plague our public schools, they have managed to educate many more students than they have failed to educate.

School is neither heaven nor hell. It is an environment where once one knows the rules, one can get by. The avowed goal of schooling is to "educate" the student. To some extent, education involves teaching the moral prescriptions of our society—along with the family and the church. It is also supposed to transmit technical information that is necessary for students to become successful functioning citizens. By the time an adolescent completes high school, he or she is expected to know how to read and write, know how to solve basic mathematical problems, be aware of the greatest artistic achievements in our culture, and be physically fit. Finally, and not least important, the person has learned how to get along with his or her peers. But there is also another level of education that occurs within schools. This "hidden curriculum"[3] consists of things like sex education, drug use, dirty jokes, how to deceive parents—topics that children have taught each other through the ages.

In the United States, the idea of education is taken very seriously. For well over a century Americans have been committed to providing an education to every child. This progressive view of mass education was not accepted in Europe until much later. This difference can still be seen in regard to postsecondary education. Most Americans believe that all young adults should have the opportunity to attend a college or technical school if they wish. (The various grant and loan programs that are available support this.) In other nations, only a small minority attend any kind of post-high-school program, and there is no general sentiment that they should be entitled to.

Given the United States' intense commitment to mass education, it may seem strange that schools are not controlled on the federal level, but by local communities. Even with the federal government's increased involvement (for example, a series of regulations school boards must follow if they wish federal aid), most decision making still occurs within the local school districts.

Obviously, a school system that aims to educate its entire child population necessarily must have several levels of emphasis, unlike a school system that only trains the elite. American education has tried to meet this challenge with "technical education." In addition to learning the Three Rs, many students are also taught a trade. This vocational emphasis is also found at the postsecondary level.

Schooling can be seen as a functional social institution that unifies society by teaching similar values and knowledge to the mass of young people. Some people see schools as a melting pot in which students with different backgrounds are treated in nearly identical fashion, thus producing a common national culture among the graduates.

In contrast, those people who accept a conflict perspective of society see other outcomes of schooling. They do not see education as a homogenizing process. There are real differences among schools, particularly between those that have a middle-class set of values and those that do not. The question of the effects of school facilities on educational achievement is, perhaps, debatable. The 1966 Coleman report[4] found that the school's characteristics had only a slight effect on a child's achievement. On the other hand, within schools, children from different backgrounds do get treated differently. Teachers who expect particular children to do well often find that these children actually do better than their peers. This disturbing example of a self-fulfilling prophecy is known as "the Pygmalion effect,"[5] after the Cockney flower girl in George Bernard Shaw's play *Pygmalion* (later turned into *My Fair Lady*) who recognizes that what she could be depends on how she is treated. Children who are poor, African American, or who have reputations as being disciplinary problems may find themselves with at least one strike against them.

Conflict theorists take the functionalist view of schools as a mechanism by which society can continue to be stable and turn it on its head. They see schools as a means by which a class system reproduces itself and maintains social inequality. The children of those who are dominant will become dominant themselves, while the children of factory workers find themselves directed toward the factory and may even receive hidden messages that they should drop out.

As noted at the beginning of the chapter, education does not occur only within school. Many talented people continue their education after they leave school, and some people leave school early to create their own education. Some people even charge that a school as currently formulated is not a good place to become educated. While schools (including colleges) are able to teach masses of facts, other life experiences may be equally effective in producing insight and creativity. Schools are learning institutions from the top down; that is, they are bureaucracies founded on the authority of degrees. For some people, that degree is an important credential; for others, the truth can be found on a summer breeze.

■ Question:

Should Books in Public Libraries Be Censored?

Few among us would like to be known by that rather pejorative title "the censor." This phrase dredges up images of the blue-nosed Puritan, the little old lady in tennis shoes, the dour dowager, or the extremist crank who finds traitors under everyone's bed. At the same time, most of us would like to be known as people of discerning judgment. We wish to be known as people who can separate the wheat from the chaff, the trash from the genius, the pearls from the swine. This is part of the paradox of the debate on censorship. It is the difference between "censorship" and "selection." Censorship is what the other guy does; selection is what we do.

What would a library without "selection" look like? It would either purchase every book that is published or, more feasibly, it would purchase books by random selection. Imagine the chaos in the library system if books were chosen by sticking pins in the pages of book catalogs. Clearly someone must make decisions, but how?

Political scientist Harold D. Lasswell defines censorship as "the policy of restricting the public expression of ideas, opinions, conceptions and impulses which have or are believed to have the capacity to undermine the governing authority or the social and moral order which that authority considers itself bound to protect."[7] This definition takes the motivation of the "censor" into account. In this definition, a librarian who decides not to purchase the autobiography of the leader of the Communist Party of America would be engaging in censorship, while one who decides not to purchase the autobiography of Lee Iacocca would only be making a selection. It is easy to see how such a definition systematically favors those books that challenge the system, as opposed to books that support it.

The selection process is supposedly designed to ensure that a library purchases the "best" books, those that the community would be most interested in and most "needs" and those books that provide a diverse collection. Yet these criteria may lead librarians to purchase some books over others on ideological grounds. Styles and subject matters pass in and out of favor; definitions of what the "community" is interested in depend on a librarian's perceptions, stereotypes, and prejudices; and what makes for a diverse collection is a matter of judgment. (How well represented should Communist, racist, Nazi, or fundamentalist Christian works be?) A librarian has considerable leeway in such matters, and it is this latitude that makes some argue that censorship and selection are synonymous. While we might be willing to concede, in some cases, that different motivations are involved, selection and censorship have precisely the same result: Certain books are not put on the shelf.[8] If censorship consists of removing books already purchased, we must admit that librarians do this all the time for such "appropriate" reasons as a work becoming outdated. Even this can be a matter of ideology; for example, what constitutes scientific progress is never certain.

Crucial to the definition of censorship is the role of the librarian. Some see librarians as dedicated professionals striving, despite inadequate budgets, to provide a diverse array of knowledge to the public; they are in constant battle with outsiders who wish to limit what people can read. Contrast this to the view that librarians are government bureaucrats, responsive only to those political functionaries who appointed them and to the universities that trained them. These librarians try to enforce a particular, biased set of views. When members of the public (who support the library through their taxes) object to a particular book, the librarian is unwilling to understand that in a democracy citizens have a legitimate right to help select books. These two images give widely different perspectives on the legitimacy of selection and censorship. Librarians, like members of most white-collar occupations, think of themselves as professionals, with the authority of doctors and lawyers. Those outside the occupation see librarians as government employees whose primary function is to serve the wishes of the public. Library selection, from this viewpoint, is *always* government censorship, because a government employee is choosing what the public will be able to read. The question of censorship becomes a question of who has power to make decisions.

The idea of censoring library material is not new and is parallel to other attempts to suppress material thought to be immoral or subversive. The first major flowering of moral crusaders in the United States occurred in the aftermath of the Civil War,[9] with the establishment of Anthony Comstock's New York Society for the Suppression of Vice in 1873. To this day, "Comstockery" refers to the vigorous suppression of material deemed to be obscene or immoral. Similar societies grew in number and in influence throughout the latter part of the nineteenth century, and they managed to pass legislation that significantly limited what could be sent through the mails.

During the twentieth century, censorship attempts have continued. The list of authors whose works someone has wanted to ban is impressive: William Faulkner, James Joyce, Mark Twain, J. D. Salinger, J. R. R. Tolkien, Alice Walker, and William Shakespeare, to name a few. Although it is fair to say that the mood is more tolerant now than earlier in the century, cases still arise in which some citizens wish to have materials taken off library shelves. In the period from September 1, 1990, through August 31, 1991, the Office for Intellectual Freedom of the American Library Association reports that there were over 500 reports of people or groups attempting to censor books. They estimate that for each report they receive, perhaps four attempts are not reported.[10] Of course, this statistic alone does not tell us much since the seriousness of the challenges is not indicated. (You could, if you wish, challenge the Bible.) It does suggest, however, that there are still some people who would like to see books removed from libraries. In recent years, attention seems to have focused particularly on school libraries and curricula. People for the American Way, a social democratic advocacy group, claim that challenges to public school material quadrupled from 1983 to 1990.[11]

Knowing that they might be challenged makes some librarians more careful about the controversial titles they purchase. A 1983 survey of North Carolina librarians indicated that 42 percent engaged in "self-censorship" because of the fear of public controversy and a desire to keep their jobs.[12] A Canadian study found that even though librarians were personally "liberal," their behavior was cautious.[13] For good or ill, librarians engage in self-censorship in the name of selection. Political scientist Oliver Garceau describes how the issue of censorship becomes obscured: "The censorship of library holdings does not often become a public issue, largely because it is an intramural activity. As a member himself of the white collar middle class that uses his library, the librarian has a green thumb for cultivating those books that will be popular and an equal knack for weeding out what will be considered dangerous."[14] There are far too many books published for a librarian to read even a small portion of them, so they rely on book review journals. In 1970, thirty-six thousand books were published, but the *Library Journal*, the widest read book review journal, reviewed only about nine thousand of these,[15] and one would guess that fewer than half of all the books published are reviewed anywhere. Thus, these book review journals serve as *gatekeepers*—mechanisms that provide entry (or rewards) to selected things or persons. If a publisher does not get his or her books reviewed, for all practical purposes, these volumes are shut out of the library market. To the extent that such journals do not review religious literature, radical political tracts, racist books, or pornography, it is easy to see why, despite the proclamation of diversity, libraries reflect mainstream thought.

The Libertarian Point of View

The extreme libertarian believes the government has no business running libraries since these institutions do not provide for the common defense or internal peace. For them, the issue of public library censorship is moot. Libraries should be privatized.

Leaving aside this extreme position and recognizing that there always will be public libraries and librarians who will make decisions about books, the libertarian is deeply offended by limits to public access to any type of writing. For the libertarian, the library is a free marketplace of ideas; those ideas that are offensive or incorrect will fall by their own weight. Consider the comment made by nineteenth-century libertarian philosopher John Stuart Mill:

> The peculiar evil of silencing the expression of an opinion is that it is robbing the human race: posterity as well as the existing generation; those who dissent from the opinion still more than those who hold it. If the opinion is right, they are deprived of the opportunity of exchanging error for truth; if wrong, they lose what is almost as great a benefit, the clearer perception and livelier impression of truth, produced by its collision with error.[16]

Some believe there should be a "freedom to read"—a right as vigorously upheld as any. For libertarians, this right follows directly from freedom of speech and the press. There is a right to be a passive recipient of ideas and not just an active disseminator of them. The American Library Association has articulately expressed this in a document adopted in 1953 and revised in 1972:

The freedom to read is essential to our democracy. It is continuously under attack. . . . We trust Americans to recognize propaganda, and to reject it. We do not believe they need the help of censors to assist them in this task. We do not believe they are prepared to sacrifice their heritage of a free press in order to be "protected" against what others think may be bad for them. We believe they still favor free enterprise in ideas and expression. . . . Every silencing of a heresy, every enforcement of an orthodoxy, diminishes the toughness and resilience of our society and leaves it the less able to deal with stress. . . . We believe that free communication is essential to the preservation of a free society and a creative culture.[17]

The image of the marketplace of ideas is a central metaphor for libertarians, and they support the free market here as elsewhere. Libertarian economist Milton Friedman sarcastically proposes that the government may wish to do with books what it has already done with cigarettes—require a warning label on them: "Reading is dangerous to mental health and may cause death from revolution and other disturbances."[18]

In addition, there are many technical problems with censorship. What is obscene to one person is not so to another. Attitudes of acceptability keep changing. Defining what is offensive or obscene is impossible. And how do we prevent censorship from leading to thought control? Libertarians often argue that any censorship will lead to total censorship. Censorship represents a slippery slope: As one porno shop operator commented, "If they succeed in [censoring] pornography, you'll see all future Pentagon Papers and all future Watergates suppressed."[19] Harriet Pilpel, the co-chair of the National Coalition Against Censorship, claims that "the First Amendment can not be compromised, because, once censorship creeps in, censorship takes over."[20] Some might argue with this fearsome claim, noting that we have long censored material, and yet we still maintain a lively literary and political scene.

Libertarians have a visceral hatred for others telling them what they cannot do, and so they become incensed when pornography is attacked, even though most libertarians are no more readers of smut than are the censors.

Are there really to be no limits? Some librarians and other libertarians believe that a free and open library should have hard-core pornography and other sexual material in its open stacks. The American Library Association's Task Force on Sex Related Media is attempting to provide reviews to librarians on materials dealing with sexuality.[21] Radical political scientist Mulford Q. Sibley opts for a totally open library purchasing policy in order to picture the world more perfectly:

Perhaps a certain proportion of supposedly obscene literature, other things being equal, should not only not be excluded but rather positively included as indispensable in every library collection. . . . Our grasp of reality is imperfect and if it is ever to approximate "truth," all forms of expression must not only be tolerated but encouraged. Once we begin making exceptions—for obscene or other supposedly evil literature—we have given up the quest for understanding and have in effect arrogantly set ourselves up as those who know what is absolutely true and right.[22]

For the libertarian, a library will not be entirely free of censorship until all types of published material are included: pornographic, fundamentalist, racist, and that written by obnoxious, ignorant, illiterate people. That day has not yet arrived.

The Conservative Point of View

Although conservatives are more likely than others to support censorship,[23] not all conservatives totally support it. For example, when the Boston Public Library was under attack in the 1950s for carrying Communist literature, Herbert Philbrick, a leading anticommunist, telegraphed: "Shocked to hear that the Boston Public Library has under consideration the suppression of vital information concerning the methods, nature, and extent of the Soviet conspiracy against the United States. Such suppression would be directly in line with the current policy of the Communist Party in the United States to conceal the true aims of the Party from all except its trusted members."[24] He argues that it is important to know about those you abhor.

Other conservatives, however, see a justification for controlling what is provided in libraries. Whatever else one might think about Iran's late Ayatollah Khomeini, no one can deny that he cared about literature. Salman Rushdie's *The Satanic Verses* mattered enough that the Ayatollah determined that the author deserved a death sentence. Similarly, Senator Jesse Helms and other opponents of the National Endowment for the Arts believe that obscenity can make a difference. These critics give literature its greatest compliment. They claim that books matter, that they change people—for better or for worse. It is common to hear people argue that "good books" can have positive effects on their readers, and for this reason reading is important. The censor carries this one step further by saying that if good books have beneficial effects, does it not logically follow that "bad books" have negative effects, and shouldn't we do something about it? Many literate societies have feared books, and columnist Nat Hentoff observed wryly that the impulse toward censorship may be stronger than the sex drive.[25]

After all, conservatives note, citizens subsidize libraries through their taxes; should they not have some right to say what is in them? Why should government-employed librarians not be held accountable to the people who pay their salaries; are they always above reproach?[26] Whereas libertarians are likely to emphasize the part of the First Amendment that mentions freedom of speech and the press, conservatives stress the last phrase: "the right of the people . . . to petition the government for a redress of grievance." Surely removing an objectionable book from a library constitutes a "redress of grievance." While citizens only have the right to *petition*, objections to books fall under the First Amendment.

The conservative believes that access to some books may have significant negative effects, which a government may legitimately wish to control. Control may increase the level of civility in a society since some writings may lead to a debasement of moral standards. Harry Clor, an advocate of some forms of censorship, argues: "We know of no civil society which has yet established its fundamental law or ethical code upon the affirmation that any man may do just as he likes and live just as he pleases as long as he avoids 'violence, constraint or fraud.' This is hardly a mere accident of history, for the human community is always interested in something more than the prevention of violence, constraint, and fraud."[27] Some books, particularly those that are felt to be obscene, weaken the bonds of civilized society. Some theorists believe that society needs consensus and moral agreement in order to function and reject the argument that a wide diversity of opinion makes for a stronger, freer social system. Some beliefs may undermine the basic institutions of society: the church, the family, and the community. The *Dallas Times Herald* editorializes that pornography may blunt our moral sense:

> Pornography is not morally neutral. It has to do with man the savage, man the naked ape (to borrow C. S. Lewis' phrase), man shorn of the restraints and inhibitions which alone make possible civilized existence. The danger is that we should cease to think of this sort of man as abnormal. That which we hear and see again and again and again, we become inured to. But do we wish to become inured to behavior which runs counter to Judeo-Christian tenets?[28]

Unlike libertarians, who reject the notion of moral or cultural absolutes, conservatives believe that such absolutes exist. They worry about a society that is eager to separate religion from education but is willing to allow anything in the name of freedom of the press. Conservative columnist George Will, in discussing the removal of prayer from school, presents this unfortunate paradox this way: "It is, by now, a familiar process: people asserting rights in order to extend the power of the state into what once were spheres of freedom. And it is, by now, a scandal beyond irony that thanks to the energetic litigation of 'civil liberties' fanatics, pornographers enjoy expansive First Amendment protection while first graders in a nativity play are said to violate First Amendment values."[29] The paradox is even more ironic to the conservative when it is remembered that both the schoolhouse and the library are paid for by taxes and are run by government functionaries. The conservative sees no reason why the people's institutions cannot express popular values.

The Social Democratic Point of View

Most people who adopt "left" or "liberal" stands in American politics agree with the basic thrust of the libertarian point of view on library censorship. This may be the case because, in the past, most of the censors have been conservatives and much of what has been censored has appealed more to the left or liberal social principles. *The Wall Street Journal* sees censorship as a battle between the proponents of the traditional culture, "the bedrock Americans" (conservatives) and the "cosmopolitan Americans" (libertarians and social democrats).[30]

Despite this, some social democrats believe that censorship is justified to prevent attacks against minority groups and the disadvantaged. Should we permit a full flowering of "hate speech" and hateful writing—a topic of real concern on many college campuses? It is this set of arguments that will be examined here.

The social democrat, unlike the libertarian, does not accept freedom as an absolute. There are competing freedoms. People do not have the right to discriminate, nor do they have the right to deceive or to harm others (to cry fire in a crowded theater). Morris Ernst, a prominent civil liberties lawyer, makes a distinction among ideas, sedition, and merchandising words.[31] Only the first of these is protected, claims Ernst. But some would go further and ask, since we do not permit libel of individuals, should we allow libel of groups? Why should we permit literature that attacks Jews, African Americans, or women in our libraries? To give such works a place on the shelf gives them a legitimacy they do not deserve. While Hitler's *Mein Kampf* deserves a place as a historical document, contemporary Nazi tracts do not deserve any recognition. This, of course, presumes we are able to distinguish among those writings that are "politically correct" and those that are not. While this may seem troubling, the social democrat contends that librarians continually sell books that are considered outdated and wrong. Just as a fact can be shown to be wrong, so can an opinion.

Among the groups that have made a special attempt to indicate their disapproval of certain types of literature are the National Organization of Women and the Council on Interracial Books for Children. They condemn such books as *The Story of Doctor Dolittle, Mary Poppins*, and *Hansel and Gretel* on grounds of racism, ethnocentrism, and sexism. These groups justify their demands by noting that their position is based on the Fourteenth Amendment's guarantee of "equal protection of the law." Author Melvin Berger warns that books can have real (and harmful) effects: "If a book presents a poor image of some group of people, it deprives them of equal protection and may lead others to treat the group in a different way, which also violates the Civil Rights Act of 1964. . . . Books that show such bias are contributing to discrimination. . . . and are thus justly criticized."[32] Although most of these groups do not support censorship as such (certainly not by that name), they recommend that the textbooks chosen and purchased present desirable images.[33] This directly affects publishers and means that fewer "incorrect" books will be published. For example, a supposedly racist children's book, *Jake and Honeybunch Go To Heaven*, was refused by many libraries, even though they had other books by this popular children's author.[34] Raising the consciousness of librarians so they self-censor books has also long been a tactic of the conservative.

Radical feminists who are concerned about the effects of pornography recently have raised one of the more interesting arguments in the debate over censorship. Andrea Dworkin, author of *Pornography: Men Possessing Women*, ably presents the feminists' view that pornography sends an ideological message to women:

> The major theme of pornography as a genre is male power, its nature, its magnitude, its use, its meaning. Male power, as expressed in and through pornography, is discernible in discrete but interwoven, reinforcing strains: the power of self, physical power over and against others, the power of terror, the power of naming, the power of owning, the power of money, and the power of sex. These strains of male power are intrinsic to both the substance and production of pornography, and the ways and means of pornography are the ways and means of male power.[35]

While feminists and conservatives both oppose pornography, they do so on quite different grounds. The conservative sees the obscene as undermining morality, whereas the feminist sees pornography as an affront to the civil rights of women. Indeed, the City of Minneapolis passed an ordinance (subsequently vetoed by the mayor) that defined pornography as a form of sexual discrimination against women, violating their civil rights. Under this ordinance, a person could sue those who display pornography (which could include libraries).[36] The offense is to a minority group, as opposed to an attack on the moral fiber of the society as a whole. Ironically, defining pornography in terms of its political components seems to give it additional dignity and makes it fall clearly under the rubric of the First Amendment. Dirty books have become moral philosophy.

Pornography and Social Research

As actors in the political drama, pornographers do not have too many admirers. Nevertheless, until quite recently, there was no substantial social

scientific research that demonstrated that this "art form" could have negative consequences. At one time, academics were among the most vocal
opponents of censorship, arguing that there is little evidence that pornography leads to violence against women. Although the major battle about
library censorship is not about the purchase of explicitly pornographic
materials, libertarians believe that such materials should be included.

Discovering the effects of sexually explicit material on public behavior
is not easy. Rapists are surely different from lawful persons on more than
their reading and viewing habits. Nor are potential rapists likely to reveal
candidly their inner secrets to prying social scientists. As a result, most of
the research on the effects of pornography has involved laboratory experiments conducted with college students. Perhaps the leading advocate of
this approach to studying pornography is social psychologist Edward Donnerstein. Donnerstein's research is especially concerned about the relationship between pornographic films and violence to women.[37]

The basic methodology in Donnerstein's numerous experiments[38]
uses a male student in an introductory psychology course who signs up to
participate in an experiment to earn extra credit toward his final grade in
the course. When he arrives at the laboratory, he meets a second subject,
who is actually a confederate of the experimenter. He is told by the experimenter that the research is designed to study performance under stress.
The student is asked to write an essay that is to be evaluated by the other
"subject" who may shock him if the essay is a poor one. After completing
the essay and regardless of the quality of the writing, the student is shocked
a set number of times. Presumably, he believes this judgment has been made
by his fellow subject. Then, in a "break" in the experiment, the subject is
asked to rate and provide physiological measures about a film that is
supposed to be used for a future experiment. Some of the films are pornographic; some are not. After the film, the original experiment begins
again. The subject now gets to shock the experimental confederate after the
confederate performs a task. Finally, the subject is given a short question-
naire, and the real purpose of the experiment is explained.

Among the conditions tested in this methodology is whether there is
a different response to a male or female confederate, whether the amount
of shocks received by the subject (his level of "anger") affects his response,
and whether the content of the film (pornographic or not) affects his
behavior. This is supposed to measure aggression, which is measured by
the level of shock he decides to give to the confederate when it is his turn
to punish, which is supposed to be a surrogate for rape.

Laboratory experiments sometimes seem to compete with the best of
the Broadway stage in the intricacy of their plotting. We never learn exactly
what the subject *believes* he is experiencing, only that he reports being angry
when expected to be and aroused when that is called for. These "manipulation checks" suggest that the experimental manipulations are having some

effect, presumably the one that is intended. The control the experimenter has over the situation is one of the most potent advantages of this methodology. Nevertheless, we cannot be certain how the subject is defining the events he is experiencing. By focusing on the experimenter's view of the world, this methodology is alien to interactional methods, yet is congruent with both functionalism and conflict theory. Since Donnerstein is examining the feminist issue of the relationship between pornography and violence toward women, we can tentatively label his research as falling within the conflict theory approach.

In a recent book, Donnerstein describes eight of his most recent experiments in this area, a style of presentation that is often found among experimental social psychologists. The assumption is that each experiment leads to the next as the experimenter tests related questions. The results of one study provide questions for the next. Each experiment further refines the experimenter's theory and eliminates hypotheses that are demonstrated to be false. Thus, experimental social psychology may be closer to the model of "natural science" than any other sociological methodology.

It is not possible to describe Donnerstein's whole series of experiments. The following only briefly summarizes some of his most salient conclusions. Basically, his findings support the view that watching pornography, even for short periods of time, even by "intellectual" college students, can increase the level of violence toward women. This is not, however, the case with all pornography, only that which also shows aggression toward women—such as a film in which a man rapes a woman and in which she appears to enjoy it. In such a situation, Donnerstein suggests that the male's inhibitions against violence toward women are lowered. Angry male subjects are particularly likely to shock female confederates after seeing a film that is both aggressive and pornographic. Even some films that are "merely" aggressive toward women (with no overtly sexual content) can, in some instances, provoke higher levels of shock to females. Aggressive pornography does not appear to produce heightened aggression toward other male subjects.

Such experiments provide troubling indications that material potentially found in libraries (in this case films, not books) can have unsavory effects. Even though Donnerstein does not argue for censoring such materials, it is significant that the proponents of the antipornography ordinance in Minneapolis brought in Professor Donnerstein as a witness to testify about his research. His approach is perceived as being supportive of feminist activists who wish to limit pornographic violence. These findings certainly add weight to those social democratic arguments that claim pornographic material is an assault on women.

Censorship and Education

In part, the arguments raised in this chapter boil down to questions about trust. How much should we trust ourselves? How willing should the government be to trust its citizens? Americans believe that education can have positive effects on those who are educated. Few would ever question this belief. But if there is positive education, is there also negative education? Are there some things that are harmful to us as individuals and to the society of which we are a part? Is learning a kinky sexual technique likely to make us or our partners immoral? Are there some things that would be better for us not to know? Those who see individual human beings as naturally good and rational (the libertarians) argue that a person can make his or her own choices. But if we agree with the conservatives that human nature is basically fallible, we might wish to opt for some measure of control.

The long-term effects of communication are very difficult to determine. If we could somehow arrange a random group of subjects that had been exposed only to pornography (or televised violence or comic books) and compare them to another random sample that had no exposure, we could better understand the nature of cultural effects. Unfortunately, this is not possible. People who choose to read pornography are different from people who do not, in many ways, so it is virtually impossible to get any definitive effects of long-term exposure. Also, the effects of pornography may be so subtle that it would require very large groups to notice any difference. Perhaps only 1 of 1,000 people are affected by pornography in a harmful way.

A second set of questions concerns who should do the controlling. We can expand this question from the issue of library censorship to that of education as a whole. Is it right and proper for the government (even a local government) to run schools? How can these institutions, populated by government employees, help but pass on the government line? While this line may not be inflexible, the very fact that teachers are certified by the government and are paid through public taxes makes them prone to accept the rightness of state power. Can you imagine a school that kept as much distance from the state as public schools must keep from the church?

Education in a free society is dangerous. Education implies the teaching of beliefs, ideas, norms, and values. But in a democracy, what should be taught? We want to teach our children the truth, but we cannot always agree on what the truth is. Do we agree sufficiently on a political or moral system to permit one truth to be taught? Should we teach our children that communism is wrong, even though some think it is right? Should we teach them to respect their fellow citizens, even though we may feel some do not deserve respect? Should we only teach evolution, or should we also teach creationism? And in the age of AIDS, what should we do with sex education, teach it as fundamentals of human plumbing? The more the members of a society share a view of the world, the more agreement there will be on the content of education. Perhaps, then, we should relish our disputes about what children should learn; surely it indicates we are still free.

Questions

1. What is the difference, if any, between selection and censorship?
2. Should librarians have the sole responsibility for deciding which books to purchase?
3. What kind of input should citizens have in the book-selection process?
4. On what basis should books be purchased for a small public library?
5. Is there a "freedom to read"?
6. Should obscene works be censored by the government?
7. Should hard-core pornography be purchased by libraries?
8. Should children be prevented from reading some books?
9. Does a diversity of opinion lead to freedom or the breakdown of order?
10. Should libraries purchase books that are racist or sexist?

For Further Study

Berger, Melvin. *Censorship*. New York: Franklin Watts, 1982.

Boyer, Paul S. *Purity in Print: The Vice-Society Movement and Book Censorship in America*. New York: Scribner's, 1968.

Busha, Charles H. *Freedom Versus Suppression and Censorship*. Littleton, CO: Libraries Unlimited, 1972.

Clor, Harry M. *Obscenity and Public Morality: Censorship in a Liberal Society*. Chicago: University of Chicago Press, 1969.

Dworkin, Andrea. *Pornography: Men Possessing Women*. New York: Perigee, 1981.

Office for Intellectual Freedom of the American Library Association, *Intellectual Freedom Manual*. Chicago: American Library Association, 1974.

Thomas, Cal. *Book Burning*. Westchester, IL: Crossway Books, 1983.

Zurcher, Louis A., Jr., and R. George Kirkpatrick. *Citizens for Decency: Antipornography Crusades as Status Defense*. Austin: University of Texas Press, 1976.

Notes and References

1. Mary and Herbert Knapp, *One Potato, Two Potato . . .: The Secret Education of American Children* (New York: W. W. Norton, 1976), p. 173.
2. The National Commission on Excellence in Education, *A Nation at Risk: The Imperative for Educational Reform* (Washington, D.C.: U.S. Department of Education, 1983), pp. 8–9.
3. Barry Glassner, "Kid Society," *Urban Education* 11(1976): 5–22.
4. James Coleman et al., *Equality of Educational Opportunity* (Washington, D.C.: U.S. Government Printing Office, 1966).
5. Robert Rosenthal and Lenore Jacobson, *Pygmalion in the Classroom* (New York: Holt, Rinehart, and Winston, 1968).
6. Ivan Illich, *Deschooling Society* (New York: Harper & Row, 1971), pp. 1–24.
7. Harold D. Lasswell, "Censorship," in *Encyclopedia of the Social Sciences* (New York: Macmillan, 1930), vol. 3, p. 290, quoted in Charles H. Busha, *Freedom Versus Suppression and Censorship* (Littleton, CO: Libraries Unlimited, 1972), p. 83.
8. Leon Carnovsky, "The Obligations and Responsibilities of the Librarian Concerning Censorship," In *The First Freedom*, Robert B. Downs, ed. (Chicago: American Library Association, 1960), p. 312.
9. Paul S. Boyer, *Purity in Print* (New York: Scribner's, 1968), pp. 1–5.
10. Personal communication from the Office for Intellectual Freedom of the American Library Association, January 1992.
11. "School Censorship on the Rise," *Newsletter on Intellectual Freedom* 39(1990), p. 201. We do not know whether this increase is due to better reporting or more incidents.
12. Judi Lawson Wallace, "What Kids Read—Who Decides?" *Ms.* 10(April 1985): 21.
13. Bernadette Schell and Lionel Bonin, "Factors Affecting Censorship by Canadian Librarians," *Journal of Psychology* 123(July 1989): 357–367.
14. Oliver Garceau, *The Public Library in the Political Process* (New York: Columbia University Press, 1949), p. 132 in Busha, *Freedom Versus Suppression and Censorship*, p. 87.
15. Busha, *Freedom Versus Suppression and Censorship*, p. 75.
16. John Stuart Mill in Carnovsky, "The Obligations and Responsibilities of the Librarian Concerning Censorship," p. 313.
17. Office for Intellectual Freedom of the American Library Association, *Intellectual Freedom Manual* (Chicago: American Library Association, 1974). Part 2, pp. 14–15.
18. Milton Friedman, "Book Burning, FCC Style," *Newsweek* (June 16, 1969): 86.
19. Editorial, *Arkansas Gazette*, June 27, 1973, printed in *Editorials on File*, 4 (January–June 1973): 844.
20. Harriet Pilpel, "American Thought," *USA Today* 117(January 1989): 85.
21. Gordon McShean, *Running a Message Parlour: A Librarian's Medium-rare Memoir About Censorship* (Palo Alto: Ramparts Press, 1977), pp. 229–232.
22. Mulford Q. Sibley, "Intellectual Freedom, Suppression, and Obscenity," in *Intellectual Freedom in Minnesota: The Continuing Problem of "Obscenity,"* Nancy K. Herther, ed. (Minneapolis: Minnesota Library Association, 1979), pp. 14–15.

23. Louis A. Zurcher, Jr., and R. George Kirkpatrick, *Citizens for Decency: Antipornography Crusades as Status Defense* (Austin: University of Texas Press, 1976), pp. 242–243.
24. James Rorty, "The Attack on Our Libraries," in Downs, *The First Freedom*, p. 304.
25. Erwin Kroll, "Bookburners," *The Progressive* 49(December 1985): 4.
26. Cal Thomas, *Book Burning* (Westchester, IL: Crossway Books, 1983), p. 80.
27. Harry Clor, *Obscenity and Public Morality* (Chicago: University of Chicago Press, 1976), p. 199.
28. Editorial, *Dallas Times Herald*, June 22, 1973, printed in *Editorials on File* 4 (January-June 1973): 838.
29. George Will, quoted in Thomas, *Book Burning*, p. 22.
30. Editorial, *The Wall Street Journal*, June 27, 1973, printed in *Editorials on File* 4 (January-June 1973): 841.
31. Clor, *Obscenity and Public Morality*, p. 103.
32. Melvin Berger, *Censorship* (New York: Franklin Watts, 1982), p. 65.
33. Ibid., pp. 64–65.
34. "Black Folklore Controversy Erupts: Farrar Questions Selection Policies," *School Library Journal* 29 (March 1983): 68.
35. Andrea Dworkin, *Pornography: Men Possessing Women* (New York: Perigee Books, 1981), p. 24.
36. Jean Bethke Elshtain, "The New Porn Wars," *New Republic* (June 25, 1984): 15–20.
37. Edward Donnerstein, "Pornography: Its Effect on Violence Against Women," in *Pornography and Sexual Aggression*, Neil M. Malamuth and Edward Donnerstein, eds. (New York: Academic Press, 1984).
38. Edward Donnerstein and Gary Barrett, "Effects of Erotic Stimuli on Male Aggression Toward Females," *Journal of Personality and Social Psychology* 36(1978): 182–183.

CHAPTER TEN

Work and Organizations: Should Corporations Be Allowed to Give Employees Lie Detector Tests?

■ Perhaps no other word in our lexicon provokes such ambivalent reactions as "work." We feel that work is ennobling and personally fulfilling, and we judge people by their work and the skill with which they do it. We sometimes describe our species as *homo faber*—man the maker. Throughout much social theory, notably in the writings of Karl Marx, human beings are conceptualized as being first and foremost workers; transforming nature makes us who we are.

However, some days we are not so rapturous about work. Many people find that work does not express their "selves," but is merely a way of earning what they need to express their "selves" on Saturday nights. As Marx recognizes, many workers are "alienated" from work—they feel powerless, isolated, and psychologically separate from their tasks. A person who is too caught up in work is considered abnormal: a workaholic. Is work addictive?

All work is not created equal. Some work is honored; other work is considered "dirty work"—work that is outside the bounds of proper society,[1] but which someone must do for the society to function. This includes sanitation, cleaning, and killing (persons and animals). Honored work receives high status and is rewarded either with an honorific title (such as doctor or reverend) or with monetary rewards, such as those received by models and investment bankers. In some high-status occupations, those we call professions,[2] the workers themselves control (or attempt to control) the conditions and rules of their employment. We expect factory workers to obey their supervisors, while doctors make their own rules and "govern" themselves. Of course, it is never that simple: No group is totally free, and outside forces can restrain professionals, through client control, bureaucracy, or government regulations. Further, many occupations attempt to gain the mantle of "professional" for themselves, and the debate over occupational "worth" may be vigorous, as it involves power. Are nurses "professionals," are social workers? I do not ask whether they are *competent*, but whether they should have occupational autonomy, free from outside influence.

We assume that everyone in our society should be in the labor market, with the exception of married women who have the choice of working outside the home (at a "job") or inside the home. The divisions between types of work contribute mightily to the development of social classes and status levels. Not only is an individual's work important for him or her, but it is equally crucial for society. We think of a primitive society as a group in which all persons do all jobs. There are no specialists, only tribesmen. Often the reality was not as egalitarian as the image: There were gender and age differences in work, and often there were ritual specialists (e.g., medicine men) and political specialists (e.g., chiefs). Still, the "occupational" distinctions were not as extensive as those distinctions that occur in modern, industrial societies. Consider the range of modern occupations: tape librarians, urban planners, tree pruners, oven tenders, punch-press operators, silk-screen cutters, actuaries, efficiency engineers, and occupational therapists. Sociologists speak of this as constituting the "division of labor," a term that became prominent in the writings of the French sociological theorist Emile Durkheim.[3] For Durkheim, who mistrusted modern life, the division of labor posed problems for social solidarity in that different occupations give individuals different values and norms, undermining the consensus found in less complex societies. This can lead to normlessness, or what has been called *anomie*, and radical individualism. Still, complex societies provide *options* for behavior and *tolerance* for self-expression that may be unavailable in smaller and less complex social systems.

A related feature of modern society is the tendency of persons to form groups or organizations to achieve some end. While such groups occur in all spheres of human activity (consider Little League baseball teams or Mothers Against Drunk Driving), I focus on organizations that structure work: companies or corporations. Groups can achieve things that individuals (even numerous individuals) cannot. In some cases, such as hunting bands, several people may be required to accomplish a single task; in other cases, such as sailing a ship, people band together to do different tasks for a common end. On a ship, the captain makes the final decisions and assumes ultimate responsibility, while officers are assigned specialized tasks. Within the organization, a division of labor based on expertise exists.

As societies become more complex, local, face-to-face groups (churches, farms, villages) are replaced by larger organizations. A major difference between the small groups of the past and the large organizations of the present is size and its implications. In a small group, a person is known personally and knows those who provide services. In a large, bureaucratic organization, people are clients, and the people serving them are likely to be anonymous and impersonal. Yet, large organizations may be functionally necessary to achieve desirable social goals and to produce things efficiently. What large organizations lose in friendliness, they may make up in efficiency or *economy of scale*. This phrase refers to the idea that it may be cheaper per unit to produce many objects than it is to produce a few. The small widget maker must purchase the same machine as the large widget maker, yet the small widget maker uses the machine only part of the day, while the competition uses the machine constantly. Since the machine is the same price for both manufacturers, it is easy to see why producing many widgets is cheaper than producing a few.

If it is impossible for large organizations to be personal, then perhaps they should just try to be more efficient. Sociologists refer to these large organizations as *formal organizations*. They have a consciously planned structure that is organized to achieve socially valued goals. Often these organizations have detailed *organizational charts* showing how employees are connected to each other. These plans, in effect, describe the rights and responsibilities of members of the organization and suggest the proper patterns of communication among the parts of the organization. These charts show in detail the "vertical" hierarchy (who supervises whom) and the "horizontal" divisions (the range of activities in which employees are engaged).

Interactionists correctly emphasize that an organization rarely functions in exactly the manner specified in an organizational chart. Rather, an informal structure exists that gets things done through agreements and tacit understandings. Interactionist sociologist Anselm Strauss refers to this as the *negotiated order*[4] to set it apart from the formal structure.

Taken together, both the structure and the flexibility of the organization facilitate work. Organizations are typically hierarchical and depend on authority, but they also permit workers to form communities of interest and class. The organization can be thought of as a social world in miniature.

■ Question:

Should Employers Be Permitted to Use Lie Detectors?

Guilt carries Fear always about with it; there is a Tremor in the Blood of a Thief, that, if attended to, would effectually discover him; and if charged as a suspicious Fellow, on the Suspicion only I would always feel his Pulse, and would recommend it to Practice. It is true that some are so hardened in Crime that they will boldly hold their Faces to it, carry it off with an Air of Contempt, and outface even a Pursuer; but take hold of his Wrist and feel his Pulse, there you will find his Guilt; . . . a fluttering heart, an unequal Pulse, a sudden

Palpitation shall evidently confess he is the Man, in spite of a bold Countenance or a false Tongue.
    —Daniel Defoe, "An Effectual Scheme for the Immediate Prevention of Street Robberies" . . . , 1730[5]

The truth is a precious commodity. Sometimes it may also seem to be a rare commodity. Studies have indicated the difficulty in establishing whether a person is lying or telling the truth.[6] Knowing "for sure" whether a person is lying is of considerable use in many spheres of life—from marriage to law enforcement to personnel offices. We look in other people's eyes, watch their palms, and listen to the timbre of their voices to determine whether they are consciously deceiving. Such interpersonal observation is widely practiced but with uncertain skill. Experimental research suggests that law enforcement agents, supposedly trained in distinguishing truth from falsehood, were no better able to separate the two than were untrained college students.[7] These researchers believe that each of us will develop our own "pet theories" for determining honesty.

As a consequence of this uncertain prediction, it is not surprising that we have attempted to create tests and to build contraptions that give us answers as to whether our colleagues are fibbing or are worthy of our trust. Torture has been a perennial favorite method for discovering "the truth." Pain supposedly encourages honest report, although it must be fairly noted that some would sooner die than confess and others would sooner confess than maintain their real innocence. More subtly, the ancient Hindus asked suspects to chew a mouthful of rice and then spit it onto a leaf of the sacred Pipal tree. The liar would find rice stuck to his or her tongue and palate. Such a primitive test is based on sound psychological and physiological principles. Fear diminishes the flow of saliva and makes it stickier in consistency.[8] If the subject believes that the test will work, it will. Early students of dishonesty looked for sweating, blushing, trembling, an unsteady gaze, and a rapid pulse.

And then we invented lie detectors (also known as polygraphs). The principle of lie detectors is simple, even if the machinery appears complex. The assumption is that when people are lying, they are anxious, and the effects of anxiety can be measured physiologically: the pulse changes, hands sweat, and even the voice may sound different. We believe that the body is a window into the soul. The important, if obvious, point is that the machines do not measure *lying*, they measure bodily changes that are caused by anxiety, not by lying. We have no machine that can measure lying (or truth telling) and we will not have such a machine until we find some objective reaction that characterizes the acts of lying or truth telling. The Truth Verifier, a common image in science fiction, seems far from reality.

The lie detector is a twentieth-century American invention, traditionally more widely used in the United States than elsewhere, perhaps because of American faith in technology. Harvard Ph.D. (and the creator of the *Wonder Woman* comic strip) William M. Marston is credited with inventing the original machine and its label, "lie detector," during the first two decades of this century.[9] The original impetus for Marston's work was his interest in criminal apprehension and counterespionage. In both areas, lie detectors remain in the arsenals of authorities. In the past century, the machines have become more sophisticated, but the basic principle of measuring physiological changes produced by anxiety remains constant. Its success has been helped enormously by a related factor that helps to create anxiety—the belief that the machine works.

If you don't believe that a lie detector can detect lies, you would have no reason to be anxious! The readings would likely be meaningless. As a consequence, examiners sometimes play tricks on those they test, asking them to choose a card from a deck made up of fifty-two Queens of Hearts. When the machine "learns" that the respondent's card is a Queen of Hearts, she or he is impressed and, perhaps, a bit scared. Information that undercuts the credibility of the lie detector is doubly damaging—damaging because it questions the validity of the test and because it makes the test less effective if we don't trust it. As former President Richard Nixon noted, lie detectors "scare the hell out of people."[10]

An obvious weakness of the polygraph is that individuals can be anxious for many reasons, and some people can deceive without wavering. To cope with this problem, a lie detector operator doesn't merely ask the central, relevant questions and examine the measures based on your response, but compares responses to these questions to other, control questions. If you are being investigated about a particular crime, you might be asked whether you have ever lied, cheated on your taxes, or taken anything without permission. Many people will lie to those questions and this gives a base reading for your response when you feel secretly guilty. You might also be asked about a fictitious crime because a response that indicates dishonesty might simply be because you secretly believe that you are guilty of everything. The operator *compares* your answers with other answers that you have given.

While lie detectors are still used in criminal detection and in national security investigations, until recently they were widely used in another way: by companies as part of their hiring procedures and in determining whether workers should be fired. Significant differences exist between criminal and security investigations and employment tests. Some argue that national security is so important that even if innocent people are denied employment, every technique should be used to trap the guilty. In criminal investigations, detectives focus on whether a particular act did or did not occur, rather than predicting whether the person is "generally honest." A person may be denied employment because of a history that is only marginally relevant. Lie detectors are highly controversial in personnel testing and employee control.

During the 1980s, lie detection became increasingly popular in pre-employment hiring decisions. Figures on the number of tests given vary, but estimates in business range to over two million tests each year.[11] Three-quarters of these are used in pre-employment screening, according to the American Polygraph Association,[12] often in an attempt to reduce internal theft that has been estimated as costing from $5 to $40 billion annually.[13]

One wonders how accurate polygraphs are. This is not an easy question to answer. A lot depends upon the qualifications of the tester, the type of machine, the kinds of questions asked, the conditions of stress, the degree of belief in the machines, and the proportion of truth tellers and liars being studied. A "natural" test in which people have reason to hide information is impossible to construct, because how does one ever know the truth? One study indicates that most liars (about 80 percent) are caught by the machine and some are not; most truth tellers (about 60 percent) are exonerated and some are not.[14] Is this good enough? It might be if you were an employer attempting to cut losses by avoiding taking risks in hiring; it might not be if you were one of the honest 40 percent denied a job because of a machine. Is the lie detector a fire alarm that often goes off by mistake?

During the 1980s, reactions to lie detectors grew increasingly hostile as their use increased by employers. In 1983, the U.S. Office of Technology Assessment released a report that suggested that, while the polygraph was useful in criminal investigations, it was worthless for screening workers. By 1986, thirty-two states had laws restricting polygraph use.[15] Responding to this hostility, Congress, prodded by the unlikely coalition of conservative Utah senator Orrin Hatch and liberal Massachusetts senator Edward Kennedy, passed a law, signed by President Reagan, that sharply limited the use of lie detector tests in pre-employment screening by employers involved in interstate commerce. As a consequence, the use of polygraphs for employment declined dramatically, although government employees and criminal suspects still will be subject to them. Applicants no longer need to fear these machines, but now fear paper-and-pencil tests, drug screening, and background checks.

The Libertarian Point of View

It would be nasty to suggest that libertarians like to lie, but there is something that is profoundly liberating about lying. Lying is, after all, an act of free will—not letting facts fetter you. One's own thoughts are, by rights, private, and that privacy should not be lightly invaded. The concern of employers should be whether a worker is a good, diligent, and honest; we should judge behavior and not thoughts.

The libertarian sees this fundamentally as a civil liberties issue: the right of privacy. Could this lead to governmental thought police—one reason that politicians such as Jeane Kirkpatrick and Jack Kemp are suspicious of polygraph use? Conservative columnist William Safire, blasting the "Sweat Merchants," calls the lie detector "the modern equivalent of hot lights and truncheons of the 'third degree.'"[16] Libertarians agree with Pope Pius XII that lie detectors "intrude into man's interior domain."[17] Or as Robert Ellis Smith, the editor of *Privacy Journal*, put it, "Even if polygraphs were regarded as totally reliable, I would still oppose their use as lie detectors, just as I oppose the use of wiretaps. Wiretaps, after all, are totally reliable, but they still violate individual privacy."[18]

The danger to individual privacy is evident in a set of questions that Coors Beer once asked their employees, including questions about their sexual behaviors ("Have you ever done anything with your wife that could be considered immoral?") and political attitudes ("Are you a Communist?"). Workers found these questions so objectionable that they went on strike.[19]

The libertarian believes deeply in a zone of personal privacy to which institutional forces should not have access. Even if this might mean that fewer "criminals" or dishonest people are caught, this would be worthwhile in an open society. The libertarian believes in the concept of "free minds." Institutional control is secondary to individual rights in the libertarian framework.

There is a second theme in the libertarian suspicion of polygraphs that deserves note: These machines are "inhuman." Clearly, the machines are nonhuman and, just as clearly, the operator is "human." But is the process dehumanizing? Some writers think so and object to it, just as the Luddites in England in the early nineteenth century wished to destroy machines that threatened to change the nature of work. This argument is put dramatically by law professor E. A. Jones:

> If the lie-detecting polygraph were indeed to be what it is *not*—a monument to technological infallibility—if it were a chrome-plated, flickery-lighted, superefficient computerized conduit of discovery, linked to the sweaty wrist and breath-gulping, heaving chest of an evasive, guilt-worried, fault-smothering, self-excusing human being, . . . I would still come down on the side of exclusion [from court evidence]. Each of us is too imperfect and fragile a creature to sustain such rigorous thrusts of suspicion and rejection into our being and yet maintain that sense of personal worth and higher purpose—and recurrent resolve to do better—which is indispensable to dignity and accomplishment. I think it is far preferable that a fellow human, concededly imperfect in the capacity to perceive calculated falsehood, be the assessor of credibility than to achieve a mechanical perfection akin to Orwell's *1984* and Huxley's *Brave New World*.[20]

For Jones, and for those with a libertarian orientation, it may be preferable for the discovery of truth to be a game, rather than a science. Certainty about truth implies total control over the actions of individuals.

Anecdotes about affronts to "honest" individuals are part of this argument. Everyone can find someone who has been wrongly accused, and this adds piquancy to the attack on technology and corporate control. Consider the tragicomedy, sarcastically reported by attorney Irving Kaler, of his son not being hired as a stockboy in the pet department in a local discount store:

> As a condition of his employment, Michael was subjected to a lie-detector test. After all, the pet department must be protected from unwittingly giving employment to a possible guppy snatcher or a goldfish filcher. But Michael, who is only 16 and who has never had any altercation with the law, became understandably agitated when asked questions such as how many times he had been married (none), and how many times he had been arrested. . . . Now, thanks to this incident, I almost feel as if I have joined the company of Ma Barker in the pantheon of wicked parents.[21]

In fairness we should note that we have only Mr. Kaler's account of the sterling qualities of his son, and, further, a competent examiner would compare Michael's responses to questions about his marital status with questions that are more relevant, such as his treatment of his pets.

But, ultimately, our response doesn't depend on the specifics of the case, but to general sentiments about the rights of individuals and the role of modern technology. In the words of Irving Kaler, "It is absolutely incomprehensible that we rely upon some goofy, Rube Goldberg-type contraption to make sensitive decisions. . . . Men and women of America, it is time we rise in indignation against this untrammeled invasion of our humanity! After all, we should possess a greater power to reason than some cold and merciless machine which, in all likelihood, hates rabbits, puppies and even those limpid-eyed guppies."[22] While the libertarian may believe that companies have the *right* to conduct such tests, the lie detector challenges the dignity of the human being.

The Social Democratic Point of View

Social democrats are not friends of this "cold" machine, but object to it for different reasons. For them a lie detector is a technique of management power—an unfair means by which employers control employees. The humanity of the worker is being denied by these intrusions.

Why do corporations use lie detectors? A key reason is to save money from employee theft. But often, as in employment screening, they are not catching those who have committed an offense, but screening those who are judged "likely" to commit an offense. By eliminating all possible sources of trouble, many good people are denied jobs. The social democrat is likely to emphasize the relative lack of validity of these machines. While I do not discuss the extent to which lie detectors are accurate, more innocent people are judged guilty than the reverse, and polygraph evaluations are less accurate in "real-world" settings than they are in the controlled arena of the laboratory.[23] Thus, their "unreliability" counts against them, although the question of how accurate they would need to be to be considered "reliable" is rarely addressed. Polygraphs are considered sufficiently suspect that the American Psychological Association prohibits members from administering tests.[24] Psychologist Leonard Saxe suggests that it is "shocking that such unreliable measures are being used to decide the fate of innocent people."[25] Senator Edward Kennedy terms them "twentieth-century witchcraft."[26] Often, polygraphs are attacked because some people are highly anxious at having to take the test (or because their children are ill or they are going through a divorce); however, as noted, if a person's own responses are being compared to each other, this generalized anxiety should cancel itself out.

More significant is the charge that, given the level of inaccuracy, these tests are used because they are easy and cheap to administer. They are a "quick fix" that substitutes for careful background checks. As Montana Democratic congressman Pat Williams suggests, lie detectors are popular because:

> They're convenient. They save employers money that otherwise would have to be spent creating good personnel practices and a good personnel department. It's a lot easier to give five dozen employees a lie-detector test than to do a good personnel check on them. There's a line in a song by the Western singer named Tom T. Hall, "If you hang 'em all, you'll get the guilty." Unfortunately, some American businesses have found that it's cheaper to hang them all than it is to really seek out the guilty.[27]

Beyond this concern is the belief that employers can use lie detector tests to fire those workers who are honest but troublesome (such as being active in unions), refuse the sexual advances of their supervisors, or are members of minority groups. It is seen as a means of arbitrarily firing people. One former government employee notes that "if you don't have the right WASP profile and weren't born in a medically sealed bag which was opened just before the polygraph, you won't pass."[28]

In some instances, lie detectors may be used deliberately to fire workers who management wants fired. Consider the account by a former manager of a southern department store chain:

> According to Blews, his district supervisor told him that blacks "just don't work out" and ordered him to dismiss two black women workers. Blews said that

when he refused, the supervisor remarked, "We'll have to show you how our polygraph test works around here." The women were subsequently fired after their test results indicated "a sign of a possibility of deceit." His bosses also turned down the only two blacks whom he had ever recommended for management trainee positions, again on the basis of the polygraph test.[29]

There is evidence that African Americans fail pre-employment polygraph tests more often than whites. Critics of the test suggest that this is not because African Americans are more likely to lie but that the races may react to stress differently. Failing a test can have long-term consequences if a new employer learns of the old test results.

It bothers the social democrat that the fired worker can only appeal with difficulty. After all, the company can claim that the firing was due only to the fact that the machine (or its operator) claimed that the worker was a thief. This places too much power in the hands of private employers for the social democrat, and it is no wonder that social democrats were particularly pleased when Congress passed strict regulations on the practice.

The Conservative Point of View

Not all conservatives support the use of lie detectors. As noted, conservative senator Orrin Hatch of Utah sponsored the bill limiting lie detectors that President Reagan eventually signed, and many successful companies do not use them. However, it is probably fair to suggest that conservatives are more sympathetic to the private use of lie detectors than are other groups. Remember that the conservative believes that human beings are naturally imperfect and that various forms of social control are justified. They may be tempted to believe that "if you have nothing to hide, you have nothing to fear."[30]

The conservative (and the libertarian, too) believes that employers know their own best interests without direction from Congress.[31] If the technique were not effective, it wouldn't be used. The conservative notes that thefts from employers hurt profits and may bankrupt small businesses. Larry Talley, vice president of risk management for Days Inns of America reports that in 1976 his company lost more than $1 million from employee theft. Since instituting the polygraph in 1977, it lost no more than $115,000 each year. He notes further: "Especially in the hotel, day-care and nursing-home industry, companies have been sued for hiring people who later committed crimes against a guest or a patient or someone in their care. If used properly, polygraphs help screen out such people."[32] With large legal liability judgments, companies avoid taking chances on employees. Employers will attempt, and always have attempted, to judge the honesty of their employees. Why shouldn't they develop a relatively objective, unbiased, accurate test, rather than use an idiosyncratic interview that can easily be manipulated? The conservative suggests that polygraphers should be licensed to set standards, making the tests better and fairer. A licensing standard may protect employers from liability suits and would increase the public's confidence in the power of these machines to get the "truth."[33]

Ultimately, the conservative says, the lie detector can help to stem the tide of lawlessness and immorality. For example, one study found that one-third of all applicants lie about their job credentials.[34] These tests may reek to some of totalitarianism, but others find them a bracing breath of discipline. Consider the words of polygraphers R. J. Ferguson and A. L. Miller:

> Complacency and toleration, with respect to crime and moral conduct, is the deadliest of diseases. If a deadly disease is not checked, death results—in this case, the death of a nation. No matter how hard it is to accept, a democracy such as ours, like less libertarian systems, cannot grant all freedoms to individuals and leave none for itself to use in the interest of its own preservation.[35]

Conservatives are willing to give up some freedoms that libertarians prize for their own prize of social order. The lie detector is one imperfect tool in this effort.

Organizational Control and Social Research

In this section I do not discuss research that bears directly on lie detectors, but retreat to a period before these machines, nineteenth-century England, to examine how employers attempted to control their employees. A major change in sociological research over the past two decades has been an increasing interest in historical sources—what is often known as *comparative/historical sociology*. Why should we limit ourselves to our own time and place for understanding human nature and social organization?

William Staples decided to examine the records of a British hardware firm (a firm that made metal pots and pans, doorknobs, and nails) located in the English Midlands, near Birmingham.[36] He perused documents and records from the company, Kendricks, for the period 1791–1891. Such data have considerable advantages and real disadvantages. Staples wants to explore the development of the modern factory system and how the economic structure affects the condition of work in the factory. With this topic, historical data are essential. Staples can depict the sweep of history and the effects of social change in ways that would have been impossible had he studied a modern factory. Nineteenth-century factories are different from modern ones; these differences are more than historically interesting, they are also theoretically significant. Blending historical detail and sociological theory creates a robust area of research.

Of course, this research has limitations. Unlike interviews or participant observation, we cannot ask these historical figures what they meant by their actions and words. We have an incomplete historical record; one that cannot be increased. Once a document is destroyed, it is forever unavailable. Staples, despite help from this company, is limited in what he can know. Further, he may be uncertain of the meaning of certain ideas. When we consider child labor, it is difficult not to conceive of it through the lens of contemporary values. But attitudes toward child labor changed throughout this century, and one must attempt to take the perspective of those actors.

Staples argues that "factory" work changed dramatically in the nineteenth century in its mechanisms of control—what he calls the "factory regime." This represented a change from a system of patriarchical control to one of paternalistic control. What does he mean by patriarchical and paternalistic control? In the former, describing factory work until around 1867, work was organized through (adult male) internal subcontractors and their families. Thus, in different areas of the "factory" groups worked partially independently from other groups. In effect, the owners arranged with these men to produce what they needed. The factory was a collection of families.

The later system, that of paternalism, is quite different. Here the owners feel obliged to involve themselves in the lives of the workers. They are almost "parents" to their "worker-children." No longer do subcontractors run things, and owners give themselves authority to tell workers what they should be doing, within and outside the factory. This system unites family, work, and community life, combining the interests of management and labor—as seen from the standpoint of the owners, of course. Ultimately, this system led to the subordination of labor to "capital" (i.e., management).

The change in the factory regime in the 1860s was in part a function of state involvement. Staples suggests that prosperity led to "enlightened" reforms, notably changes in rules regarding child labor and a shortened work week. The family employment of the earlier period was severely criticized; yet, Staples suggests that this was not a function of increased morality, but rather that favorable economic conditions made this morality possible. These reforms gave management an opportunity to "rationalize" their production, make it more uniform, and gain more direct control over their workers. These changes and other economic conditions also helped to limit competition for those firms, such as Kendricks, that survived, giving workers fewer options. Companies provided money for schools and health care and increasing wages in certain areas, which, while seemingly desirable, also made workers more dependent on the company. What might have been seen on the surface as a set of changes favorable to labor limited employees'control over their work and made a series of technological innovations possible later in the nineteenth century, reducing the need for skilled craftspeople. Sometimes all changes seem to work for the benefit of those in charge. The changes in the late nineteenth century in Great Britain eliminated the vestiges of domestic production and helped to create the modern factory.

Staples operates out of a conflict theory perspective—some might call it neo-Marxism—that examines the relations between state, capital, mode of production, labor, and markets. He wishes to trace how workers lost control of their own labor, despite the gains in their material position and despite state involvement on their behalf. This analysis of business is congruent with the social democratic perspective that argues that state involvement in the economic system is not only legitimate, but necessary. Yet, Staples adds a cautionary note: Sometimes state involvement that on the surface may seem beneficial to labor has surprising after-effects. Management, with all its resources, is very effective in turning the new rules to its own advantage. This applies to limits on child labor as well as limits on the use of lie detectors in hiring.

Work and Organizational Control

Most workers do not have the luxury of being their own boss; control is part of a hierarchical workplace. As anyone who has been their own boss can attest, hierarchy is not always bad. It is nice to know from where one's next check is coming. Yet, our bosses expect things from us and may attempt to manipulate us in ways that are in their interest, but not ours.

Functionalists and conflict theorists disagree about the utility of the hierarchical control of workers so characteristic of capitalistic enterprises. The functionalist can point to the enviable success of the Western capitalistic economies. The factory system is an orderly, efficient system that, when coupled with vigorous collective bargaining, can preserve basic rights of workers. Workers are not slaves, but they do need to be directed. Without supervision by someone who has an overview of the factory and of the role of production in the economy, too few or too many widgets might be made. Without controlling labor costs, goods would be too expensive, and, eventually, workers would be unemployed. Managers are, from this perspective, necessary for the successful use of labor.

Conflict theorists have a different view. They note that the accident of birth has a considerable influence on whether you will be giving or taking orders throughout your work life. They agree that capitalistic enterprises often make a profit—but for whom and on whose shoulders? Is it fair that some, with access to capital, should control the destiny of others, particularly when those with access to capital do not engage in productive labor themselves. They invest instead of working. Some workers find their humanity demeaned by the desire of bosses to make a profit—through long hours, unsanitary working conditions, or having to submit to lie detector tests. The managers' drive for profit—some might label it "greed"—leads to a demand for change. This change can occur through government involvement (as social democrats demand), government ownership of industry (as democratic socialists demand), or worker ownership of the means of production themselves (the forms of communism). Those systems would at least be *fair*.

Interactionists note that the relationship between management and labor is not fixed. In fact, it is always negotiated in practice. The precise amount of time workers have off, their opportunities for conversation, and their personal autonomy result from local, situational conditions. This, of course, downplays the conflict argument that the negotiating groups may have quite different amounts of power. Interactionists have tended to ignore the economic conditions that lead to these decisions but, recently, interactionists have argued that the structure of the economy has "interactional" effects because managers and workers assume the *images* or *symbolic meaning* of the economy and organizational structure in their interaction.

With all its imperfections, the organizational structure of Western nations remains productive. Third World nations emulate the work relations found in industrial countries, and some seventy years after the Russian Revolution, leaders of the former Soviet Union have discovered that the love of a good profit might motivate better than worker solidarity.

Questions

1. How much control should employers have over their employees when on the job?

2. Should employers be able to control the private lives of their employees?

3. Should lie detectors be used to screen applicants for employment?

4. Should the federal government prevent the use of lie detectors to screen applicants for employment?

5. Should workers in sensitive areas (e.g., nursing homes, child care) be subject to polygraph tests?

6. Should polygraph tests be used to test workers with access to classified information?

7. How do you think you would respond to a polygraph test? Could you fool the machine? Would the machine feel you were lying if you told the truth?

8. If your professor found a final exam stolen, should students in the class be given a polygraph test?

9. What techniques should employers use to prevent employee theft?

10. If a lie detector could be made perfectly accurate, when should it be used?

For Further Study

Friedson, Eliot. *Professional Dominance*. Chicago: Aldine, 1970.
Gugas, Chris. *The Silent Witness*. Englewood Cliffs, NJ: Prentice Hall, 1979.
Jussim, Daniel. "Lies, Damn Lies—and Polygraphs." *Nation* 241 (December 21, 1985): 665, 682–684.
Lykken, David. *A Tremor in the Blood*. New York: McGraw-Hill, 1981.
Miller, Gale. *It's a Living*. New York: Free Press, 1987.
Reid, J. E., and F. E. Inbau. *Truth and Deception, The Polygraph ("Lie Detector") Technique*, 2nd ed. Baltimore: Williams and Wilkens, 1977.
Staples, William. "Control and Organization of Work at a British Hardware Firm, 1791–1891." *American Journal of Sociology* 93(July 1987): 62–88.
Strauss, Anselm. *Negotiations*. San Francisco: Jossey-Bass, 1978.

Notes and References

1. Everett C. Hughes, "Work and Self," in *The Sociological Eye* (Chicago: Aldine, 1971), pp. 338–347.
2. For discussions of the meaning of the concept of professionalism, see Ernest Greenwood, "Attributes of a Profession," *Social Work* 2(July 1957): 45–55; Julius Roth, "Professionalism: The Sociologist's Decoy," *Sociology of Work and Occupations* 1(1974): 6–51.
3. Emile Durkheim, *The Division of Labor in Society* (New York: Macmillan, 1933).
4. Anselm Strauss, *Negotiations* (San Francisco: Jossey-Bass, 1978).
5. Quoted in Donald T. Lykken, *A Tremor in the Blood: Uses and Abuses of the Lie Detector* (New York: McGraw-Hill, 1981), p. vii.
6. Paul Ekman and W. V. Friesen. *Unmasking the Face: A Guide to Recognizing Emotions from Facial Clues*. (Englewood Cliffs, NJ: Prentice Hall, 1975).
7. Bella DePaulo and Roger L. Pfeifer, "On-the-Job Experience and Skill at Detecting Deception," *Journal of Applied Social Psychology* 16:249–267.
8. Ibid., p. 26.
9. Clarence D. Lee, *The Instrumental Detection of Deception: The Lie Test* (Springfield, IL: Charles C Thomas, 1953), pp. 11–14.
10. Quoted in Daniel Jussim, "Lies, Damn Lies—and Polygraphs," *Nation* 214(December 21, 1985): 683.

11. Guy Halverson, "'Honesty Tests' Replace Lie Tests in Job Screening," *Christian Science Monitor* (December 22, 1988): 10.
12. Jussim, "Lies, Damn Lies—and Polygraphs," p. 665.
13. Constance Holden, "Days May Be Numbered for Polygraphs in the Private Sector," *Science* 232(May 9, 1986): 705.
14. "Lie Detectors Can Make a Liar of You." *Discover* 7(June 1986): 7.
15. Holden, "Days May Be Numbered for Polygraphs in the Private Sector," p. 705.
16. William Safire, "The Sweat Merchants," *The New York Times* (February 29, 1988): A19.
17. Quoted in Lykken, *A Tremor in the Blood*, p. 40.
18. Ibid., p. 39.
19. Jussim, "Lies, Damn Lies—and Polygraphs," p. 682.
20. Ibid., p. 39.
21. Irving K. Kaler, "A Mole Among the Gerbils?" *Newsweek* 105(March 11, 1985): 14.
22. Ibid., pp. 14, 15.
23. Holden, "Days May Be Numbered for Polygraphs in the Private Sector," p. 705.
24. Stephen Dujack, "Polygraph Fever," *The New Republic* 195(August 4, 1986): 10.
25. Donna Demac, "Sworn to Silence," *The Progressive* 51(May 1987): 32.
26. "Lie-Detectors: Bearers of False Witness," *The Economist* (March 12, 1988): 31.
27. "Bar Lie-Detector Use by Private Firms?" *U.S. News & World Report* 100(February 3, 1986): 81.
28 Demac, "Sworn to Silence," p. 32.
29. Jussim, "Lies, Damn Lies—and Polygraphs," p. 682.
30. Lykken, *A Tremor in the Blood*, p. 40.
31. "Lying in Congress," *Fortune* 116(December 7, 1987): 186.
32. "Bar Lie-Detector Use by Private Firms?", p. 81.
33. Jussim, "Lies, Damn Lies—and Polygraphs," p. 684.
34. Halverson, "'Honesty Tests' Replace Lie Tests in Job Screening," p. 10.
35. Quoted in Lykken, *A Tremor in the Blood*, p. 38.
36. William G. Staples, "Technology, Control, and the Social Organization of Work at a British Hardware Firm, 1791–1891," *American Journal of Sociology* 93 (January 1987): 62–88.

CHAPTER ELEVEN

Aging and Medicine: Should Euthanasia Be Permitted?

■ For most of us a time occurs when a looming birthday brings not joy and new privileges, but fear and regret. The tipping point varies, but our fortieth birthday is rarely met with the joy of our tenth. This reminds us that while aging is natural, our reactions are learned as to what particular ages mean. In our culture, the ages thirteen, eighteen, twenty-one, forty, and sixty-five have been invested with significance that other ages do not have—symbolism that is not universal.

Many have noted the special symbolism—the stereotyping—that many in American society apply to the elderly. In our society the elderly are often seen as frail, inflexible, cantankerous, and unreliable. These beliefs make it difficult for the elderly to be hired or to be treated with the respect we accord those who are "middle aged." The denigration of the elderly in industrial societies contrasts with the great status that older people are often assigned in preindustrial societies.[1] We speak of "old people" as having a "second childhood," and, so, we feel comfortable treating them as children. Some critical theorists suggest that being elderly makes one a member of a "minority group," which suffers from a form of discrimination known as *ageism*. As with other groups, there is debate about what to call these Americans: the elderly, old folks, senior citizens, geezers, the aged, older persons. I shall call those over sixty-five "the elderly."

Note, however, that age itself does not confirm infirmities. For every frail senior there is a George Burns or Ronald Reagan. If we accept sixty-five as the entrance to "being old," some of our fellow citizens will be "old" for over thirty years. Just as people change from birth to age thirty, so they change from sixty-five to ninty-five. With increases in life expectancy to approximately seventy-five years of age, the number of people who are elderly will continue to climb. In 1940, only 9 million Americans (6.8 percent) were sixty-five or over; by 1987 the figure was nearly 30 million (12.2 percent).[2] In addition, the elderly tend to vote at rates higher than young voters, and those with resources spend money to support their political beliefs. (Today, perhaps as a result of living through the Depression, senior citizens tend to vote Democratic more than younger voters.) The nation's largest "special-interest" group is the American Association for Retired Persons.

Of course, there are special physiological problems that parallel chronological aging. One cannot hope to become biologically "young" again, and these medical issues are real and traumatic for individual elderly citizens. But from the sociological perspective, isolation and all that it implies is the major challenge of aging. With the decline of the nuclear family and the generally weakened state of family relations, elderly Americans may feel cut off from society. This is often compounded by two common features associated with aging: the loss of one's spouse and the loss of one's job, sometimes through choice and sometimes through mandatory retirement. This isolation is, in itself, harmful, leading to extremely high rates of suicide, especially among men. When isolation is coupled with poverty (about 14 percent of the elderly live below the poverty line), the effects can be especially severe. It is not that the elderly are poorer than the rest of the population, but rather that when they are, they may find fewer resources. This is what makes Social Security such a symbolic issue; it is, in effect, the Bill of Rights for the elderly.

Some social scientists see the different positions given to age groups as proper and functional for society.[3] Rather than having to decide who should be forced to retire (imagine having to tell a long-term employee, like Willy Loman in *Death of a Salesman*, that his time is up), wouldn't it be better to allow impassive chronology do that instead? Functionalists suggest that "disengagement" may be in everyone's best interest and that disengagement is mutually desired. Such a system provides an "orderly" change from age categories, just as having an eighteen-year-old voting age (why not determine whether young people can vote on their individual merits) or a twenty-one-year-old drinking age (some sixteen-year-olds may be able to drink responsibly). This disengagement may also allow the elderly, with less energy, to husband their resources.

Conflict theorists have vigorously objected to this characterization of the elderly and their alleged desire for disengagement. Such a system clearly is functional for those who are younger, but evidence has not given much support to the desire on the part of the elderly to be cut off from society. For the conflict theorist, this is an example of "discrimination," pure and simple. The middle-aged want, for their "selfish" purposes, to wrest resources from those who are older. A change in the position of the elderly depends on a reordering of power relationships within society.

The interactionist focuses on the symbolic meaning of aging and the stigma associated with it. Since one's age is not marked on one's forehead, it is possible to "pass" as someone younger, just as teens attempt to "pass" as older. Likewise, interactionists note that many of the studies of prejudice depend on asking about "old people" in general; when we interact with an elderly person, we are interacting with a specific person and build up a relationship with that person that may be quite different from our beliefs about the elderly as a group.

Of all the social institutions that are important in the world of the elderly, medicine may be the most important. More than 75 percent of those over sixty-five years old suffer from chronic health problems. Although they constitute a little over one-tenth of the population, the elderly fill a third of all hospital beds and take a quarter of all medicines.[4] In fact, most diseases—from AIDS to measles to Alzheimer's—have social and age patterns associated with them.

With the decline of religion in industrial society, some have suggested that the closest we have to a priesthood are our "medicine men." Dressed in white lab coats, surrounded by instruments that appear magic to many of the rest of us, these men and women cure mysterious pains and ailments. We in turn come to them in supplication, displaying a pattern of behavior that sociologists call "the sick role,"[5] which is culturally patterned even though different ethnic groups may announce their aches in different ways.[6]

Most societies choose a set of specialists to cure illness, and typically these individuals are accorded high status. Yet, the nature of this work is subject to change. In the United States we have seen a change in the past forty years from doctors who were basically solo practitioners—family doctors—to the situation today in which it is more common for doctors to be affiliated with hospitals, clinics, health maintenance organizations, or group practices. As in so many other parts of our society, medicine has become specialized, in part a function of a need for increased technical expertise and in part because errors can lead to malpractice suits. Whereas once doctors were paid by their patients, today this is rather rare. Even though, unlike many industrialized nations, we do not have socialized medicine, we do not have a free market in medicine either. Most bills are paid by third parties: government, health plans, insurance plans. You may well have no idea how much your last medical encounter cost, and, had you known, you might have become sickened. When our son was hospitalized for two months, it cost "us" two years salary, which fortunately we did not have to pay. Can one make economically sound judgments when the price tag is hidden; further, do we want to make economically "sound" judgments or do we insist on the very best care for everyone.

Just as airlines are deregulated, medicine is becoming increasingly regulated, and it is difficult to imagine a true free market in which consumers and doctors both participate. Some middlemen are needed. The "crisis of health care" turns out to be a set of economic crises: how to contain costs, how to make sure that everyone is covered, how to protect doctors from court settlements arising from "honest" mistakes, how to protect patients from incompetent doctors, how to ensure that medical care is justly distributed.

■ Question:

Should Euthanasia Be Permitted?

Whose life is it anyway? Thus was titled a powerful play about the dilemmas confronting a young artist, incapacitated in a traffic accident, as he argued lucidly for the right to take his own life. If a woman has the right to control her own body so that she can abort the fetus inside her with the aid of a trained medical staff, shouldn't adults have the same right to decide and receive the same outcome as that fetus? Perhaps we should not make too much of this analogy—some say that the fetus is not "fully" human. But the critical point remains whether society has any right to tell a person how his or her body should be treated, and the participants in the euthanasia debate are often the same as in the debate on abortion.[7]

Euthanasia comes from the Greek *eu thanatos*, meaning "good death." Is any death good? The issue of euthanasia is a complicated one involving whether the decision must be made by the ill patient himself or herself; how ill that person must be; if "incompetent," who is the health care guardian; whether euthanasia must always be passive (not taking "heroic" measures to save a life) or whether it can be active (e.g., giving a lethal injection to someone in pain). I wish to touch on the following questions: (1) Is euthanasia ever justified? (2) Should people be allowed to write "living wills," specifying what treatment they wish to receive and which should be withheld if they are incapable of making decisions and are terminally ill or incapacitated? (3) Can doctors or family members make decisions to withhold treatment from terminally ill patients who cannot decide on their own? (4) Should doctors ever actively hasten a patient's death?

From time immemorial societies have let unwanted children (often female children) die. Protecting every human life is not always seen as necessary. The abortion debate, while framed differently, can be seen in this light. Some children who might have been born are not through the active intervention of doctors. In *The Republic*, Plato calls for deformed infants to be killed. In our society, the debate on euthanasia typically concerns the elderly, but it can include babies with birth defects, those in comas, or even those who are paralyzed or in great pain.

Unlike the other topics I analyze, euthanasia is a matter of life and death, but more than that, it depends on how you see life. Is it so sacred that it must be continued even in the face of enormous pain or without any comprehension that one is living? Should people without brainwave activity be considered living if their lungs work and their hearts beat, or are such "human beings" warm corpses? In part, we are victims of our own technology; machines can now keep lungs breathing and hearts beating indefinitely. Once a heartbeat was the sign of life, now most states have made "brain death" the key for determining if a body is alive. Surrounding this is the fact that we live in a society that does not wish to admit that death can win.

Survey results suggest that the public does support euthanasia in some form. While Americans (by a 93 to 6 margin) do not think that people have a right to end their lives if they have dishonored their family, a 52 to 45 percent majority do believe that this is justified if they have an incurable disease. Further, Americans believe by a better than 2 to 1 margin that if a patient has an incurable disease, doctors should be allowed by law to end that life if the patient and his or her family request it.[8] According to a 1990 Gallup Poll, a startling 84 percent say that if they were on life-support systems and had no hope of recovering, they would want treatment withheld.[9] The suicide rate of those over sixty-five years of age is approximately twice as high as for the rest of the population and can be attributed, at least in part, to euthanasia. Unlike suicide rates in general, the rate of suicide among the elderly has been increasing in the past decade.[10] Indeed, the American Hospital Association estimated that the timing of 70 percent of the deaths in the United States is determined by a decision not to use certain medical technology[11]—most deaths are "negotiated."

The issues surrounding euthanasia become even more complicated when we consider individual cases.

Consider the well-known case of Karen Ann Quinlan. In 1975, this twenty-one-year-old slipped into a coma after ingesting a combination of alcohol and tranquilizers. After a year on a respirator, her parents successfully forced her hospital to turn off the respirator after a lengthy and controversial court hearing. Such are the mysteries of life that Ms. Quinlan continued to breathe on her own until she died ten years later. One might have asked whether, given her irreversible coma, doctors should have removed her feeding tubes. Or should they have given her an injection to end her life and the costs to taxpayers? Did Ms. Quinlan die with dignity? What would she have wanted? Should anyone have had the right to stop her treatment?

Then there is the case of Roswell Gilbert, seventy-five, who pumped two bullets from his 9mm Luger into his wife's brain as she lay on the sofa.[12] Emily Gilbert, seventy-three, was diagnosed with Alzheimer's Disease, which causes severe mental confusion, and osteoporosis, a bone disease that causes fractures and pain. Mrs. Gilbert was *not* terminally ill in the sense that her death was imminent. She might have lived for decades. But with what quality of life? Mr. Gilbert was found guilty of first-degree murder. Was the jury decision fair? Should a husband have the right to shoot his wife, even for noble causes? They shoot horses, don't they?

Finally, consider the case of Janet Adkins. At age fifty-four, she learned that she had Alzheimer's Disease. After considering her options, she contacted Dr. Jack Kevorkian, a physician who believes in doctor-assisted suicide. Dr. Kevorkian, known to critics as "Dr. Death," built a suicide machine, which Mrs. Adkins used to send poison into her veins. At the time of her death, although some symptoms of the disease were appearing, she was still able to beat her son at tennis and might have been lucid for months or years. Suppose the next day Mrs. Adkins would have been "miraculously" cured? Suppose a new treatment was discovered? Suppose the diagnosis was wrong? Is there a moral difference between ceasing treatment and deliberate suicide?

These cases collectively reveal the problems that have come with our increased openness to taking life. The attempts to institute "living-will" laws similarly address this question of autonomy. As a consequence of these laws, which by 1989 had been enacted in thirty-eight states and the District of Columbia, people can prepare legal documents that detail the type of medical treatments they wish and do not wish in the event they are severely ill or incapacitated. Such laws would have been unthinkable before publicity about Karen Ann Quinlan led us to recognize that we could be in her position sooner than we might think.

To understand where we might wind up, consider the Dutch. Each year Dutch doctors "actively" kill 3,000 terminally ill or incompetent patients. While active euthanasia is not technically legal, it is an accepted legal defense for a doctor accused of killing his or her patient, when certain conditions are met: (1) the patient must express his or her desire for euthanasia; (2) the patient must be fully informed about his or her condition; (3) the patient must be afflicted with an irreversible illness that causes "unbearable" suffering; (4) there must be no acceptable alternative; (5) a second doctor must be consulted, and (6) the doctor must inform the local coroner that euthanasia has occurred.[13] Some Dutch physicians argue that a quick, painless death is more humane than removing all life support and waiting for the patient to die. Others wonder whether physicians, like medical James Bonds, should have a "license to kill."

The Conservative Point of View

The conservative, believing in the power of community and moral standards, is very troubled about the possibility of deliberate death. In Judeo-Christian ethics, isn't life sacred? Although there have been revered martyrs who have given their lives for God, it is God who decides the proper span of our lives. The conservative believes that our reverence for life should not be lightly discarded, and those opposed to "living wills" are often the same people who are in "pro-life" movements. A painful life is still a life. As an editorial in the *Worcester Telegram* contends:

> Many people have, at times, concluded that it would be better to mercifully terminate such bleak existences. But, thankfully, society and the medical profession have been slow to accept that philosophy. Traditions and teachings going back thousands of years tell us that life is not to be deliberately terminated except in the most extraordinary circumstances, such as war or capital punishment. The exhumation of bones that may be those of Dr. Josef Mengele [the infamous Nazi doctor] reminds us once again of the terrible dangers that are created when man plays God or Satan.[14]

Mary Senander of the International Anti-Euthanasia Task Force asserts that "homicides should be prosecuted, whether committed by thugs in dark alleys or doctors in bright rooms."[15]

A related argument often used by conservatives is that of the "Slippery Slope" or the "Wedge." (A wedge, or "foot in the door," allows for extending the possibilities for taking human life.) This argument suggests that once we start permitting some legalized death, other conditions in which death is permitted will follow. We will slide down that slope without being able to stop.

As Yale Kamisar writes:

> It is true that the "wedge" objection can always be advanced, the horrors can always be paraded.... One reason the parade of horrors cannot be too lightly dismissed in some particular instance is that Miss Voluntary Euthanasia is not likely to be going it alone for very long. Many of her admirers . . . would be neither surprised nor distressed to see her joined by Miss Euthanatize the Congenital Idiot and Miss Euthanatize the Permanently Insane and Miss Euthanatize the Senile Dementia. . . . Another reason why the "parade of horrors" argument cannot be dismissed . . . is that the parade *has* taken place in our time and the order of procession has been headed by killing the "incurables" and the "useless." . . . The apparent innocuousness of Germany's "small beginnings" is perhaps best shown by the fact that German Jews were at first excluded from the programme.[16]

If you give us an inch, will we take the mile? Some conservatives see the greater acceptance of euthanasia as widening the circle of acceptable negotiated deaths. Even love should not be a justification for taking a life, as in "mercy killings"; protecting the moral standards of the community should count for more than "helping" an individual. Dr. Carlos Gomez, having studied the Dutch experience, suggests that we need better pain management, not more euthanasia:

> The cries of those who die in pain and despair, amid the studied indifference of professionals whose duty it is to attend to their needs, should be heard. . . . What I ask, however, is that those desperate cries for release from pain be balanced against the needs of the voiceless, who even in their silence still have a right to live.[17]

While Catholics have vigorously opposed suicide, there is a tradition in Catholic thought that distinguishes between "ordinary" and "extraordinary" means of saving human life. Sometimes, withdrawing treatment can be defined "as acceptance of the human condition."[18] Yet, what constitutes human life? While there is a growing consensus that expensive medical technology need not be used to keep a comatose person alive, the debate has typically centered on whether intravenous feeding constitutes extraordinary treatment. Should we permit comatose people to "starve" to death? While doctors are prone to suggest that decisions about feeding are part of medical practice, opponents of living wills and euthanasia suggest that this goes too far. As Mary Senander writes:

> Anyone who has followed the living-will debate for the last few years knows that the debate is not over keeping people "plugged in"—it's over food and water via tubes or assisted by spoon-feeding. (Proponents of death by choice call this "medical treatment" and suggest it should be optional. Opponents and most ordinary folks call it lunch).[19]

The conservative believes that most people want to live; they cling to life, despite temporary wavering. If euthanasia is practiced, the deceased can never change his or her mind.

The Libertarian Point of View

As the German romantic poet Rainer Maria Rilke wrote in *The Book of Poverty and Death*, we have a right to "our own death."[20] The libertarian who mistrusts collective control believes that, most of all, life is an individual's choice and that the state or community has no compelling interest in the matter. Indeed, this was the decision of the New Jersey Supreme Court when it decided that Karen Ann Quinlan could be removed from her respirator. It is not the state's business. "If biology declares war, have people no right to a pre-emptive strike?"[21] The issue is *quality*, not *quantity*, of life.

A living will provides an opportunity for the author to make his or her free choices known prior to the time when he or she may no longer be able to do so. Think of it as part of consumer rights. As the president of the Minnesota Medical Association notes:

Patients. . . have repeatedly expressed concern, based on personal experience with friends or loved ones, that our medical system often seems unwilling to stop in the use of technological forms of treatment, even when such treatment offers very little hope of significant patient improvement. . . . They fear that these treatments will be applied to them when they can no longer say, "No!"[22]

For the libertarian, the right of the individual to say no is crucial, and organizations such as the Hemlock Society or Americans Against Human Suffering have been organized to defend the right of individuals to a "dignified death."[23] Some note that hospital attorneys and insurance managers are now in more control of the process than either doctors or patients.

Nowhere has this policy been pushed further than in the Netherlands where, as noted previously, doctors can practice active euthanasia if certain stringent conditions are met. One Dutch anesthesiologist, Dr. Pieter Admiraal, a leader in the fight for active euthanasia, believes that active euthanasia is merciful and that standing by while an individual dies slowly is really a form of homicide. For Admiraal and others, active euthanasia is connected to a belief in "free will":

> Does life belong to the individual, or can society make decisions about it? In a world where society's powers continue to occupy new areas—to the point of suffocating every right of the individual—the chance to choose one's own death acquires both ethical and political weight. It helps protect the "free will" that jurists, moralists, and theologians have upheld for centuries. If every human being's life is sacred, Admiraal asks, why shouldn't every person's death be sacred?[24]

Attempts are being made in various states by Death with Dignity groups to permit some forms of active euthanasia, along the Dutch model. While such a referendum was defeated in the state of Washington in 1991, such attempts will be tried elsewhere.

The final point that is relevant to the libertarians' approval of euthanasia involves their mistrust of technology. The image of a person hooked up to rows of machines with their inhuman "faces" causes no joy for libertarians. Is that life? Certainly it is not individual life, lived freely. Being unable to live freely, some libertarians might take the option that euthanasia permits them, as a recognition of their humanity, to make one final "free" choice. An editorial in the *Tulsa World* put it this way in discussing Karen Ann Quinlan's death:

> She was the precedent for the argument that no one can be forced to submit to the twin horrors of law and technology when used in a misguided effort to prevent the most natural of occurrences—death.[25]

The Social Democratic Point of View

For the social democrat, the problem of euthanasia is not an easy one to solve. Those who are likely to be "victims" or "requesters" of euthanasia are among our most vulnerable citizens. Social democratic thought holds that a narrowly defined religious morality should not play a role in public policy, and so living wills are not abhorrent. Citizens should be able to formulate a living will, in conjunction with sympathetic and well-meaning experts who put these decisions into effect or even help to make them. The social democrat believes that the state can act *in loco parentis* (as a parent). After all, in the case of abortion, the legitimacy of the taking of life by doctors is recognized. Yet, there is also the troubling possibility that some may be bullied into death to save money that society might otherwise be forced to spend. Let us consider each of these issues in turn.

Arthur Clough satirically suggested to members of the medical profession that they should adhere to the "commandment," "Thou shalt not kill but needs't not strive officiously to keep alive."[26] The healing professionals are devoted to human welfare and they have the expertise to know when a life is savable. While no one believes that an individual doctor should be free to take the life of a patient on his or her own, shouldn't a doctor have greater authority in making these critical decisions for the rest of us who lack such expertise? Unlike the pro-life groups who see feeding as being the "humane" thing to do, doctors see it in the context of a web of medical decisions. While the opponents of living wills call this "lunch," proponents call it "the artificial administration of hydration and nutrition"[27]—what could be more medical than that?

Famous heart surgeon Christian Barnard argues for more control by the physician in the decision-making process:

> In several European countries physicians wield a power that would shock many Americans: the right of active euthanasia. When a patient . . . cannot be saved or will be forced to endure a life that is not worth living, doctors need not merely hope that nature will quickly end the ordeal. They can give the hopelessly ill a painless release from suffering. I believe that American medicine would serve people far better if they also could exercise this mercy.[28]

Barnard's plea for more authority for the physician includes shielding doctors from "frivolous lawsuits." The doctor has professional authority, even in this sensitive area.

There is another side to this problem for the social democrat: the dangers of cost accounting. Hospital rooms and medical technology are not cheap; the "average" cost for a hospital room in 1985 was $460 per day.[29] For seriously ill patients, expenses are much higher. The cost to government doesn't bother the social democrat; we can afford to help our most vulnerable fellow citizens. The concern is that euthanasia may be a "painless" way in which to trim the budget deficit. One opponent of living-will legislation makes this point explicitly, noting:

> In 1977, Robert Derzon, head of the federal Health Care Financing Administration, issued the now-famous Derzon Memo, which boasted: "The cost savings from a nationwide push toward 'living wills' is likely to be enormous. Over one-fifth of Medicare expenditures are for persons in their last year of life." . . . Some seniors have been bullied into a distorted altruism, all too willing to accept their duty to die. Like a Pied Piper returning for the old people, advance directives will guide citizens to certain, but cost-effective, premature deaths.[30]

Just as some believe that the rising cost of welfare led indirectly to the legalization of abortion (since a disproportionate number of black and brown fetuses are aborted), some suggest that the increased cost of medical care for the aged through Medicare and Medicaid is leading to our tolerance for euthanasia.[31] Some social democrats suggest that health care reform should come before we discuss shortening life; perhaps death becomes appealing when one can no longer afford life. Ethicist Teresa Takken contends that "we have no business even talking about euthanasia here until we have health care for all and even housing for all."[32] Economic factors lead to a context in which euthanasia makes sense. Some days morality follows one's pocketbook. The social democrat, of course, views this human accounting with horror, and such a concern puts brakes on his or her enthusiasm for the practice.

Senility and Social Research

Alzheimer's Disease has been called "the disease of the century," and, while proponents of cancer, AIDS, polio, or diabetes might argue, it is certainly true that Alzheimer's Disease is a modern malady. It was "discovered" (or at least named) by Alois Alzheimer in 1906, when at first it was believed to affect those between thirty and fifty years of age and was referred to as presenile dementia. Later it was discovered that there is no biological difference between senile dementia and presenile dementia, and the label Alzheimer's Disease is now applied to both.

The disease gains its impact from the success of medical care and the increase in longevity. In 1920, the average life expectancy in the United States was about fifty-four years; by 1986, it was seventy-five years. Alzheimer's Disease becomes more common with increasing age, and there are some who claim that it does not differ in kind from "normal" aging—perhaps we all may suffer from it if we live long enough. The key difference is that it affects some of us earlier than others. Given current knowledge, there is no cure for the disease and the most effective treatments work only in the early stages of the disease.

Sociologist Jaber Gubrium, a prominent student of aging, decided to study Alzheimer's patients and their families.[33] Anyone with a person with Alzheimer's in the family quickly recognizes that the disease has two victims: the person who is ill and those around him or her who must deal with this person, often physically strong, but without "normal" mental functioning. Gubrium questioned how the mind operates "phenomenologically." While the range of phenomenological approaches in sociology is broad, all are concerned with examining core philosophical questions from the standpoint of personal experience and individual meaning. The fundamental questions are "epistemological": How do we know what we know? How do we know our world? What is the nature of experience? These questions are not as easy as they may sound—others see what we see quite differently and interpret it in various ways.

For Gubrium, Alzheimer's Disease provides an excellent means to understand how minds work and what we do when they don't follow society's rules. Gubrium approached the problem through participant observation at a small hospital for the care of Alzheimer's patients and with support groups for the patients' caregivers. He hoped to understand the world from the point of view of the patient, as much as was possible, and more simply from the standpoint of the caregiver and family. His understanding of the patients was based on rapport.

With a disease like Alzheimer's, it is a challenge to understand the self-concept, the mood, and the thoughts of the patient. Those surrounding the patient continually search for clues that the person's "real self" is still present. The mind is treated as a thing—a thing can be known and assigned by others, as when we speak of a person "losing his/her mind."[34]

In his attempt to interpret what a person is thinking, Gubrium argues that "mind" is fundamentally social—it is a concept created with the help of others. We may not recognize this when the mind operates as expected and when public expression is "normal," but it become clearer when "trouble" occurs. The mind, while hidden, must be "spoken for." A mind not spoken for and not capable of being addressed for all purposes does not exist. We do not know what an Alzheimer's patient is really "thinking" (could it be brilliant thoughts?), we only know that the expression of these thoughts is not suitable. As one caretaker put it, "How do I know that . . . behind all that confusion, [he's not] trying to reach out and say: 'I love you, Sara'?"[35] Pacing the hall may be taken to mean that the person is anxious; withdrawing may mean that the person is scared. But always it is up to us to determine what that mind is attempting to express. Even for those without the challenge of Alzheimer's, putting things "into words" is not always easy. We allow others, through our expressions, to help us with the task.

Ultimately for Gubrium, the mind is "dialogic." It is the property of an individual—and its operation represents an "internal conversation" that we have with ourselves. Yet, simultaneously it recognizes that mind is also a "social achievement." It is formed and transformed through experiences that we have with others. Neither of the two principles takes priority; each must be understood in regard to the other.[36] This is a fundamentally sociological approach: One cannot have individual existence without a community. The community is made meaningful only because of the individual actor. When we ask "How can we *really* know?", the answer is that because knowing derives from the relation between minds—there is no greater reality. Alzheimer's Disease, admittedly a dreadful and special case, provides us with a window into a mental process that is little thought of when all is well.

Gubrium's research operates from an interactionist perspective, which should place it closer to libertarian thought, but Gubrium downplays the role of the minded *individual*, as he emphasizes that mind is a communal phenomenon. This would suggest that he is conservative, as we have discussed it. He underlines the hidden dignity of the Alzheimer's patient, while also stressing the role of the patient's support network. With the double emphasis on self and moral community, Gubrium's research straddles libertarianism and conservatism.

Aging, Medicine, and Euthanasia

Sometimes we are victims of our own success. Suppose we could someday create a machine that would permit a human heart to beat forever. Should we let it? When is enough enough? When a person is in enormous pain or faces a life of impending death, what does society have to gain from preventing that individual to make his or her own choice? For some, society has a lot to gain. With more people living longer, with AIDS constantly hovering, with babies "saved" while several months preterm, the issue of life support has taken on increased urgency. The extension of life expectancy and the triumphs of medicine combine to pose thorny problems.

For the libertarian, problems arise only when a person (of whatever age or condition) cannot make a decision. It doesn't have to be a good decision, a moral decision, or even a rational decision, it merely needs to be a decision. The libertarian can live with free and open suicide. We have no right to judge the decision of another. The problem for the libertarian is one of agency—who *else* should decide? Here libertarian theory is less clear. For very young children, perhaps parents have rights; certainly the state has none, and the libertarian would question the right of doctors to make decisions for their patients. If the patients can't speak, how can we know what they think—the problem of Gubrium's research on Alzheimer's patients.

The conservative values the tried and true and, therefore, seems to give greater weight to the elderly among us—those with the most experience to explain what has worked and what should be avoided. The elderly are valued resources, just as is life itself. The conservative, with his or her moral reverence, is most likely to adhere to life as a virtue in itself. It is no surprise that conservative activists see their antiabortion crusade as the pro-life movement. Life is to be valued above choice. Further, the conservative recognizes that the death of an individual affects more than that individual. Indeed, we might say that this individual is the least affected. All those surrounding him or her are greatly affected—it is their loss, and ours. If we do not treat life as sacred in this instance, how can we be sure that we will treat it as sacred at other times. Our life expectancy is fated; we should not tinker with fate.

The social democratic perspective does not easily deal with euthanasia. On some level, this is not an issue in which government should be much involved. Yet, government must set the rules, and government also provides many of the resources that make medical technology possible. If the libertarian argument won the day and there was no government health care, we might not have so many elderly to worry about. Social democrats provide the support to make aging possible in a technological society. It would be criminal to shorten that life as a consequence of an accountant's green eyeshade.

Comparing our position with those of societies around the globe, we should be grateful that euthanasia is a problem we must face. Can you imagine a debate about living wills in Ethiopia, Bangla Desh, Paraguay, or Iraq? This is a social problem that results from success. It is a luxury to debate euthanasia in a population in which the fastest growing segment is those citizens who are over eighty-five and in which some of our best-paid citizens are those physicians who serve them.

Questions

1. Should people be permitted to write "living wills," specifying the types of medical treatment they wish?
2. Should family members be allowed to decide when to remove patients from respirators?
3. Should doctors be allowed to decide when to remove patients from respirators?
4. Under what conditions should doctors stop feeding comatose patients?

5. Should doctors ever practice "active euthanasia"?
6. Under what conditions would *you* wish to have medical treatment stopped?
7. Under what conditions would you stop medical treatment for one of your parents?
8. Should severely mentally or physically deformed infants be given medical treatment?
9. Should medical treatment provided by the government be rationed according to cost?
10. Under what conditions should suicide be permitted?

For Further Study

Behnke, John, and Sissela Bok, eds. *The Dilemmas of Euthanasia.* Garden City, NY: Anchor, 1975.
Charmaz, Kathy. *Good Days, Bad Days: The Self in Chronic Illness and Time.* New Brunswick, NJ: Rutgers University Press, 1991.
Freeman, John, and Kevin McDonnell. *Tough Decisions: A Casebook in Medical Ethics.* New York: Oxford University Press, 1987.
Gomez, Carlos E. *Regulating Death: Euthanasia and the Case of the Netherlands.* New York: Free Press, 1991.
Gubrium, Jaber. *Oldtimers and Alzheimer's: The Descriptive Organization of Senility.* Greenwich, CT: JAI Press, 1986.
Hochschild, Arlie. *The Unexpected Community.* Englewood Cliffs, NJ: Prentice Hall, 1973.
Humphrey, Derek. *Final Exit: The Practicalities of Self-Deliverance and Assisted Suicide for the Dying.* Eugene, OR: The Hemlock Society, 1991.
Kass, Leon R. "Death with Dignity & the Sanctity of Life." *Commentary* 89(March 1990): 33–43.
Myerhoff, Barbara. *Number Our Days.* New York: Simon & Schuster, 1978.

Notes and References

1. David Hackett Fischer, *Growing Old in America* (New York: Oxford University Press, 1978).
2. D. Stanley Eitzen with Maxine Baca Zinn, *In Conflict and Order: Understanding Society,* 5th ed. (Boston: Allyn & Bacon, 1991), p. 84.
3. Elaine Cumming and William Henry, *Growing Old: The Process of Disengagement.* (New York: Basic Books, 1961).
4. Ian Robertson, *Sociology,* 2nd ed. (New York: Worth, 1981), p. 337.

5. Talcott Parsons, *The Social System* (Glencoe, IL: Free Press, 1951).

6. Mark Zborowski, "Cultural Components in Responses to Pain," *Journal of Social Issues* 8(1952): 16–30.

7. Germain Grisez and Joseph M. Boyle, Jr., *Life and Death with Liberty and Justice*. (Notre Dame: University of Notre Dame Press, 1979), p. 1.

8. National Opinion Research Center survey, June 1986, in Elizabeth H. Hastings and Phillip K. Hastings, *Index to International Public Opinion 1986–1987* (New York: Greenwood Press, 1988), pp. 522–523.

9. Katrine Ames, "Last Rights," *Newsweek* (August 26, 1991): 41.

10. Melinda Beck, "The Doctor's Suicide Van," *Newsweek* (June 18, 1990): 46.

11. Sol Gordon, "The Right to Die with Dignity," *The Humanist* 51(March/April 1991): 37.

12. "Merciless Jury," *Time* 125(May 27, 1985): 66–67.

13. John Horgan, "Death with Dignity," *Scientific American* (March 1991): 17, 20.

14. Editorial, *Worcester Telegram* (June 14, 1985): n.p.

15. "A Very Chilling Bedside Manner," U.S. News and World Report (June 18, 1990): 10.

16. Yale Kamisar, "Some Non-Religious Reasons Against Proposed Mercy-Killing Legislation," *Minnesota Law Review* 42(May 1958): 1031.

17. Carlos Gomez, *Regulating Death: Euthanasia and the Case of the Netherlands*. (New York: Free Press, 1991), p. 139.

18. John J. Mitchell, Jr., "Knowing When to Stop," *Commonweal* 115(May 6, 1988): 272.

19. Mary Senander, "Like a Pied Piper for the Old, Living Will Brings Untimely End." *Star/Tribune* (January 26, 1989): 17A.

20. Quoted in Eike-Henner W. Kluge, *The Ethics of Deliberate Death* (Port Washington, NY: Kennikat Press, 1981), p. 9.

21. Roger Rosenblatt, "The Quality of Mercy Killing," *Time* 126(August 26, 1985): 74.

22. Quoted in Lawrence M. Poston, "Living-Will Bills Would Honor, Not Erase, Patients' Rights," *Star/Tribune* (January 28, 1989): 11A.

23. Derek Humphrey, "Legislating for Active Voluntary Euthanasia," *The Humanist* 48(March/April 1988): 10–12.

24. Giuliano Ferrieri, "Death by Choice," *World Press Review* 34(December 1987): 51.

25. Editorial, *Tulsa World* (June 13, 1985): n.p.

26. Quoted in Raanan Gillon, *Philosophical Medical Ethics* (New York: Wiley, 1986), p. 126.

27. Poston, "Living-Will Bills Would Honor, Not Erase, Patients' Rights," p. 11A.

28. Christian Barnard, "First Word," *Omni* 8(March 1986): 6.

29. *Statistical Abstract of the United States*, 1988 (Washington: Department of Commerce, Bureau of the Census), p. 100.

30. Senander, "Like a Pied Piper for the Old, Living Will Brings Untimely End," p. 17A.

31. Grisez and Boyle, *Life and Death with Liberty and Justice*, pp. 7–8.

32. Quoted in Horgan, "Death with Dignity," p. 20.

33. Jaber Gubrium, "The Social Preservation of Mind: The Alzheimer's Disease Experience," *Symbolic Interaction* 9(1986): 37–51.

34. Ibid., p. 41.

35. Ibid., p. 44.

36. Ibid., p. 49.

CHAPTER TWELVE

Social Movements/Collective Behavior: Can Civil Disobedience Be Justified?

■ "We Shall Overcome," says an old Negro spiritual, which in time, became the anthem for the civil rights movement. This song recognizes the important role that groups of citizens have in our social system. People have the right, perhaps the obligation, to protest when they feel that injustice is being practiced by the government, social institutions, or their fellow citizens.

Although Americans like to think of themselves as having a representative democracy, this represents only part of how policy is made. Elections are not the only means by which citizens do—and should—influence their government. The First Amendment to the Constitution recognizes that the right to assemble peaceably and to petition the government for redress of grievances is a protected way to bring about change. Throughout our history, citizens have attempted to change government policies through social movements and collective behavior.

A *social movement* is a collection of individuals who organize together to achieve or prevent some social or political change. Obviously, social movements differ considerably in their structure, tactics, ideology, and goals. Some social movements are centrally organized with a strong and effective hierarchy. This hierarchy may be open or secretive, democratic or authoritarian. Social movements may engage in persuasion, letter writing, voter registration, civil disobedience, or violence. Depending on a perceived need and effectiveness, people within a social movement may change their approach. Thus, some terrorist organizations may renounce terrorism when they perceive it is in their interest to do so; other groups may become frustrated working within the political sphere and choose to become more violent. There is some evidence that in the United States groups engaging in forceful action (violence or civil disobedience) are more successful in responding to repressive treatment than "meek" organizations.[1]

Throughout U.S. history, a remarkable array of social movements has existed: from the Industrial Workers of the World to the National Association of Manufacturers, from the Animal Liberation Front to the Women's Christian Temperance Union, from the American Nazi party to B'nai B'rith. These movements reflect libertarian, conservative, and social democratic ideologies, and others not as compatible with democratic ideals. The goals and ideas for which these groups choose to fight are incredibly diverse. Some groups organize to promote change and others (called *countermovements*) oppose it. Sometimes after change occurs (as after the 1973 Supreme Court decision that legalized most abortions), the roles of opposing organizations switch. Now, the "pro-choice" groups are fighting to keep things the way they are while "pro-life" groups are fighting to change the situation. Should the Supreme Court overturn *Roe* v. *Wade*, positions may change yet again.

Sociologists have proposed numerous theories to explain the emergence of social movements. An early approach suggests that members of social movements have psychological characteristics in common. These theorists, such as Gustave LeBon,[2] see a social movement as fundamentally irrational, as are its participants. Other theorists emphasize that social movements meet a need for the individual member. These approaches, however, ignore what the movement is fighting for in their haste to characterize the participants. While it seems reasonable to suggest that people who choose to be active in social movements may have different preferences than those who do not, this does not explain why a movement exists or why it arises when it does.

One explanation is the existence of "strain" in society. When a problem (a strain) is recognized, groups are likely to coalesce to deal with it. This strain may be an "objective" problem (such as the existence of guns) or a "perceived" problem (such as people feeling relatively deprived compared to others). Such a theory has considerable appeal because it recognizes that social movements are a response to what is occurring in society. Yet, some charge that strain theories rely too heavily on a simple cause-effect analogy. The problem exists and then a social movement arises to meet it. The difficulty here is that there are many potential "problems" but only a few social movements. For example, one of our most active social movements is attempting to prevent individuals from driving after they have consumed alcoholic beverages. It is by no means clear, however, that the proliferation of "drunk drivers" is a recent problem or even that it is the most pressing problem that society faces.

Resource mobilization theory[3] has been formulated to explain why some movements succeed and others do not. As the name suggests, access to resources is crucial to an aspiring movement. No social movement can grow until a committed group of individuals is willing to acquire and use resources. In the broadest sense, these resources need not only be material objects, but can also include mobilization of the press, recruitment, and use of members' social networks. These mobilizers may, at first, be outsiders, with the expertise and resources to assist in the mobilization of a movement, such as the members of the Communist Party of America who went down south during the 1930s to help organize southern workers.

Typically, social movements that are oriented toward change will not have the material resources of governments or those in favor of keeping the status quo. But one potential advantage they do have is their ability to use "bodies" in collective behavior. *Collective behavior* is the behavior of large numbers of people, which typically is unstructured and relatively unplanned. Crowds, mobs, demonstrations, sit-ins, and picket lines are instances of collective behavior. While social movements may not have much cash, they have supporters, and these supporters can make a strong argument by their mere presence.

Some people argue that crowds are, by their nature, irrational (they have a "group mind") and subject to contagious mass behavior,[4] but an alternate view sees collective behavior in a more positive light. According to the emergent norm theory,[5] crowds are not as uniform as they might appear from a distance. For example, participants may have different motives for being present: from some looking for violence to others hoping to meet a romantic partner, a few hope to pick a pocket, while still others desire to express a deeply held conviction. This approach to collective behavior suggests that norms develop through the interaction of the group. A crowd situation is usually ambiguous with most participants not certain about what they should be doing. As a result, a few outspoken members can define proper behavior by setting a framework for action. Even though the majority of the crowd may not feel strongly, it will typically go along since at the moment it seems the proper thing to do. This approach to crowd behavior is set squarely within the interactionist tradition because it assumes that what is happening will be uncertain until it is defined through the dynamics of social contact.

Whether social movements and collective behavior are helpful or harmful depends on how you evaluate their methods and goals. Functional sociologists are more cautious than conflict sociologists about endorsing the idea of collective behavior as such because it may indicate a radical restructuring of the relationships within a social system. Conflict theorists are more enthusiastic about such behavior and hope for the radical restructuring of relationships among classes and social institutions—something that would disturb functionalists.

■ Question:

Can Civil Disobedience Be Justified?

Does true freedom mean the right to say "No!" whenever one feels like it? For some, this is precisely what freedom means and, for those individuals, civil disobedience comes easy. The issue of what constitutes civil disobedience has been complex for philosophers, political theorists, and jurists. I will use a simple and rather straightforward definition of the term: "Anyone commits an act of civil disobedience if and only if he acts illegally, publicly, nonviolently, and conscientiously with the intent to frustrate (one of) the laws, policies, or decisions of his government."[6] Obviously, no society can long exist if every citizen chooses the laws he or she will accept or disobey. Of course, civil disobedience does not mean disobeying laws generally; it is a subset of all law breaking. Among the criteria usually proposed to differentiate civil disobedience from other criminal activity are that, in addition to being performed in public view, it is derived from moral principles, it avoids harm to others, and usually the law breaker willingly accepts the punishment meted out by the courts.[7] It is this last feature of civil disobedience that may differentiate some recent American protesters from the tradition of true civil disobedience since many of these people have attempted to avoid the punishment they otherwise would have received.

The history of civil disobedience is a lengthy one, populated with numerous distinguished names. Socrates and Antigone both refused to obey the state on moral grounds. Saint Augustine points to the Gospels as justification for civil disobedience to immoral laws. More recently, the example of Mahatma Gandhi in the campaign for Indian independence has proved to be an attractive model for many pacifists. Gandhi freed India from British rule with a minimum of violence; he succeeded because he had moral authority on his side and was backed by millions of nonviolently protesting Hindus and Moslems.

In the United States too, civil disobedience has had a long history. In 1755, Pennsylvania Quakers opposed taxes levied by the British to fight the French and Indian Wars. Some might consider the Boston Tea Party to be an act of civil disobedience although the protesters were not arguing that a law was immoral but that it was passed without representation—the process was immoral. Throughout the Revolutionary War there were acts of civil disobedience aimed at the British. Throughout our history, some people of conscience have refused to pay taxes for wars they considered immoral or unjust. Perhaps the most sustained period of civil disobedience during the nineteenth century concerned the opposition to acts that condoned slavery. Northern abolitionists who strenuously opposed the fugitive slave act aided and abetted slaves in winning their freedom.

The twentieth century has also witnessed considerable disobedience. The civil rights movement, and its leader, the Reverend Martin Luther King, Jr., used the inspiration of Gandhi to organize nonviolent civil disobedience. Civil disobedience continued throughout the decade with protests against the war in Vietnam, including sit-ins, draft-card burning, and tax protests. During 1971, the IRS recorded a peak of 1,740 returns from war-tax resisters (and a remarkable 70,000 households resisted the federal excise tax on telephone bills in 1972 and 1973).[8] Although the amount of civil disobedience declined during the mid-1970s, by the end of the decade and into the 1980s protest aimed first at nuclear power plants and then at nuclear arms production increased. Currently, active groups practicing civil disobedience (sometimes with a mix of other tactics) include ACT-UP Against AIDS, People for the Ethical Treatment of Animals (PETA), and the Environmental Liberation Front.[9] Philosopher Gerald Kreyche, surveying the "plethora of protests," sarcastically calls for another social movement, the New Protestants, "to protest the protests!"[10]

Most of the social movements mentioned so far are considered generally to be liberal causes, but the right also participates in this kind of activity. During the 1980s, various extreme right-wing tax-resistance protests sprang up.[11] Likewise, fundamentalist ministers disobeyed the law when Nebraska courts shut down a fundamentalist religious school. Reverend Jerry Falwell's Moral Majority endorsed civil disobedience in such cases. Perhaps the largest civil disobedience movement currently is Operation Rescue—militant pro-life activists intent on shutting down abortion clinics, aligning themselves with the abolitionists of a 150 years ago. Anyone can claim a moral objection to laws he or she dislikes. Civil disobedience often achieves change effectively. Even if people do not gain immediate satisfaction, they get publicity for their cause that exposes the ideas of the social movement to citizens who would not otherwise know about it. This represents, in the words of the Russian revolutionary Pyotr Kropotkin, "the propaganda of the deed." The act, whether or not effective in achieving the group's ends, does communicate a message.

The Libertarian Point of View

Libertarians believe individual freedom is the ultimate value; as a result, they see civil disobedience as profoundly moral. It is moral, not so much because it prevents the application of an unjust law, but because the individual stands up to an oppressive government. Although libertarians do not support random or continual law breaking, the content of the law that is broken is not as critical as it is to social democrats. The libertarian treasures the rebel who refuses to accept the rules of society. In the words of Texas columnist Molly Ivins, only half the reason the Constitution of the United States is a great and living document is because the founding daddies were among the smartest sum-bitches who ever walked. . . . The other half of the credit goes to 200 years' worth of American misfits, troublemakers, rebels, eccentrics, mavericks, anti-Establishmentarians, [and] outsiders.[11]

The most profound American theorist of civil disobedience was Henry David Thoreau, the nineteenth-century Massachusetts transcendentalist and inspiration to many contemporary libertarians. Following the lead of his friend Bronson Alcott, Thoreau refused to pay the Massachusetts poll tax as a matter of principle. Thoreau's immediate objection to the tax was Massachusetts's indirect support of slavery and the U.S. government's expansionist war with Mexico. These were only symptoms of something larger, however. Thoreau made clear that his opposition was really an opposition to all government. In July 1846, he was stopped in Concord by the local constable who asked him to pay the tax he had not paid for three or four years. When Thoreau refused to pay, the constable jailed him. By the following morning, an anonymous friend had paid his tax and Thoreau went on his way. His night in jail led to Thoreau's 1848 lecture to the Concord Lyceum, "The Relation of the Individual to the State," now better known as "Civil Disobedience." Thoreau rejected the coercive power of the state, writing:

> I heartily accept the motto, "That government is best which governs least;" and I should like to see it acted up to more rapidly and systematically. Carried out, it finally amounts to this, which also I believe—"That government is best which governs not at all;" and when men are prepared for it, that will be the kind of government which they will have. . . . It is for no particular item in the tax-bill that I refuse to pay it. I simply wish to refuse allegiance to the State, to withdraw and stand aloof from it effectually. I do not care to trace the course of my dollar, if I could, till it buys a man or a musket to shoot one with—the dollar is innocent—but I am concerned to trace the effects of my allegiance. In fact, I quietly declare war with the State, after my fashion, though I will still make what use and get what advantage of her I can, as is usual in such cases.[13]

What, then, is Thoreau's theory of government; are we to live in blissful anarchy? Thoreau's idealistic answer is that the individual con-science must take priority over the state. For Thoreau, the consent of the governed depends on each individual law and can be withdrawn at will:

> The authority of government, even such as I am willing to submit to . . . is still an impure one: to be strictly just, it must have the sanction and consent of the governed. It can have no pure right over my person and property but what I concede to it. The progress from an absolute to a limited monarchy to a democracy, is a progress toward a true respect for the individual. . . . Is a

democracy, such as we know it, the last improvement possible in government? Is it not possible to take a step further toward recognizing and organizing the rights of man? There will never be a really free and enlightened State until the State comes to recognize the individual as a higher and independent power, from which all its own power and authority are derived, and treats him accordingly.[14]

The ultimate power in a social system for the libertarian is the individual, and some libertarians even claim that their theory of government is profoundly antimilitaristic because it rejects the need for collective force. Libertarians note that many nuclear war protesters see no contradiction in government forcing individuals to support other programs. That is, many of these "hypocritical" protesters accept government power as essential. Frederick Foote, a libertarian law student, argues that a weak state is not a warlike state: "Laissez-faire capitalism, in contrast [to socialism or a welfare state], is the only social system that consistently upholds individual rights and bans the use of force against peaceful citizens. It is the only system under which no group, however large, can use force against another group, however small. *In theory and in practice, laissez-faire capitalism is the only social system fundamentally opposed to war.*"[15] The extent to which libertarians disobey laws varies; some, despite their rhetoric, are model citizens. Others try to do whatever they can to remain free of government entanglements. While voluntary compliance with the Internal Revenue Service is extraordinarily high, the IRS can enforce its will. It takes a brave, committed, masochistic, or foolish person to stand up to this might.[16] Yet, despite the difficulty, libertarians believe it is the mark of a free citizen to pick and choose which laws he or she will obey,[17] and on occasion to say, "I won't." While you may pick and choose which laws you will obey, other free citizens may choose to isolate you if they think you have made a poor decision; this threat produces cooperation and social order.

The Social Democratic Point of View

Civil disobedience is a problem for social democrats because they believe in the power of the state to do what is morally right and to enforce equality. Whereas libertarians believe that self-motivated civil disobedience is morally justified, the social democrat examines the goal of the disobedience and the nature of the government opposed. Moreover, the social democrat is likely to welcome a collective social movement more than the libertarian, who focuses on individual actions.

The nature of the government is critical to social democrats. Political scientist Hanna Pitkin writes, "If it is a good, just government doing what a government should, then you must obey it; if it is a tyrannical, unjust government trying to do what no government should, then you have no such obligation. . . . Legitimate government acts within the limits of the authority rational men would, abstractly and hypothetically, have to give a government they are founding. Legitimate government is government which deserves consent."[18] This sense of moral absolutes is found throughout social democratic writing. They believe equality and justice are concepts worth protesting for. The social democrat does not like all governments, only moral ones. Consider the words of Yale University Chaplain William Sloane Coffin, an outspoken supporter of civil rights and opponent of the war in Vietnam:

> Too often we forget that majority rule can never be equated with the rule of conscience. After all, the majority of our citizens have in the past supported slavery and child labor, and today still support various forms of racial discrimination, sex discrimination, slums, and a penal system far more punitive than curative. . . . [W]e must recognize that justice is a higher social goal than law and order. . . . Rarely do the powerful ask which side is struggling for greater justice; rarely do the powerful see what is clear to me, that a conflict for the emancipation of a race or a class or a nation has more moral justification than a law to perpetuate privileges. In other words, the oppressed have a higher moral right to challenge oppression than oppressors have to maintain it.[19]

In war-tax protest, this issue is sometimes phrased as the hypocrisy of "praying for peace and paying for war." The problem with this approach is who defines what is moral? Consider the comments of the Reverend Martin Luther King, Jr.: "[A] just law is a law that squares with a moral law. It is a law that squares with that which is right, so that any law that uplifts human personality is a just law. Whereas that law which is out of harmony with the moral is a law which does not square with the moral law of the universe. It does not square with the law of God, so for that reason it is unjust and any law that degrades the human personality is an unjust law."[20] King suggests that to disobey an unjust law reveals deep respect for *law*. But such a belief does not really solve anything. As we know from the history of religious strife, God's law is not easily interpreted by human beings. Some churches discriminate against African Americans because of their interpretation of the Bible; should those churches engage in civil disobedience to prevent integration? Should citizens who are against abortion from their moral principles stand in the doorway of abortion clinics or prevent them from being built, as others do at nuclear power plants? These are difficult questions for social democrats to answer since, presumably, not all forms of disobedience are justified from their position. If citizens share a belief in what is moral (the abolition of slavery or the prevention of nuclear war) and they can agree on which tactics help them reach that goal, then civil disobedience is morally right—both in provoking the government to act and in raising moral issues in the minds of others.

Social democrats see civil disobedience as a moral drama—an action designed to persuade and to lead to further action. David Carlin, Jr., a Rhode Island state senator, sees civil disobedience as a form of political theater:

> Civil disobedience is essentially a theatrical performance, a public action carried out in full view of an audience and with that audience in mind. Like a good play, it will exhibit character as well as plot. That is, actors will make the audience understand not simply the significance of their act of disobedience, but the significance also of the characters performing the act; for unless we understand the characters, we will not be able to appreciate their actions. In this particular play the characters, of course, will be those of exceptionally good persons—the saints or moral heroes.[21]

From this perspective it is not surprising that religious people are frequently publicized for their activity in civil disobedience. Religious leaders give the movement moral credibility by indicating that the protest is founded on justice and human values and not in selfishness.

The Conservative Point of View

Because of their love for order, civil disobedience presents a troubling moral issue for conservatives. A government must lose all shred of moral authority and democratic process before the conservative will concede the right to disobey laws. Laws in a democracy are enacted with the consent of the governed. If citizens oppose the laws, they can elect different politicians in the next election and operate within the accepted political channels. Because a political democracy allows us to change leaders, some legal authorities, such as Alexander Bickel, see all civil disobedience as coercive in its ultimate attempt to sidestep the electoral process.[22]

As one judge comments, "Every time that a law is disobeyed by even a man whose motive is solely ethical, in the sense that it is responsive to a deep moral conviction, there are unfortunate consequences. He himself becomes more prone to disobey laws for which he has no profound repugnance. He sets an example for others who may not have his pure motives. He weakens the fabric of society."[23] If someone believes the legal process is sacred (or nearly so), then any disruption becomes a very serious breach of order. Those people who civilly disobey the law may wish to define their action as obeying a higher law, but Cornell University philosopher Stuart Brown, Jr., contends that law breaking is law breaking:

> The very notion of a justified case of [civil disobedience] seems to imply a contradiction. It seems to imply the possibility of a legally permitted case of lawbreaking. For if civil disobedience, which is lawbreaking, can be justified, then surely the law ought to permit it where justified. But the law logically cannot permit lawbreaking. It logically cannot take the position that in the course of a public protest the breach of a valid law is no breach. . . . The moral beliefs and convictions of a man absolve him from obedience to the law only where the law itself allows.[24]

The conservative emphasizes the responsibility that citizens have to abide by the laws they, through their votes, helped to enact. It is too tempting for people to structure their sense of outrage and impassioned morality on the basis of whether their side has prevailed in a fair political struggle. Just as the majority may not always be right, it need not always be wrong, and there should be a strong presumption that it is correct. The conservative is likely to reject claims that the United States is not truly a democracy and not worthy of support from its citizens. Philosopher Sidney Hook sees the social democratic vision of civil disobedience as "sour grapes." He writes, "It is characteristic of those who argue this way to define the presence or absence of the democratic process by whether or not *they* get their political way, and not by the presence or absence of democratic institutional processes. The rules of the game exist to enable them to win and if they lose that's sufficient proof the game is rigged and dishonest."[25] Of course, if a person believes he or she is fighting for basic moral principles, a defeat would only support his or her questioning of the legitimacy of democratic institutions.

Conservatives also maintain that civil disobedience affects everyone in the society in that it costs the taxpayers money that could be spent elsewhere. Consider tax protests. If tax protesting ever reached significant levels, nonprotesting taxpayers might have to make up the difference that the government loses by not being able to collect taxes from everyone. Rather than preventing the government from spending money on military weapons, these protesters might only ensure that everyone else's taxes will be proportionally higher. At the present time, such redistribution of the tax burden has little practical effect, but it could. Likewise, protests of all kinds, and particularly those that involve civil disobedience, cost taxpayers money for police, court proceedings, jailing, and sanitation. One protest in Minneapolis against the Honeywell Corporation, which makes guidance systems for nuclear missiles, resulted in the arrest of 577 people. It is estimated that this protest cost local taxpayers at least $40,000[26]—money that might have been used for social service programs.

Civil disobedience is an affront to public order and, as such, conservatives can be expected to oppose it. The morality of a social movement's cause has little weight against the morality of the legitimate social institutions of a nation.

Moral Development and Social Research

For most students today, the decade of the 1960s was not an age of protest and civil disobedience, but one in which they had no part. For you, unlike your parents, the slogan "Make Love, Not War" was not a call to action, but a birthright. The first, and perhaps the most significant, of the protest movements of the 1960s was the free-speech movement at the University of California at Berkeley. Students in 1964 conducted an illegal sit-in at the campus administration building, demanding to have a wide variety of speakers on campus. As a consequence, many were arrested.

Norma Haan, a researcher at Berkeley, was curious about the moral reasoning of those involved in this controversy. In order to learn how students justified or condemned the free-speech movement, she sent questionnaires to three groups of students: students who were arrested during the protest, students who were members of conservative and/or Republican groups, and a random cross-section of Berkeley students. In this survey, she asked the participants to provide moral justifications for a set of hypothetical situations and specific moral questions about the sit-in ("Do you think it was right or wrong for the students to sit in? Why, or why not?")[27]

The hypothetical and actual moral reasoning responses were then divided by two coders into six moral reasoning categories developed by psychologist Lawrence Kohlberg.[28] Kohlberg believes that individuals progress through six stages of moral reasoning, with the first two, mainly egocentric, primarily characteristic of childhood. Stages three and four, termed "conventional" moral reasoning, focus on the role of authority in determining proper action. Stages five and six, "principled" reasoning, return the responsibility for moral judgment to the individual actor—suggesting either that the rights and duties of individuals be respected (stage five) or that transcendent moral principles be observed (stage six). Kohlberg believes that individuals proceed through these stages sequentially until they reach their highest level of moral reasoning. He suggests that only a small proportion of people will ever base their reasoning on transcendent moral principles. Haan differs from this approach to some degree because she recognizes that the context of reasoning is important. It is her concern for context that makes this study of moral reasoning fall within the interactionist approach. Moral meanings can change depending upon what is going on around you. (We must also be cautious in judging a person's capacity for moral reasoning from their answers to hypothetical issues.)

Haan's methodology might perhaps be called an "experimental survey." She compares the reactions of three different groups of subjects to two types of moral dilemmas (actual and hypothetical). She hypothesizes that there should be systematic differences between a person's reasoning about real situations and about hypothetical ones. Even though this is not the focus of the analysis, she is also able to examine differences among those with different attitudes toward civil disobedience. Haan attempts to incorporate the advantages of survey research and of experimental research. Specifically, she uses a broad sample of subjects who respond to a large set of questions, which allows her to contrast responses of groups of subjects. There is at least one weakness in her research method. Because the questionnaires were mailed to subjects, only half of the potential subjects responded and perhaps those who did were only half-hearted in their responses. And by lumping these subjects into large groups, some of the meanings of their personal situations may have been lost.

Haan's findings support the importance of context in moral reasoning. Focusing on those students who engaged in civil disobedience and were arrested (the group most pertinent to the arguments in this chapter), Haan discovered that 63 percent, a clear majority, showed an *increase* in their level of moral reasoning when discussing their justifications for civil disobedience during the sit-in as compared to their responses to hypothetical moral questions. Among the broad cross-section of Berkeley students, 54 percent of those who displayed "principled" reasoning participated in the sit-in whereas 60 percent of the nonprincipled did not—a finding that is on the borderline of being statistically significant. This finding suggests that students with "high" moral reasoning ability were the most likely to put their beliefs into action through civil disobedience. Part of the argument for this increase of moral reasoning is that these protesters were developmentally ready to increase their level of moral reasoning, and this dramatic event provided the impetus for positive change. Of course, this developmental readiness is hard to measure in advance and, furthermore, there is no certainty that the moral reasoning of these students will remain high. Even more troubling is the uncertainty that these stages of moral reasoning are actually hierarchical. Who is to say that "principled" reasoning is better than "conventional" reasoning? Conservatives would not agree that a belief in the power of legitimate authority is undesirable.

Haan's research implicitly supports libertarian theory by suggesting that civil disobedience is characteristic of students who have higher levels of reasoning. Also, by suggesting that the rationales for civil disobedience are "better" than those for other moral problems, this implies that civil disobedience is a profoundly liberating and moral enterprise.

Social Movements and Civil Disobedience

What is the relationship of the individual to the state? Is government based on the consent of the governed, and when must that consent be given? Do people have the right to press for change outside the normal political channels? Widespread civil disobedience seems to give evidence that all is not well, that a sizable number of citizens have rejected the traditional lines of authority. Although these actions may not come from an individual conscience but rather from a political movement, this does not deny their morality. Social movements can educate individual citizens and then provide a channel by which they can express their grievances.

It is important to remember, as I have suggested at several points in this chapter, that the issues on which people might engage in civil disobedience do not neatly fall in any one corner of the political arena. Abortion, school prayer, and pornographic bookstores can provide as potent a motivation for direct action as nuclear power plants, racism, or military build-ups. The theoretical underpinnings of civil disobedience are, rather, tied to how a person perceives the state. To be willing to engage in such acts, a person must concede that there are some cases in which the authority of the government is not supreme. In a democratic system, philosophical conservatives would not agree with this, notwithstanding the support of supposedly conservative groups for such action. The social democrat, with an absolute code of morality based on equality and justice, places some organized resistance above a government's right to crush that resistance; libertarians place any resistance over the government's right to intervene. For the libertarian, civil disobedience proves that individuals are still free, as the bonds of consent to the government can be broken at any moment.

We might consider a social movement to be like a collective individual. By bringing individuals with shared values together, a movement is able to express views more forcefully than any single individual could. In time, if the movement proves successful, it comes to speak for all its members, even though there are many within the group who would disagree with what is said. The National Organization for Women (NOW) is often said to speak for "women," but this is obviously a loose use of the word "women." Likewise, the Moral Majority does not represent all fundamentalist Christians. Yet, the existence of such groups allows the social order to function, dealing with these groups as brokers for their constituencies. In a society as large and diverse as ours, it is impossible to deal with citizens as individuals; thus, the ideals of libertarianism function far better in a small state than in a large one, where individualism must be given up in some measure. A social movement as a voluntary collection of like-minded individuals provides a means by which some principles of libertarianism can be incorporated into a nation state. The existence and vitality of social movements, therefore, gives legitimacy to a democratic government and permits this government to maintain the consent of the governed by providing an avenue for the expression of dissatisfaction.

Questions

1. Is civil disobedience ever justified? If so, under what circumstances?
2. Are people who engage in civil disobedience criminals?
3. Is there any circumstance in which you would refuse to pay your income taxes to protest a government action?
4. Was Thoreau right in saying that the government that governs best, governs not at all?
5. Should people who oppose the nuclear arms race blockade companies doing business with the military?
6. Is America's system of government sufficiently democratic to make inappropriate any form of civil disobedience?
7. Should protestors accept the punishment they are given or should they use whatever legal techniques they can to avoid being punished?
8. Should social movements organize and direct acts of civil disobedience?
9. Why are religious leaders frequently in the forefront of movements involving civil disobedience?
10. Was civil disobedience justified in the South during the civil rights movement of the 1960s?

For Further Study

Bedau, Hugo Adam, ed. *Civil Disobedience: Theory and Practice.* New York: Pegasus, 1969.

Brown, Stuart M., Jr. "Civil Disobedience," *Journal of Philosophy* 58(1961): 669–681.

Hook, Sidney. "Social Protest and Civil Disobedience," *The Humanist* (1967): 157–159, 192–193.

Pitkin, Hanna. "Obligation and Consent—I," *American Political Science Review* 59(1965): 990–999.

Prosch, Harry. "Limits to the Moral Claim in Civil Disobedience," *Ethics* (1965): 103–111.

Thoreau, Henry David. "Civil Disobedience." This essay can be found in many editions of Thoreau's writings.

Weber, David R., ed. *Civil Disobedience in America.* Ithaca, NY: Cornell University Press, 1978.

Weil, Robert. "Inhuman Bondage." [An account of the activities of the Animal Liberation Front] *Omni* 9(November 1986): 64–66, 124–132.

Zwiebach, Burton. *Civility and Disobedience.* Cambridge: Cambridge University Press, 1975.

Notes and References

1. William Gamson, *The Strategy of Social Protest* (Homewood, IL.: Dorsey, 1975).
2. Gustave LeBon, *The Crowd: A Study of the Popular Mind* (London: T. Fisher Unwin, 1896), pp. 54–56.
3. John D. McCarthy and Mayer N. Zald, "Resource Mobilization and Social Movements: A Partial Theory," *American Journal of Sociology* 82(1977): 1212–1241; J. Craig Jenkins, "Resource Mobilization Theory and the Study of Social Movements," *Annual Review of Sociology* 9(1983): 527–553.
4. Le Bon, *The Crowd: A Study of the Popular Mind,* pp. xiii–xxi.
5. Ralph Turner and Lewis M. Killian, *Collective Behavior,* 2nd ed. (Englewood Cliffs, NJ: Prentice-Hall, 1972), pp. 21–25.
6. Hugo A. Bedau, "On Civil Disobedience," *Journal of Philosophy* 58(1961): 661.
7. William Sloane Coffin, Jr., and Morris I. Leibman, *Civil Disobedience: Aid or Hindrance to Justice* (Washington, D.C.: American Enterprise Institute for Public Policy Research, 1972), p. 14; Charles Colson, "The Fear of Doing Nothing," *Christianity Today* 31(May 15, 1987): 72.
8. John Junkerman, "Why Pray for Peace While Paying for War?: Tax Resisters Seek the Path of Conscience," *Progressive* (April 1981): 16.
9. John Leo, "Today's Uncivil Disobedience," *U.S. News & World Report* (April 17, 1989): 64.
10. Gerald Kreyche, "Methinks They Doth Protest Too Much," *USA Today* 188(May 1990): 98.
11. "A Blue-Collar Tax Revolt," *Newsweek* (March 9, 1981): 33.
12. Molly Ivins, "Up the Rebels," *The Progressive* 51(November 1987): 28.
13. Henry David Thoreau, *Walden and Civil Disobedience* (Cambridge: Riverside Press, 1960), pp. 235, 252.
14. Ibid., p. 256.
15. Frederick C. Foote, "No Nukes—No Consistency," *The Freeman* 33(1983): 461.
16. For an example of such a person, see Junkerman, "Why Pray for Peace While Paying for War?", p. 18.
17. Burton Zwiebach, *Civility and Disobedience* (Cambridge: Cambridge University Press, 1975), p. 150.
18. Hanna Pitkin, "Obligation and Consent—I," *American Political Science Review* 59(1965): 999.
19. Coffin and Leibman, *Civil DIsobedience: Aid or Hindrance to Justice,* pp. 3–4.
20. Martin Luther King, Jr., "Love, Law, and Civil Disobedience," in *Civil Disobedience in America,* David R. Weber, ed. (Ithaca, NY: Cornell University Press, 1978), p. 215.
21. David R. Carlin, Jr., "Civil Disobedience, Self-Righteousness, and the Antinuclear Movement," *America* (September 25, 1982): 153.

22. Rodney Clapp, "Christian Conviction or Civil Disobedience?" *Christianity Today* (March 4, 1983): 31.
23. Charles E. Wyzanski, Jr., "On Civil Disobedience," *The Atlantic* (February 1968): 59.
24. Stuart M. Brown, Jr., "Civil Disobedience," *Journal of Philosophy* 58(1961): 672–673.
25. Sidney Hook, "Social Protest and Civil Disobedience," in *Moral Problems in Contemporary Society*, Paul Kurtz, ed. (Englewood Cliffs, NJ: Prentice Hall, 1969), p. 169.
26. Wayne Wangstad, "Protest Runs Up Hefty Bureaucracy Bill," *St. Paul Pioneer Press* (October 25, 1983): 8A.
27. Norma Haan, "Hypothetical and Actual Moral Reasoning in a Situation of Civil Disobedience," *Journal of Personality and Social Psychology* 32(1975): 255–270.
28. Lawrence Kohlberg, "A Cognitive-Developmental Approach to Socialization," in *Handbook of Socialization*, D. Goslin, ed. (New York: Rand McNally, 1969).